Bringing Metal to the Children

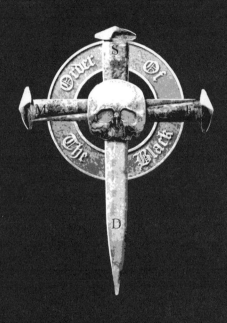

Zakk Wylde

with Eric Hendrikx

𝓌𝓂

WILLIAM MORROW

An Imprint of HarperCollinsPublishers

BRINGING

Metal

TO THE

CHILDREN

THE COMPLETE BERZERKER'S GUIDE TO
WORLD TOUR DOMINATION

HarperCollins books may be purchased for educational, business,
or sales promotional use. For information please write: Special
Markets Department, HarperCollins Publishers, 10 East 53rd
Street, New York, NY 10022.

A hardcover edition of this book was published in 2012 by
William Morrow, an imprint of HarperCollins Publishers.

FIRST WILLIAM MORROW PAPERBACK EDITION PUBLISHED 2013.

Designed by Jamie Lynn Kerner

Library of Congress Cataloging-in-Publication Data has been
applied for.

ISBN 978-0-06-200275-4

13 14 15 16 17 ov/rrd 10 9 8 7 6 5 4 3 2 1

To God and Jesus Christ for giving me life and for giving creation to the amazing cast of characters that make up the music business. Without them, life wouldn't be as insane or as much fun as it is. I also should mention Vaseline lubricating jelly—without which my ass would never have healed from the relentless pounding, hammering, fisting, plowing, and gaping joys I received from said cast of characters.

ON THE COVER: The spiked wristband I'm wearing on the cover of this book was a gift for my thirty-ninth birthday from my good friend and Black Label brother Kerry King, a true Berzerker who also calls upon the OdinForce of Valhalla to forge the Metal for his band, Slayer.

Contents

General Black Label Society Warning

Not a Single Sensical Word Exists in the Context of This Volume, Nor were Any Good Judgments or Rational Decisions Executed in Its Production. This Book was Planned, Developed, Produced, and Submitted under the Complete, Utter, and Absolute Idiocy of the Authors. In Fact, This Book is So Completely Horrendous that any Physical Contact with its Pages may cause Vertigo, Memory Loss, Nausea, Vomiting, and Uncontrollable Evacuation of the Bowels. The Authors do not Recommend that you Attempt any of the Stunts in this Book, with the Exception of some of the Really Cool Ones. Lastly, no Animals were Fondled in the Making of this Book. I look forward to Performing my own Prostate Exams each day and I Thoroughly enjoy Fucking Slamming my Meat all by Myself. I don't need no Stinking Fucking Animals. While this Book Offers Extensive Advice Intended for the Betterment of People's Lives (Because that's What I do), By No Means is it a Safe Alternative to Traditional Therapy. This Book will, However, Make your Penis Larger. If You don't Have a Penis, it Will Still Make it Larger. And if your Wife has a Penis, it will Make hers Larger as Well.

Foreword

I'VE BEEN IN SHOW BUSINESS FOR OVER TWENTY YEARS AND IN THAT time, between wrestling, music, writing books, and acting, I've met a lot of characters: freaks, geeks, sheiks, big jerks, young turks, Captain Kirks, Aussies, Ozzys, Fozzys, chicks, pricks, dicks, dicks with chicks, chicks with dicks, and everything in between. But I've never met anyone like Zakk Wylde. In a world infested with obnoxious egomaniacs, backstabbing charlatans, temperamental prima donnas (of which I confess I am one), world-class fakes, and all-around Grade-A Assholes, Zakk Wylde is *real*.

A real nice guy.

A real family man.

A real fan of music.

A real kick-ass guitar player.

And a real stinky son of a bitch.

Yeah, stinky! You want an example? One afternoon, following one of our notorious all-night drinking binges in New York City, I met up with Zakk and noticed he was wearing the exact same clothes he'd been wearing while throwing back cocktails the night before. His hair was a cross between Bozo the Clown's and Dee Snider's circa 1984, and good lord in heaven did he reek of alcohol and odors I've never smelled before or since.

"Great Caesar's ghost, Zakk!" I bellowed in disgust. "Why don't you take a shower?"

"Vikings didn't have showers, brutha," Zakk replied.

"Yeah, and Vikings didn't travel in their own private tour buses and sleep in the Waldorf hotel either. Take a shower, ya fuckin' scumbag!'"

And therein lies the genius of Zakky. He is a stellar musician and one of the greatest guitar artists of any generation, a man who has written some of the most classic riffs and songs in Heavy Metal history. He is a talented vocalist with a style completely his own and a vastly underrated piano player who can make grown men weep with his emotional ballads. But he is also a guy who considers himself to be some sort of Nordic warrior and has no problem farting in public, bragging about his sexual prowess (but only with his Immortal Beloved, Barbaranne), using more cuss words than a fleet of soused sailors, and washing that confused mess he calls his hair at best once a week, probably much less.

As I said, Zakk is real.

Really funny.

Really genuine.

Really obsessed with James Hellwig.

Really respected by one Chris Jericho.

And now really sober.

Yeah, you read that right. Sober. Zakk is one of rock 'n' roll's last true characters and the tales of his drunkocity will live on in the annals of rock history forever. I should know; I was a part of many of them. But Zakk was getting near the end of his lifetime cocktail punch card, and instead of using it up taking a seat at the bar in God's tavern with so many of his peers and heroes, Zakk chose to stop. Cold turkey. No therapy, no rehab, no Dr. Drew. He just stopped. And that's what I respect most about my friend. He recognized the problem and eliminated it. And he's a funnier, more talented, better man for it. I'm proud of him for that.

Now without the excess booze baggage, Iron Chef Zakk is out

there working harder than ever to make those doughnuts. This book explains in every way, shape, and form how he has created those delicious treats for the last twenty-plus years and how he will continue to do so for decades to come. Zakk discusses what it takes to become an SDMF-certified Berzerker and will take you step by step through the mind of a Truuuuu Rockaaaaaa!!

So sit back and enjoy. Pay attention; read slowly and maybe you'll find out a little of what makes our intrepid protagonist tick. And maybe you'll understand why he always wanted to be a *Solid Gold* dancer.

And that's for real.

Chris Jericho
October 4, 2011
Lady Gaga's dressing room

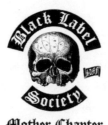

Mother Chapter

TO ALL CHAPTERS OF
THE BLACK LABEL SOCIETY —

HOPEFULLY THIS BOOK FINDS YOU
WELL N AIDS YOU IN THE MANY FACETS OF
YOUR LIFE WHERE "WORLD TOUR DOMINATION"
MAY COME IN HANDY — IN YOUR MARRIAGE,
ON A TRIP TO THE SUPERMARKET, WHILE
TAKING A SHIT, MAYBE EVEN IN THE SACK
WHILE IMPALING YOUR IMMORTAL BELOVED
SPOUSE WITH YOUR CROTCHAL HAMMER OF
THE GODS. I'D LIKE TO SAY THAT I
MADE UP MOST OF THE FANTASTICALLY
PATHETIC STORIES OF ROCK "N" ROLL
ENRICHMENT THAT YOU ARE ABOUT TO
READ, BUT UNFORTUNATELY THEY ARE
ALL TOO REAL. I ALSO WISH I
COULD SAY THAT THE EXCESSIVE
AMOUNT OF SHIT STORIES INCLUDED
WITHIN THIS GLORIOUS BINDING ARE
ALL THAT THERE WERE TO TELL.
TO BE HONEST, WE COULD HAVE
DONE AN ENTIRE BOOK ABOUT
SHIT STORIES, BUT WE NEEDED TO
LEAVE SOME SPACE FOR JAMMING,
PUKING, FUCKING, N MAKING FUN
OF JD —

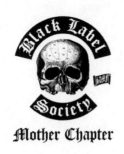

Mother Chapter

ALL SHiTTiNG ASIDE, I HOPE
YOU ENJOY THIS BOOK AS MUCH
AS I ENJOYED WRITING IT.
THE ALMIGHTY BLACK LABEL ARMADA
IS WELL ON ITS WAY TO DOOMTROOPING
WORLDWIDE AND I TAKE PRIDE IN
SAYING THAT EACH AND EVERY ONE OF
THE BLACK LABEL CHAPTERS PLAYED A
BIG ROLE IN ITS SUCCESS. NOW GET TO
READING SO THAT YOU CAN MAKE IT TO
THE PUBS N GET COMPLETELY BERZERKED
IN PURE BLACK MOTHERFUCKING LABEL
FASHION ——

GOD BLESS
STAY STRONG
BLEED BLACK LABEL ——

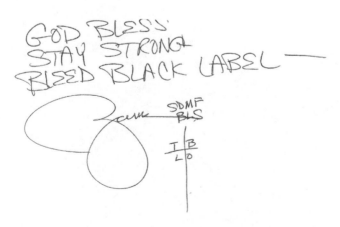

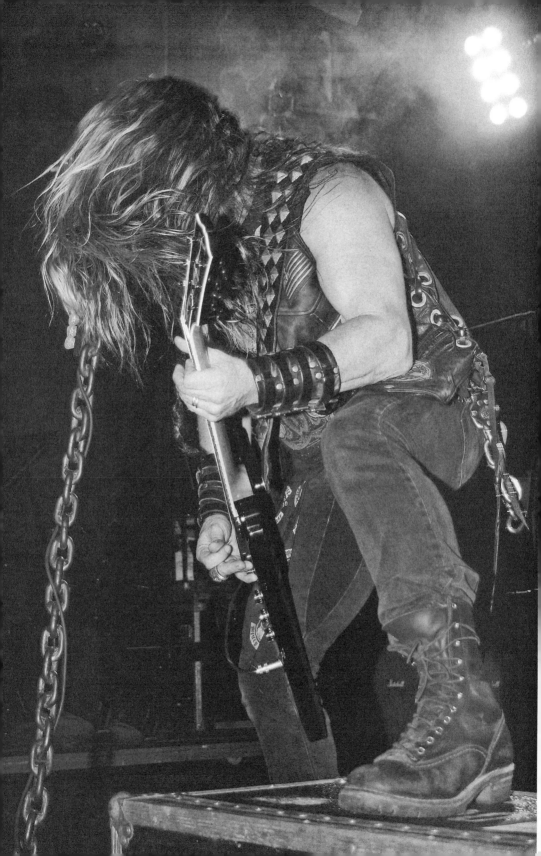

Preface

METAL. DID IT COME FROM THE BOWELS OF THE EARTH FULLY FORMED?
Or was it a gift from the god Odin, handed down from Valhalla,
forged into his son Thor's mighty hammer, known as the Mjöllnir
(a hammer that would one day inspire the title of the telltale book
Hammer of the Gods)? Or was Metal birthed across the ocean by
Led Zeppelin and Black Sabbath and driven across the world on the
iron-horse track they laid for every Metal band to follow?

Because this is my book, I'm going to start where I believe Metal
begins in all of us, and that is the exact spot where your stomach ends
and your bowels begin. That twenty-eight-some-odd feet of smaller
and larger intestines that end at your colon is what I'm referring to
here. I'm sure you are familiar with the phrase *Metal up your ass*. I
stand here before you in true testimony—they weren't kidding.

You go into Metal wanting to be the best musician you can be,
practicing until your fingers bleed and grow calluses, studying the
masters of your newfound craft. You shell out for the best gear your
wallet will allow, and you associate with others in search of that same
holy grail. But beyond that, the rest is one unbelievably rude wake-up
call. Anything that you actually take seriously, that you hold sacred to
your heart, goes straight through your bloated sack and right into the
fuckin' shitter, and your lower intestine actually disembowels itself.
That's when you know you've made it in the world of Metal.

But fear not, my fellow Berzerkers and Berzerkerettes, for you shall receive no such colonic intrusions here. Much like Jesus bore the cross so that all of us wouldn't have to suffer his burden, I've already taken it for the team so that none of you have to endure the monstrous ass-reaming of rock 'n' roll. Well, I haven't taken all of it—you'll get your fill of musical cock and balls. And when you get poked and prodded in all the wrong ways, hopefully, after reading this book, it will be more like Jenna Jameson's pinkie rather than Brock Lesnar's fist. I'm about to share some of my musical conquests and follies and a few words of advice to help shorten that lengthy path of musical doom you are about to embark upon.

There is one thing I want to mention before you embark upon your quest for the holy grail of Metal. And that is the ongoing theme throughout the pages of this book: the numerous degrading, belittling, and morally unpleasant references to one John De-Servio. My comments are obviously not to be taken seriously. JD and I have been best friends since we were kids and I love him like a brother, which is exactly why I like to ridicule him to no end, with as many cheap shots, punches to the rib cage, and insults as I can drop upon his pathetic and fatigued person in my book. And someday when JD gets his own book, which would most likely be titled *How to Ruin Everything*, I would expect nothing less from him than a full-blown, cover-to-cover literary retaliation. Although I know in my heart that pigs will spread wings on the day that JD actually gets a chance to write a book, and his odds of successfully mocking my greatness are even less.

At this time, you might feel inclined to ask me, "Hey, Zakk, where did you learn to become the mighty Berzerker you are today?" Well, I studied in school just like everybody else did. But instead of Berklee College of Music or MIT, I'm a Delta Tau Chi graduate from the University of Ozzy Osbourne. And now I'm working on my PhD in Black Label Global Domination.

Everybody would like to get signed at eighteen years old, sell twenty million fucking records, and throw down for massive crowds at Donington, but that ain't the way it works. This is when fantasy ends and the harshness of Metal reality begins. You know that shitty taste of tinny metal you get in your mouth from some piece-of-shit beer can of whatever the hell you're drinking? That's where it started for me.

Welcome to the Wonderful World of Showbiz

MY MOTHER WAS IN SHOW BUSINESS. SHE USED TO DO CASTING CALLS TO place kids in commercials. You know how the BFGoodrich commercials use little babies to show that *their* tires will keep your kids safe? Stuff like that. She was responsible for many of the Oscar Mayer wiener kids as well. I can still hear the jingle ringing in my head: "Oh I wish I were an Oscar Mayer wiener . . ." Just glad she never placed me as one of the kids desiring to be a wiener—even though since childhood I have thoroughly enjoyed pounding my wiener into submission until I'm legless and in complete vertigo. But she did get me my first gig as a musician.

My cousin Karen, who had been working at the Playboy Mansion in the Pocono Mountains, had brought home this guy named Jerry. I didn't know much about cocaine at the time, because my buddies and I were just into drinking beers and playing music. A few of them might have smoked weed, and I remember one or two of them snorting Freon or some stupid air-conditioning shit like that. Freon and weed were the only drugs I'd ever seen. Obviously I knew what cocaine was, but I was never interested in that shit and even if I was, none of us ever had the money to afford it. So I had never actually seen the abundance of sweat that pours from the body of a true GAC hound—a bona fide fuckin' cokehead.

My mother and father came from the Sinatra generation and my dad was a World War II veteran. The only thing they knew about copping a buzz was drinking highballs, and the stories they'd heard about marijuana were from the Vietnam generation. They knew fucking nothing about drugs.

That said, Karen brought home this drug-riddled motherfucker she had met at the Playboy estate. I've never seen anyone polish off as much booze as this motherfucker! He literally cleaned out the liquor cabinet that was usually reserved for fifty people coming over for the holidays. Later in life I learned that any of my friends who did do cocaine could fuckin' drink until the cows came home and never cop a buzz! They could drink all fuckin' night, drink Jack Daniel out of booze if they had enough cocaine to hold the story—a *Titanic* full of fuckin' whiskey—and not even get the least bit sloppy.

So this cat was telling my folks that he was a producer and about how he was making a record at the time. These were big words flyin' around for my mom, her being in showbiz and having a sixteen-year-old son who played the guitar. Obviously my mom jumped at the opportunity to let him know that her son played the guitar. And he instantly invited me to be on his record.

I had never been in a recording studio before. I had always dreamed about being a professional musician, but I never had a clue how to make that happen. And now my mom had just booked my first gig. I figured this, the recording studio, was where all my dreams were about to come true, where all the "magick" happened, where the Wizard of fuckin' Oz existed, and this Dorothy was on her way to the Emerald City.

Jerry gave me the address and the date and told me to meet him at this place to record some guitar tracks. So me and Barbaranne, now my wife and mother of our three children, made the excursion up north toward the Poconos and ended up getting to this big-ass mansion-type house. I grabbed my amplifier and guitar, we knocked on the door, and it was opened by this guy with his dick hangin' down to his fuckin' knee! He was completely naked, and Barb was standing there staring at this guy's schlong!

"Do you want some of that?" I asked her.

"Yeah," she said, "you go play with your guitar and I'll play with this massive pussy-gaping cock of his." It's moments like these that reassured me of my deep penetrating love for Barbaranne. Good times indeed.

Despite Dirk Diggler and his dangling dong show, we still went into the house, not really knowing what to expect. The next thing you know, we saw people fucking everywhere! It was like we had just walked onto the set of *Caligula*—people were on the floor, on couches, even up on the tables, just fucking everywhere.

We were led into this room where a full-on recording studio had been built. Not only was the studio outfitted with a nice-looking mixing board, but the console came complete with a rock 'n' roll–sized mountain of cocaine piled up at the end of it. It looked as if Scarface was engineering the damn thing on a porn set.

Once again I found myself staring at this fucking cokehound Jerry, still sweating profusely, like he was in the fuckin' Sahara desert or something. Mind you, the air-conditioning was blasting, and to me and Barb it felt like we were in a meat locker, but this guy was still sweating his fucking balls off. That's what happens when you're gacked to the motherfucking gills.

It turned out that the record was for Ginger Lynn, a famous porn star—she was basically the Jenna Jameson of her time. They were trying to have Ginger cross over from porn into music, you know, and have her become the next Madonna. Well there I was, my first "professional" recording session ever (since I got paid for it), and I was knocking out tracks for a porn star's album.

We laugh about that now, and the funniest thing is that my *mother* was the one who sent me, her son, to the gig! I can hear her now, saying shit like, "Oh, my little Jeffrey is making a record! I'm so proud of my Jeffrey . . . ," as she sent her son out on a quest to the land of cock and balls, and pussy and ass and tits—cum and cocaine everywhere. "That's my boy!" Mind you, Barb couldn't walk a straight line for two weeks after that. Once again—good times indeed.

Welcome to the wonderful fucking world of Metal.

> Yay, I'm on my way! I'm gonna make it!
> Congratulations, asshole,
> Zakk

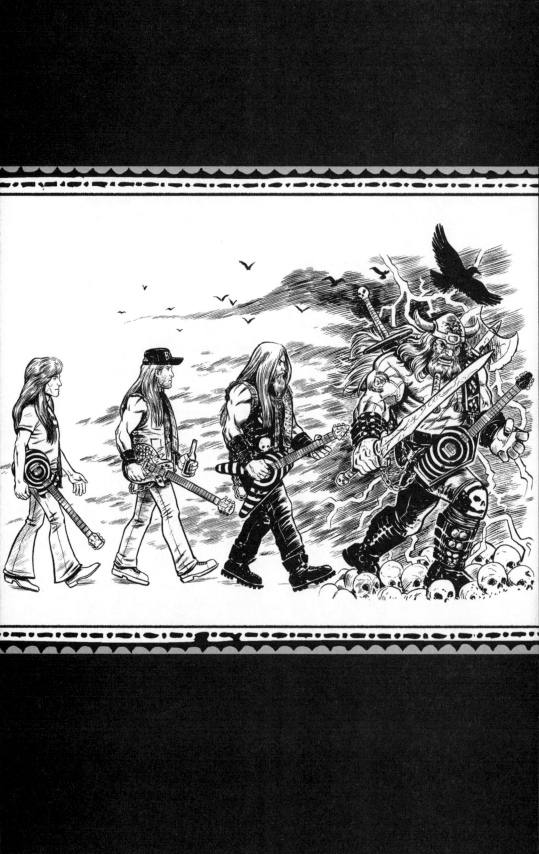

CHAPTER ONE

The Berzerkers of Asgard

To my Brothers and Sisters, Berzerkers and Berzerker-ettes, for the Immortal Beloved sayeth, do we not reside in Asgard?! For the immortal strength of the OdinForce shall carry them to victory and make all of Asgard Proud! And we shall celebrate with drink and feast, another glorious day in our holy lands, brimming with the enlightenment and enchantment of Rock.

And whilst I break away from the highest peaks of Valhalla, where I forge the Metal of the Gods, after once I hammer the Immortal Beloved with mine crotchal Mjöllnir, thou shalt don thine axe and join me in allegiance as we wage war against the enemy that has brought Vaginal countenance to our sacred rites!

So shall I return to Asgard victorious or upon mine own shield. And I shall once again drink from the cup and savor the Nectar of the Gods!!! What sayeth thee, mine battle-ready brethren? Shall we march forth in unison to the measures of the sounding drums? For the quakening of the earth is near upon us, and all shall hail the flags of Asgard! Let us beseech the blessing of almighty God as we begin this great and noble Black Label Crusade!

Zakk, you are so cute when you imagine yourself a Viking.
—BARBARANNE WYLDE

Note from Zakk: Trust me, I don't think I'm a fucking Viking. But the fact that everybody keeps throwing this shit in my face 'cause I've got long hair and a fucking beard—all the while taking the fucking piss out of me—I guess we'll just run with it. With all the little chuckles I hear from you motherfuckers, you guys seem to be enjoying yourselves.

The Berzerkers were the most crazed motherfucking Vikings that ever lived. To give you a little history lesson on these ancient warriors, they fought in a nearly uncontrollable, trancelike fury, much like the Incredible Hulk on a cocktail of steroids and acid. They battled in the name of Odin, chief god of war and ruler of Asgard, one of their mystical Nine Worlds. In battle, many Berzerkers fought bare-chested to prove to the enemy their immunity to iron weapons. And if they had to wear clothes it was surely pelts from bears or wolves. These motherfuckers were fearless and brutal, eating their enemies and toasting with the blood of their foes. On a side note, this kind of behavior also exists in my home. When my wife, Barbaranne, comes at me with an iron weapon, I simply expose my manly chest and she freezes in astonishment. Mind you, it's probably from my sheer patheticness, but she freezes nonetheless.

Going "berserk" back then usually happened during the heat of battle, but the condition could also kick in during heavy labor. Men, who were chosen by the OdinForce to become berserk, were capable of crazy, superhuman feats. The condition would begin with tremors, chattering of the teeth, and finally, a deep chill would set in; then their faces would swell up and turn red with fury. These symptoms of mightiness developed into an all-encompassing rage, under which the Berzerkers would howl like wild animals, bite the edges of their shields, and cut down everything and everyone in their paths with their mighty blades, and without discriminating between friend and foe. It took up to several days for Berzerkers to come down from the adrenaline. These warriors were so infamous that many of the Viking kings chose to use Berzerkers as their personal bodyguards. They were so ferocious and uncontrollable that they were even afraid of themselves. And I'm positive that's why Barb married me. She thinks I'm her personal Viking bodyguard, with some extra benefits, one being my Crotchal Mjöllnir, and she has given it many endearing nicknames—bather of conquest, hole puncher, rod god, labia stretcher . . . you get the idea.

To get ready for battle, the Berzerkers would lose their fucking minds by powering down fistfuls of hallucinogenic mushrooms and buckets of booze spiked with a spice called bog myrtle. This battle brew was known to maximize aggressive behavior but left them with massive hangovers. The Berzerkers also drank wolf's blood, believing that it helped to really kick in the frenzy.

Raging, alcohol-fueled warriors with relentless determination, battling in the name of the Metal god Odin—yeah, that was something our boozed-up, pilled-up brothers and sisters heading out to their children's school PTA meetings could get behind. The Berzerker moniker fuels our pursuit of wreaking havoc across the globe, tearing new assholes, stealing farmers' daughters, and drinking all the towns' whiskey—just to live up to our merciless Viking namesakes.

Note from Zakk: Listen, don't literally go around wreaking havoc, tearing new assholes—as opposed to old assholes—stealing farmers' daughters, or whatever other goofy-ass shit Father Eric is talking about here that might get your ass kicked, killed, or put in jail. Don't listen to Father Eric here. Eric is a fucking idiot, okay?

We love him. But he's an idiot nonetheless. Trust me, he has never done any of the ridiculous bullshit he's talking about here—maybe with his GI Joe doll collection, but that's about it. Why do you think he doesn't have a girlfriend? What chick in her right mind is ever gonna hook up with a guy talking stupid shit like this with a GI Joe doll hanging out of his back pocket? Don't be like Eric. Which literally means: Don't be a fucking idiot.

P.S. Love you, buddy! :)

Bleeding Black Label

JAPAN, 1991: I WAS WITH OZZY FOR THE *No More Tears* TOUR. ONE insane night, while firing off some really heavy riffs next to the Boss, I swear Odin came straight down from Valhalla and shot a fucking lightning bolt right up my ass. It was either that or I got shocked by my own gear, and since this is my book I'm going with the Viking story. I mean really, for all you know I could have been zapped backstage in the dressing room while plugging in my makeup kit to apply some rouge before the show. Just pay attention, I'm only five sentences into my book and we're all over the fuckin' map with it already.

There I was onstage, pummeling through these heavy fucking jams with Oz and the guys, getting zapped in the rectum, and then the vision came to me. All of a sudden I saw the crowd not as what they were but as what they would become—a legion of Berzerkers, or as my manager would prefer to call them, "cash crops with legs." And as Ozzy and I continued blasting out songs from *No Rest for the Wicked, No More Tears*, and some of the works of genius that Lord Iommi, Saint Rhoads, and Father Lee blessed us with, I could not stop these *electrified* visions. And neither could my manager, as he was already making phone calls to place a down payment on a new mansion in Malibu. One second I was looking at a row of cheerful fans, singing along to these musical masterpieces of doom and head-banging to the complete Armageddon of Metal, the next second I was looking on as my manager placed his order for a new Maserati, loaded to the hilt with all the options. The audience looked like a horde of battle-ready Vikings awaiting the command to attack. As I was cranking the shit out of my Marshall wall of doom I could see on the horizon the day of the Berzerker Nation. That was the first night I was drawn into the OdinForce and the first night my manager was drawn into the nearest Prudential real estate brokerage. It also dawned on me during this pinnacle moment of genius that not only do cowboys like Jon Bon Jovi come from New Jersey, but *Vikings* are from New Jersey as well—along with a high teen pregnancy rate and an even higher involvement with alcohol and getting high by inhaling Freon.

The further we got into our show, the more I could see the Berzerker Metal madness grow, as well as the sheer enlightenment and joy on my accountant and manager's faces, not so much over the mountains of Valhalla, but over the mountains of potential earnings and 401(k) contributions, as they envisioned paychecks that dwarfed anything they had conceived of. The thought of the piles upon piles of dollars upon dollars set their eyes gleaming like the stars on Orion's Belt. I was literally blinded by their money-grubbing glares, and the audience was illuminated by the intensity. Each and every fan had an inner warrior, armed and ready to explode into a frenzy of rock 'n' roll–infused destruction and debauchery. Wait . . . Is this a rock show I'm talking about or the Festivus miracle going on inside my wife Barbaranne's babymaker? It wasn't about me, it was about bringing all Metal fans into one family, one horde, one society, and one womb. All of us joining forces against the world in hopes of keeping JD out of the unemployment line—a line in which he has spent most of his adult life.

And so began the almighty Black Label Society.

And much like Jimmy Page was called upon by the spirit of

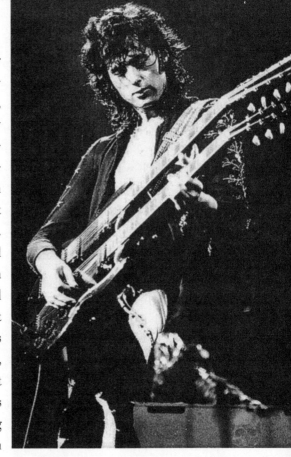

the dark poet Aleister Crowley to lead mass services in the name of Rock, I was called upon by my boss, the produce manager of Fine Fair, to restock the Granny Smith apples before I clocked out for my ten-minute break. Jimmy is a living god, and much more than *just* a guitar player. He conjured his art on the guitar, but he also took the lead as a songwriter, producer, mixing engineer, and art director—his band was his baby, his calling. Playing in the Yardbirds put him on the map, but it didn't sum him up as an artist. Jimmy wandered deep into the forest of dark souls to master his craft and create the heart that would one day beat in the name of Led Zeppelin. His journey was otherworldly. Unlike my journey, from the stockroom to the produce aisles. From Pope Page's conversations with Crowley in the netherworld, he gathered the ingredients he needed to brew the mind-altering compositions that live on today. And from my direct order from the produce manager, I gathered the freshest and greenest Granny Smith apples I could obtain from the produce gods in the back of the store.

Note from Zakk: Again . . . "Forest of dark souls"? "Netherworld"? I have no fuckin' idea what the fuck Eric is writing about here. Gimme a fucking break—the guy just loved music. We'll let Father

Eric run with his illustrious bullshit though, since he is a Black Label brother—and I use the term *brother* in the loosest way. I do, however, still enjoy a fine Granny Smith apple from time to time. Try them with caramel, kids, and if you want to really live on the edge, combine it with peanuts—its netherworldly.

Page formed his band, a concept far greater than himself, and they circled the earth, converting ordinary masses to his rock 'n' roll religion. And let me tell you, it's quite the religion—what the fuck this religion advocates is completely wacked. I'll just say this—morals and overall cleanliness don't rank too high in this religion. Anyway, moving on . . . So this is what the Nordic gods intended for the Berzerkers and what one cattle-prodding deity beckoned for me to create . . . one global nation of merciless motherfuckers intact with all the insanity and comedy one could possibly hope for.

The Berzerker Empire was founded upon the most important elements of life: God, family, music, and fearless drinking—unlike my manager, whose foundation is Satan, selfishness, dead silence, number crunching, and the utter fear of ending up spiritually broken and penniless. Hold on a second, my manager has no fucking spirit. In fact, he's completely soulless when it comes to pillaging the pockets, wallets, and purses of anyone he comes in contact with. And that, kids, is exactly why I hired him. It didn't take long for the concept to progress, for the good word to spread, and for people to gather. Although the foundations of Black Label are expressed in the music, the message is much deeper than drinking and listening to epic tunes. It is greater than the band and the show. It is a family, a brotherhood, a unity, a mind-set, and a way of life. And as long as the money keeps rolling in, management, record companies, and whoever else is on the Black Label payroll will let me believe whatever bullshit BLS represents to me in all that is sacred and holy.

We live by a creed—Strength, Determination, Merciless, Forever. Our code, honest and meaningful, is rooted more than a thousand years deep. That is, unless you go by my manager's timeline, because then it goes back to the first time someone discovered that they could pawn some useless horseshit off on some dumb motherfucker and come out on top. Just like the minute the Indians started selling fuckin' pelts, it was *game fuckin' on*. Getting back to our Viking ancestors, among whom physical, mental, and spiritual strength ruled all and each individual was part of an indestructible fortress. We are relentless in our pursuit, merciless in our behavior, eternal in our hearts. And with the gods of Valhalla watching over our Order, and my manager, wife, accountant, and team of lawyers watching over my expenditures, we stride forward on our path of global domination, spreading the word to the masses at our nightly Black Label church services. Our venue is our electrified cathedral, our music is our sermon, and all who attend are our family. And if you happen to spot a truly shady-looking character passing around the collections basket during our Black Label masses, that would be my manager, lining his fucking pockets with silver and gold to keep up his fleet of Mercedes and to complete construction of a fully equipped wet bar near his heated outdoor pool in Malibu.

SDMF: Strength, Determination, Merciless, Forever

(UNLIKE JD's MOTTO: WEAKNESS, AMBITIONLESS, HEARTLESS, SHORT-lived.)

I placed this motto on a crucifix, just like INRI, which is often on crucifixes but means "Jesus of Nazareth, King of the Jews." And when you see me play, you might notice that I do the sign of the cross twice, once for the Father, Son, and Holy Spirit, and then again for Strength, Determination, Merciless, Forever. While I'm onstage counting my blessings and thanking the good Lord for the strength he gives me and my Black Label family to continue following our passions, my manager is counting his blessings as well—eight homes, sixteen cars, lucrative offshore investments, and a time-share in Aspen, Colorado. God bless him.

Strength has always been my foundation—physically, mentally, and spiritually—that and the short string of belief that I cling to each day, the hope that my wife and children actually care about me. I began my strength-building routine after the first time my wife beat me up and embarrassed me in front of our children and I finally decided it was time for me to giddyup. Every morning after powering down my Valhalla java I head into my gym, the Doom Crew Iron Dungeon, and throw around some chunks of iron. I even bring a weight set with me when we're out on deployment so I can get in a good pump each day before we hit the stage. I also like to get in a good pump with my wife, or if she's not havin' it, with my right hand.

Although I do all sorts of exercises in the gym, squats are my favorite. Just that repetitive motion of grinding up and down, lunging and throbbing, sweating and clenching, greasing and buttering, gripping and stretching, gaping and . . . Oh wait, time out. What the fuck happened? Where am I? Oh yeah, I drifted back into the music business again, where greasing, buttering, ass-gaping, and backstabbing are bodily functions like pissing and shitting.

Aside from the heavy-hitting squats, I also follow a strong regimented workout that I designed over the years and that works well for me. It's basically the same as the routine of most power lifters and bodybuilding champions, except for the results. Then I drop in an hour and a half of cardio daily, whether it's on the treadmill or while blasting through a Black Label set onstage. I also have a high-protein diet, taking in up to three hundred grams of protein a day, depending on how many grams of protein I dumped on the Warden that morning, or again, if she wasn't havin' it, how many loads I splattered on the bathroom stall down at the venue. Replenishing my loads of doom is really easy, being that I'm in the music business. There is no shortage of motherfuckers I gotta suck off in order to keep the almighty Black Label Armada rolling. With the amount of music biz cock-gobbling I've gotta perform, between my manager, agents, band salaries, per diems, bus drivers, truck drivers, my wife's personal trainer (who I'm sure she's been fucking while I'm out here killing myself, bleeding Black fuckin' Label every waking second . . . mind you, I couldn't really give a shit as long as she's got a smile on her face; you know how it goes—the girls don't like to be disappointed!), the bright side is that my vocal cords are eternally lubed. Gotta stay positive! Fuck it—Merciless. (What that means, we'll get to soon enough.)

I don't do steroids, but I should. Then I'd have an excuse for all the pissy fits, road rages, tantrums, outbursts, yelling at my wife, then forgiveness flowers, screaming at my children, then forgiveness allowances—not to mention all the douchebag lead-singer shit I pull on the guys in the band. That said, I think it's fucking hilarious when people say that I'm on the juice. They see a picture of me at 249 pounds and a shot of me when I was eighteen years old at 140 pounds, and they assume it all happened overnight after a magical injection straight out of Barry Bonds's medicine cabinet. But if I did use steroids I wouldn't need Barry. I'd have my own team of shady gym owners and back-door physicians who would supply me with a black-market *Titanic*-load of growth hormones, Dianabol and Winstrol—enough to have any pancreas, liver, or pair of kidneys screaming for mercy.

They don't think of the twenty-plus years in between 1987 Zakk and 2011 Zakk where I was training all the time and eating healthy (though drinking professionally). The only supplements I take are protein shakes and vitamins. I don't bother with anything else. With the blood-thinning medication I'm on these days to avoid blood clots, I don't know how certain supplements will react. I'm no fuckin' nuclear physicist, but I do play one on television. And what if I do take creatine and it doesn't mix well with the shit I have to take for my blood, and I fucking croak in my sleep? I'll tell you what would happen. It would set off a nuclear chain reaction of money-hungry scavengers hoping to squeeze any remaining drops of blood from my deteriorating corpse.

I can picture it now—Barbaranne, management, and the accountants would all meet at Spago in Beverly Hills for a nice lunch and to begin planning how they are going to repackage all of the Black Label Society catalog and also release every fucking recording I've ever made, in a studio or on a cassette tape, and then probably even try to release some shit that I had nothing to do with. Back-alley meetings would take place with a black-market taxidermist to have me stuffed and preserved so that they could prop me up and continue selling meet-and-greet packages to the Black Label family. Barbaranne would sell the compound and run off with a failed NBA player. At seven foot two, with a relentlessly hammering, pounding cock of doom, and the life insurance money, and whatever Black Label shit the wife and management can pawn off, his basketball skills really won't fucking matter at that juncture, nor what college he claims to have graduated from.

Next my manager would place an order for his own corporate jet, and it would be one big party for all. I guess everything is fair game once I'm up in God's tavern with the rest of our fallen saints. But seriously, as I sit here writing, there is a vulture sitting impatiently on the back of my chair staring down at me like I'm a giant fleshy sack of cash, its insatiable drool spilling over the pages of my manuscript, just waiting to get the proceeds from this book and every other motherfucking thing I've ever done. Anyway, about the steroids, fuck all that noise. The last time I checked, I'm doing just fine by lifting weights and eating clean proteins.

Besides being physically fit, you've also got to keep your mind strong. If you don't believe in what you're doing, no one else is going to. That's why I have to believe Barbaranne when she tells me that she's not cheating on me and that our three children are really ours. Mind you, we didn't have sex during the two years prior to our youngest being born, but Barb told me that Immaculate Conception is a real and common occurrence. Lucky for her I'm a devout Catholic and not a devout atheist. Otherwise, I'd ask her if she filmed herself fucking the other guy so I can at least jerk off to this shit. Once again—gotta stay positive, kids.

And having religion won't hurt either. There are so many choices out there, it can't hurt to pick one of the nicer ones and run with it. Being a soldier of Christ, I believe in Jesus and everything he represents. Having compassion for others, giving to those who are less fortunate, protecting the innocent, empowering others as opposed to enslaving, making sacrifices for the benefit of others, and bringing someone other than yourself happiness. And through Jesus, the crucifix represents unconquerable and everlasting strength, sacrifice, blood, commitment, and faith in all that is good. Then I just ask the good Lord, why have you put JDesus in my life? Why? Why, beloved Father? Why?

Now, if your religious leader tells you to go out and murder a bunch of innocent people because they think the Stones are better than the Beatles, or that Lady Gaga can bench-press more than Madonna could when she was the same age—try to stay away from this religion. As history has shown, in the poker game of life, when you try to explain to a judge that your religious leader told you to murder innocent people over a Stones vs. Beatles debate, you will usually find that the law carries a royal flush over your religious leader. If you need any proof, ask the Manson girls—as their long-awaited album and tour has been pushed back so many times at each passing year's parole meeting. It makes Geffen Records look like they got off easy with *Chinese Democracy*.

The next religion I would try to persuade you to stay away from would be the one where the religious leader tells everybody that a meteor is coming to take us all away. But before we jump on board the meteor to go to the promised land where the McDonald's two-for-one is eternally on, we each have to put a Hefty bag over our head and seal it around our neck, suffocating us, while we slice off our fucking genitals! Now, this religion and religious leader can put a goliath fucking damper on all of your rock 'n' roll dreams. For not just one but four terrible reasons:

1. Putting a Hefty bag over your head to snuff the life out of you is bad.
2. What happens if your favorite football team is making a push for the play-offs after several bad seasons?
3. You find out that Carvel ice cream is reintroducing the legendary ice cream cake that is Cookie Puss.
4. Your wife tells you she wants to do the threesome with her girlfriend who you think is slammin'.

Well, guess what? Forget your football team holding up the Lombardi trophy. Forget having that crazy birthday party with all of your friends while enjoying Cookie Puss. And definitely forget about throwing back some Viagra and pounding and dominating the living shit out of your slammin' wife and her hot girlfriend. You ain't got no cock and balls, you dumb motherfucker! Oh, and another thing, Einstein—you're fucking dead.

In the end, find a religion that enriches your life and the lives of others and try to avoid religious leaders who land you in jail for thirty years to life. It is also advisable to keep sharp objects away from your genitals—they don't like that.

Determination only comes with you straight out of the womb. You can't learn determination. You either have it or you don't. That's why as hard as I try to beat it senselessly into JD's body, I'll never be successful. His body is already full, but with holes and emptiness that befuddle all laws of physics. Just like you can't fill a colander with water, you also can't fill JD's body with an ounce of determination. Whereas the Black Label creed is stronger than death, JD's is *weaker than life*. His heartless, soulless, lifeless, and friendless existence is an astonishing anomaly that will always amaze me.

That being said, the two most determined guys on the planet I've ever known are my father and Ozzy. These are two guys who lead by example and who've been there, done that. They had their asses handed to them repeatedly and never played the role of a victim. Instead, they said, "Fuck this," and never stopped pushing forward. If I ever needed advice in my life I could always look up to Dad or Oz—and that advice would always be, "Start drinking heavily until the pain subsides, only to awaken sober, realizing that you're in a rock band with a wife and three children who you need to provide for. Then keep drinking, trying not to remind yourself how much your wife and children are going to cost you, continually asking yourself why you couldn't have taken up another hobby, such as basket-weaving or crochet."

You think I'm fucking kidding? That's what they both actually told me. After that, they asked me to lean a little closer toward them, and then poked me in the fucking eye. Blinded and confused, I asked my wise elders, as they stood there laughing at my misfortune, "Why did you do that?" And they answered, "We're not really sure either. It fuckin' hurts though, doesn't it?"

I started listening to Ozzy's music when I was twelve years old. If I had a crappy day at school or whatever, I could get off the school bus, go home, and listen to Sabbath albums, and it would just lift my spirit. Then I would come crashing back down to earth when I realized I was actually forty-four years old and still living at home with my mommy and dada, plus the rude awakening that my allowance hadn't gone up since I was twenty-eight. So Ozzy's actually been a part of my life the whole time, far before we ever met or started jamming together.

I've seen it a thousand times in my life: The musicians who were determined and had faith became successful, and those who were only looking for a paycheck are no longer around. When I actually auditioned for Ozzy, back when I was nineteen years old, some of the other guys trying out were a lot older than me. They were waiting their turn, saying, "I hear the gig pays pretty well . . . ," and shit like that. That was the whole motivation for their being there. I would have taken the gig with no pay. I had shrines back home dedicated to Ozzy, Randy, and Black Sabbath. So when I realized that a slew of guys were there looking only for a payday, my attitude changed from nervous to "Fuck those guys, I'm going to get this gig!"

The first time I ever sat down with Ozzy he set me at ease. He said, "Zakk, just play with your heart, man, that's all I want you to do." His next piece of advice was for me to go into the kitchen and make him a ham sandwich. "And don't fuck it up by going in heavy with the mustard," he counseled me. I took his musical words of wisdom, and his instructions for the perfect lunch, to heart. With these treasures and my love of the music, I landed a gig that changed my life forever.

Determination: You can't manufacture that shit, it's gotta come from the heart. A lion doesn't choose to be a lion, that's just what he is. He knows what's expected of him, and he gets it fuckin' done. Kind of like JD—we expect nothing from him and that's exactly what we get.

Merciless—to me *Merciless* means to be relentless in your pursuit, whether it's for the love of your wife and kids, or for your passions and goals. You never give up on what's important to you. If you want your band to be successful, or if you want to open the best fucking ham sandwich deli in town, you need to be Merciless in that quest. Just make sure you don't *go in heavy* with the mustard—words of wisdom from the Sandwich Tao of Oz.

Black Label Society is going to continue to make records and will never stop kicking ass and tearing across the globe like a nuclear assault vehicle . . . Fuck it—MERCILESS!

If I have to light myself on fire and eat my own shit onstage to outdo the other bands . . . Fuck it—MERCILESS!

If I have to get one more sex change after the three I've already undergone to keep selling Black Label records . . . Fuck it—MERCILESS!

If I gotta hang a forty-pound plate from my labia majora to impress some record company executive, if that's what it takes to keep moving the Black Label Armada forward . . . Fuck it—MERCILESS!

If while doing those special engagement Black Label family meet-and-greets I have to rub all my fans' shoulders and then finish them off with a happy ending . . . Fuck it—MERCILESS! (Remember—it keeps the vocal cords lubed anyway! Stay positive!)

On my first date with my wife, Barbaranne, the two of us went to see the movie *Urban Cowboy*. I tried going up her shirt several times and got shut down. But I continued my relentless pursuit of fondling those luscious melons and today we have three children . . . Fuck it—MERCILESS!

Forever—We always say that Black Label is beyond forever. No one has ever been fired from or quit Black Label. Once you're in, the door is always open. Long after I settle in for my dirt nap and I'm hangin' up in God's tavern, people will be listening to Black Label Society, wearing the colors and raising their glasses in the name of kick-ass music—some may argue that it would have to be no music that I've ever been part of.

That's the true essence of Black Label Society and its creed, SDMF. The creed is our foundation, and from that place of strength, the concepts continue to grow and develop. And with all of us fuckin' idiots involved, it can also be interpreted as Stupid Dumb Mother Fucker—you included.

The Three Black Label R's: Revenge, Retaliation, Redemption

FACE YOUR FEAR, ACCEPT YOUR WAR, IT IS WHAT IT IS. . .

Being a Berzerker and part of the Black Label Society is also about accepting the responsibility of the Three Black Label R's:

Revenge—The idea is that you are taking revenge upon your failures through your own achievements. You're not going around beating anyone's ass or being a dick because you're pissed off that you're not succeeding at life—I do that. Remember, I'm the lead singer fronting this two-bit fucking operation.

Nobody can *make* you fail; they can create more obstacles and force you to have to be more resourceful, but that just means you have to keep working it. Bottom line is that if you fail at something, if you get knocked down, then you gotta get the fuck back up and any desire for vengeance you feel has to be channeled through yourself into productive energy. Look at me; even with all the times I got shot down by Barbaranne I was still able to plow her sugar walls, dominate her baby maker, and bathe her in conquest enough times to kick out three children.

Retaliation—Revenge is the energy and retaliation is the set of actions you take to exact that revenge. Again, always retaliate upon yourself, because you are the only one who can carry out the steps toward your goals. Lawsuits and jail are no fun.

Redemption—Once you've sought revenge and followed through with your plan of retaliation, then you get to take home the prize, the redemption. You have succeeded; you've challenged yourself and come through on the other side. Face your fear and accept your war. It is what it is. And after all, life is a test and life is tough—let's see how motherfucking tough you really are. Remember, nothing stuffs a behemoth brass-knuckled fist up your detractor's ass more than when you succeed.

I should actually add a fourth Black Label R: **Remove**—as in please remove JD from my life. Yep. Now there are four. Moving on.

We pray for war and we pray for adversity, because we bleed for a challenge—something that's bigger than us. You can either get discouraged and crawl into a corner and cry about it, or you can come out dick fuckin' swinging. That goes for the ladies as well. Yeah. You heard me right. Around this camp, it's not out of the ordinary to have a few of them motherfuckers rolling around—a nice round apple-bottom power-ass of doom—only to turn around swinging a cock bigger than the migraine I get from hanging out with JD.

Remember, life's a mountain and we're either going over it, going around it, going through it, or completely dismantling it.

Final score: Mountain—0, Black Label Order—1.

Flying the Colors

Now, you've heard stuff like "These colors don't touch the ground," like with the American flag and other patriotic or revered

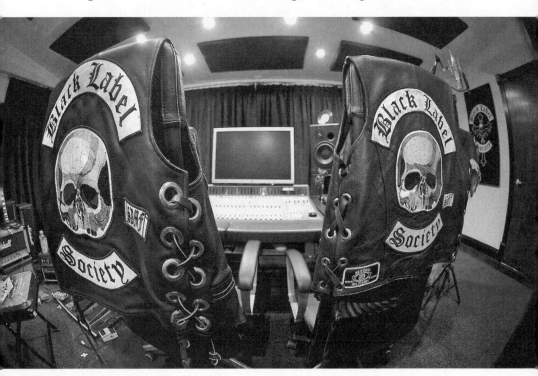

symbols. Well with Black Label, our colors do touch the ground. Sometimes it feels like they've been pounded into the ground and then shit on, but they *always* get back up again. The Black Label colors themselves represent family and unity. I've always referred to our fans as our *fams*. That's what Black Label is, one gigantic extended family—something bigger than yourself and bigger than a band.

Back Patches—The original BLS patch set started with a bowling ball and pins to represent all of the shenanigans and the true concept of Black Label—

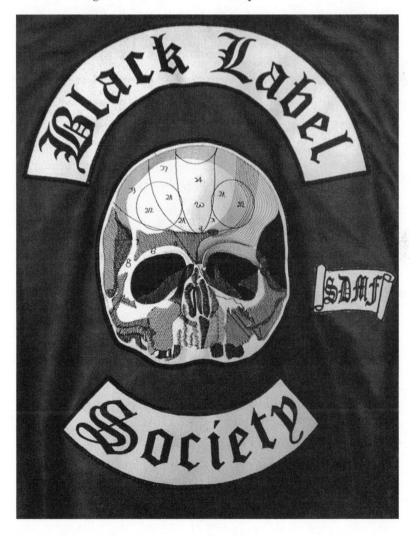

that of a secret Illuminati bowling society. We had the bowling ball and pins in the center, and then "Black Label" across the top and "Society" below. As the concept grew, more patches were added to the front of the vests. Eventually we came up with a few different back patches as well. Each patch reinforces a different virtue of the Berzerker.

Skully—I chose Skully from an old medical manual, mostly because he looks like my favorite actress and the most handsome woman in show business—Bea Arthur. She ran the *Golden Girls* ship with an iron fist. There are numbers and locations on different areas of Skully. And the joke in our band has always been that the locations are the parts of your brain that are affected by booze, weed, painkillers, and stuff like that—not that we take any of that shit. One time someone in the Doom Crew suggested that the two circles and shaft near the top of the head look like a set of cock 'n' balls on Skully's forehead. And it's ironic, because JD often accuses us of tea-bagging him while he's sleeping on the bus. The problem is that his only proof is having a forehead that smells like an unwashed nut sac—that could come from anywhere. Between all the cock pumps (which you'll be hearing about later) and all the jerkin' off and porn that goes on in this outfit, I guess we really do have cock 'n' balls on the brain!

If you take a look at the lyrics in the song "Berzerkers" (*Drinking, puking, pissing, and fighting—Starting all over again*), that's the way the guys live. With the amount of pain pills going down, the amount of booze, and God only knows what else flyin' around, things get a little crazy. But in the end, no matter how banged up you get, you gotta answer the bell the next day. That's how the acronym *GIFD* was born.

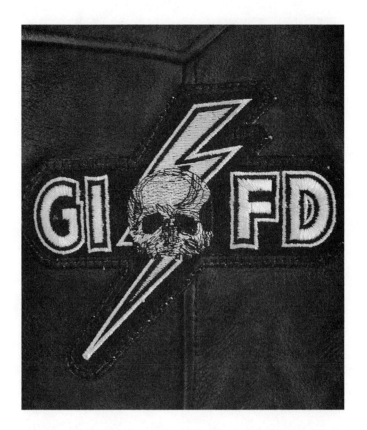

GIFD—Get It Fucking Done. Elvis coined the acronym *TCB*, "Taking Care of Business." He had the lightning bolt going through the TCB. We added the lightning bolt going through Skully on the GIFD patch, in the spirit of the King and out of respect for the Memphis Mafia. It's a way to pay homage to Elvis's work ethic and his relentlessness in keeping his operation moving forward. No matter what obstacles he faced, how many zeppelins jam-packed with narcotics flew into Graceland, how many televisions he shot, or how many late-night fried peanut-butter-and-banana sandwiches he devoured, the King was pure Black Label, always *getting it fuckin' done.*

Chapters—The chapter patches identify where each Berzerker lives. Mine says "Los Angeles Chapter." JD is

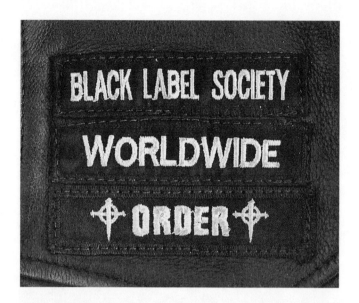

in the Jersey chapter. Nick is in the Pittsburgh chapter—
you get the picture. The idea is that a couple of guys
from the same chapter can meet up, start a bowling
team, come up with a cure for children's cancer, end
up millionaires, and bring joy to countless families
across the globe. Or you can end up just like JD and his
chapter—shoot heroin, share dirty needles, and bitch
and moan that you all got nothin' except that you're
in the same chapter and you now have the same blood
type.

Berzerker Casket—Once you're
a Berzerker, you're a lifer, as long as
you're bleedin' it and you're committed. That's the mentality you live with,
living life full-bore, stronger than
death (or as I mentioned earlier in
JD's case, weaker than life—God bless
the Mongoose)—a term of endearment
we have long since bestowed upon the
little fella. You're a Berzerker long after

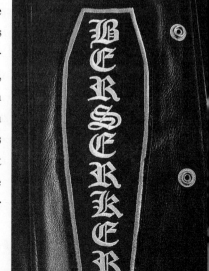

they shovel the dirt on top of you and that's the reason we have the word on a fuckin' coffin.

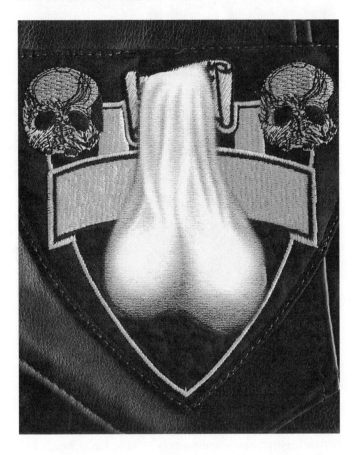

Silhouette of My Testicles on a Shield–This is not a patch on the vest at all, it's a silhouette of my nut sac. I tried to get this particular image printed with a scratch 'n' sniff effect, but we were unable to reproduce the correct scent, so you'll have to use your imagination or just sniff your own nut sac. We were originally going to use this design for our crest shield patch, but after a band vote, the idea was completely shut down.

BLS Crest Shield–The shield of strength represents family heritage. In the Black Label family crest you'll

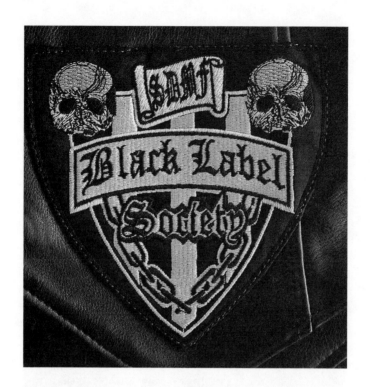

see everything that Black Label is: the unbreakable chains to represent determination and faith; *SDMF* between the two images of Skully, which represent strength in numbers; and the black and white colors illustrating that there are no gray issues. There's only yes and no, right and wrong, as in *"Yes,* Barb, I would love a blow job this morning," and *"Right,* I haven't bathed since the deployment of our tour over six weeks ago."

When you're on tour, your goal is to get yourself from point A (your hotel room) to point B (the rock show that night). Everything in between is the gray area that nobody gives a fuck about. You get a flat tire on the way to the gig, you stop by the liquor store and get shot at, and your dog eats your fucking homework. Nobody wants to hear about all that stuff. Just get it fuckin' done. Get yourself from point A to point B and handle your business. Black and white.

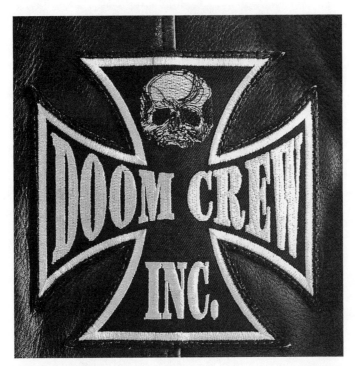

Doom Crew Iron Cross–The Doom Crew patch honors the hardworking crew involved in keeping the Black Label Armada rolling.

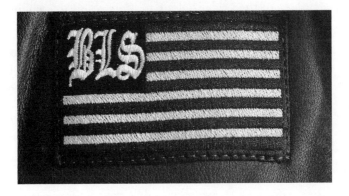

BLS Nation Flag–Represents the BLS Nation and everyone that belongs to it, including all you Society-Dwelling Mother Fuckers!

The Black Label Order–The Order is a lot like the Illuminati–it's a secret religious order with its

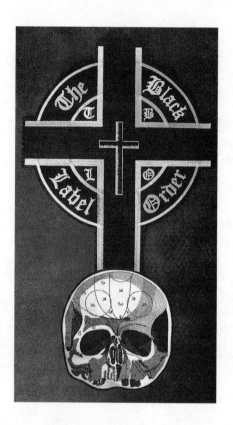

foundations deeply embedded in the Black Label code. Members of the Order belong to their respective chapters worldwide, signified by the crucifix and the unbreakable circle that supports the cross standing in front of it. As the circle represents everlasting faith and commitment, the crucifix represents unconquerable strength, blood, and sacrifice. Skully is at the bottom, representing the foundation and the true secrets of the almighty Black Label Order.

Basically, it's so secret that we don't even know who we are. Truth be told, only Bea Arthur from *The Golden Girls* knew our most sacred and core secrets. And if you go back and watch some of those old episodes you can clearly see Saint Bea blinking and signaling codes that will reveal the truth of the Order.

All of the symbols and acronyms that make up the colors stand for something meaningful to me and all those who wear them. They represent a philosophy on how to approach life, with the music of Black Label providing the enchanting hymns and melodious anthems for those within the Almighty Order.

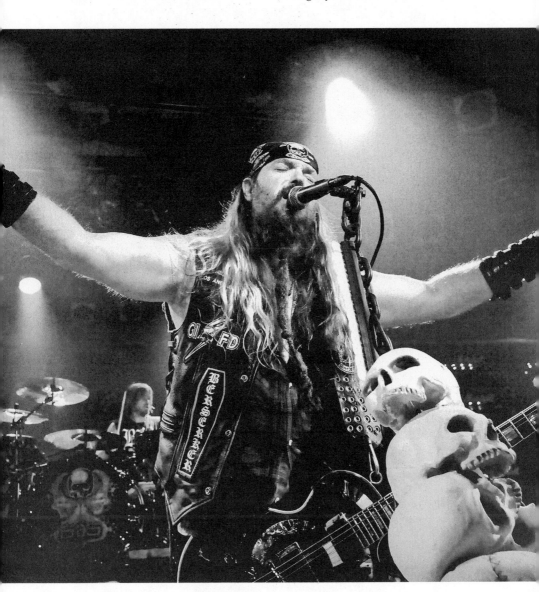

In Witness of Unity

BY ERIC HENDRIKX

SAN BERNARDINO, 2002: THE BLACK LABEL SOCIETY TOUR bus rolled up to the Blockbuster Pavilion. Within a few hours of their arrival every single ticket holder at the venue was made aware of their presence.

Sirens pierced through the scorching desert air, instantly setting the tone to one of terror and aggression. It was a warning signal identical to the alarm for incoming air raids heard during the kamikaze attacks on Pearl Harbor. The alarms clutched the attention of every society dweller within their reach. But this time, the alarms were not sounded to warn people that their lives were in danger. Instead they were fired up from the Ozzfest main stage to alert fifty thousand crazy motherfuckers that Black Label Society was about to pummel their eardrums with the Metal sounds of Valhalla. The crowd gathered below the stage with fists and devil horns raised by the thousands in anticipation of the fury about to be unleashed.

And then it began.

Draped in denim, leather, and unbreakable chains, the Viking Zakk Wylde, graduate of Jackson Memorial High School in New Jersey, class of 1985, marched to the center of the stage, raising his battle-axe of choice above his head for all to behold, a Bullseye Les Paul guitar. His heavy brow and jaw, Hessian hair (which was washed and double conditioned using Gee, Your Hair Smells Terrific), and paralyzing stare into the eyes of his audience were all testimony to his uncontested command. And while the alarms continued to rupture the air, his band commenced with the pounding of thunderous drums and bass. Taunting guitar harmonies bled through stacks of Marshall cabinets as Wylde and his evil twin guitarist Nick Catanese cranked their Marshalls up and stroked their first chords.

"How many of you motherfuckers believe in rock 'n' fuckin' roll?"

The San Bernardino Berzerkers roared as Zakk yelled back, "So do I! And that's why I still live at home with my mommy and dada, and occasionally sleep on the floor of my buddy Andy's van—down by the river!"

The crowd roared like a pride of lions as the band tore into what sounded like war between the gods of Olympus and Titans of Tartarus.

The mosh pit beneath the stage flowed with reckless abandon. Berzerkers who populated the circling masses of Metalheads had donned the same attire as the band. Their black leather and denim, with *BLS* emblazoned upon their clothing in Old English lettering, was testimony to their loyalty to the Metal giants before them. Just then, Black Label manager Bob Ringe whipped out his trusty calculator and started counting heads among the sea of Black Label T-shirts, headbands, and vests—and started to beam with sheer unbridled enthusiasm, knowing he was that much closer to purchasing a forty-thousand-square-foot home sitting atop beachfront property in Malibu.

The band began doom-trooping into "Battering Ram," "Graveyard Disciples," "Bleed For Me"—as each song merged into the next, Wylde challenged the Black Label family to raise the bar and bleed even more. Mosh pits formed by the crowds throughout the modern Colosseum. "13 Years of Grief," "Demise of Sanity"—the open lawn of the venue looked like a dusty swarm of locusts where hordes of moshers circled to the hostile rhythms of the music.

Wylde's fixation was unbreakable as he ripped through guitar solos with precision and speed. One hand continued to play while the other worked to empty a can of beer down his throat, foaming down his long beard, all over his clothing, before he crushed the can into his forehead and chucked it into the crowd. His voice could be heard for miles as he delivered line after line of his lyrics through the main stage's PA system.

Leading in with his wicked bass line, Trujillo fired up the anthem of the Berzerkers as Wylde pierced the ear canals of his listeners, screaming, "Let me hear you, motherfuckers!" and then went into the final jam before hurling his guitar into the sky, allowing its inevitable crash into the stage floor. Feedback and resonance struck listeners as the band took its exit.

And as I wiped the dirty sweat and blood from my eyes and brow, I gazed around at the rest of the moshers in the pit with whom I'd shared the last forty-five minutes of physical chaos, forever bonding with those who also beamed with pride and sonic satisfaction. My colors were soaked with the sweat and blood of hundreds of other diehards who had joined in the success of what just took place. We looked like we had emerged from the trenches of a desert war, having just survived a fury of colliding bodies and flailing limbs, animated by the sounds of Black Label Society. Our union was much more than that of ordinary fans. We were Berzerkers.

Note from Zakk: By the way, this bullshit about me throwing my fucking guitar in the air and it coming crashing down is an utter load of garbage . . . never fucking happened. Like the majority of this waxed-poetic load of bullshit—"emerged from the trenches of a desert war"? Here's my question: When was the last fucking time Eric got laid? And did he write this crap in between playing with his Star Wars dolls or whatever make-believe shit he comes up with when he's all by himself? One word: wow.

World Tour Survival Technique: Play What You Love and What Moves You

It's safe to say that a large number of you Berzerkers are not only interested in learning about my majestic world of Metal, you are also interested in carving a slice of this musical beast for yourself. That is to say, you play guitar or another instrument of rock, and you plan to attempt some global domination of your own. My first words of advice for you are: Don't Do It, Save Yourself, Run for Your Life, Turn in Your Badge, Sell the Farm, Run and Pray! That's what I opted to do when I realized that I would be surrounded by JDesus and his odor for the rest of my life—but to no avail, as his stench still permeates the buses, hotel rooms, and stages wherever I go. However, if you decide to travel down the same imminent Road of Doom that I have, a road of countless back-door reamings, sleepless delirium, and tour buses that smell like prison ass, then I have a few pointers to help you out along the way.

People always ask me, "Hey, Zakk, got any advice for me or my kid about starting a band?"

Yeah, here's some advice—play what you love and what moves you. The running joke, I always say, when me and the rest of my Black Label brethren have driven thirty hours, crossed the sea in a ferry for another seven hours, and arrived in some rat-and-piss-infected shithole, is you better love the music, 'cause sometimes the music doesn't love you.

But getting back to playing what you love and what moves you—it sounds easy, right? Well it ain't.

I knew a guy, a friend of mine, who would basically change his image more often than I change the blades in the razor to shave my wife's back, chest, and stomach hair. (Barb told me this is the norm so she probably won't mind that I mention it here.) In the eighties, when the whole Hair Metal thing was going on, the guy threw on the full look: the big hair, bright clothes, and leather jacket—the works. Then when grunge hit, he switched it up to the flannel shirts and beanies and shit. When the Green Day thing hit, I shit you not, I saw him cruisin' with a green fuckin' Mohawk! (This is also something I considered for my wife's back, chest, and stomach as she looks fantastic in green—it really brings out the color in her eyes.) As each phase of music came and went, so did my buddy's personal style. He had no real identity of his own or belief in what music he enjoyed listening to, let alone playing.

If you're doing that shit, you're pretty much startin' out a day late and a dollar short. When Hair Metal was big, the grunge guys, like Alice in Chains and Soundgarden, were already doing their thing. When grunge came in, the Green Day guys were already being who they are and playing their music. All of these musical movements were happening underground, while the popular music was going on. If you're modeling yourself on whatever is the new thing, then you've already missed the boat and don't even know it! So to prevent this from happening to you, just play the fucking music that gets your dick hard—or your labia swollen.

I remember when I played in a called band Zyris. We were playing our songs and at the end of the show one night we played "Rock and Roll" by Led Zeppelin. Right then and there, I asked myself, "How come our music doesn't move me like this? We should be doing kick-ass fucking music like this instead of music that we think is gonna get us a recording deal or on the radio that has absolutely zero fucking passion in it." So ask yourself, "Why am I doing what's popular when I can't stand playing this shit?" When you play what you love, then it's fucking real. You'll know the difference. Lesson number one—don't ever forget that.

While you're finding your signature sound, you've also gotta have the balls to stick to your game plan. What would have happened if Chris Cornell had turned on the radio and heard "Cherry Pie" by Warrant and went for what he thought would be popular at the time? Instead of Soundgarden it would have become

Spandex-Hairspray Garden. He may have known what the fuck was going on, but he was like, "I can't stand this shit." He played and wrote the shit he dug and steered the ship steady. Nothing for nothing, so did Warrant. They didn't give a fuck what anybody thought about them. They were like, "This is us. You don't like it? Go eat a bag of fucking dicks."

Not to get sidetracked, but since we mentioned Chris's name here, I've got a pretty fucking funny story.

I remember getting completely hammered and making the usual roll-through-your-fucking-phone-book-until-somebody-will-deal-with-your-drunken-bullshit phone call. Well, on this occasion, I happened to get Father Edward Van Halen on the other end of my stupidity. Anyway, Ed told me that he had been recording a bunch of new shit and was really happy with the way it was coming out.

"Awesome, I can't wait to hear you killin' it, as always, Father Edward!" I said.

At this point, Gary Cherone was no longer singing with the band. So I asked Ed, "Who's singing?"

Ed said, "We're thinking about having Chris Cornell be the new lead singer."

"Oh cool," I said, "Chris is fucking unbelievable!"

And then it dawned on me: "Wait . . . How in the fuck is this gonna work?" Then I'm trying to picture Father Cornell jumping around in spandex, doing splits off the drum riser, and then walking up to Eddie and going, "Ah . . . I reach down in between my legs, ease the seat back . . ."

You gotta be fucking kidding me! It would be a toss-up to see what the fuck would be funnier, this musical comedy delight or seeing George Carlin do his stand-up routine. I love David Lee Roth; nobody can do it like Dave. Chris is the complete fucking opposite of DLR.

I said, "Cool, Ed. Chris is the man." I wasn't about to piss on Ed's parade by saying, "Ed, have you heard some of Chris's lyrics? *Nail in my hand from my creator. You gave me this life, now show*

me how to live. You know . . . then just transition into *Got a drink in my hand, got my toes in the sand, all I need is a beautiful girl*—fucking classic! Hopefully between the fucking spandex and the titanic vats of booze and weed, nobody will notice a fucking thing. After I pissed and shit my pants from envisioning this musical comedy that could only be rivaled by *Chappelle's Show,* I thought, "Why the fuck stop here?"

Hey, Chris, if you're reading this, here's a short set list that me and your army of fans would all love to hear you sing. These are very much in the spirit of the musical stylings we would expect to hear from you. These songs obviously represent every ounce of integrity for which you've worked so hard for throughout your career:

> "She's Only Seventeen," Winger
> "Unskinny Bop," Poison
> "Talk Dirty to Me," Poison (They're so fucking badass,
> I had to list Poison twice!!!)
> "Cherry Pie," Warrant
> "Wango Tango," Ted Nugent

Now, if your life has been sucking balls lately and you're contemplating committing fucking suicide, trust me, after you hear Father Cornell singing these classics Cornell-style on an acoustic guitar, all of your troubles will just melt away, as your only problem will be trying not to die from fucking laughter. The point is, all of these artists that I mentioned are successful. Whether it's talent, hard work, luck, or whatever the fuck it is that gets you to Madison Square Garden, there's one thread that ties all of these artists together—they love and believe what they're playing. Remember, you gotta play what you love and what moves you. Which brings me to another classic moment in the music business history of *unimportant people making important decisions.*

Unimportant People Making Important Decisions

THIS WHIM OF STUPIDITY HAPPENED TO BEFALL ME SOMEWHERE RIGHT around the birth of the almighty Black Label Society.

At this point, I had signed with Geffen Records after the multiplatinum success of *No More Tears* with the Boss. I was kind of viewed like a number one draft pick in the NFL—I had all these meetings with all the legendary record company people and everybody in between. It was wonderful, with everybody blowing smoke up my ass and telling me how great I am and asking how one human could possibly contain all the cute and cuddly and flat-out fucking adorable qualities that I possess—and telling me that their record company would be the best home for me.

When all this goofy business shit was settled, me and Barbaranne decided Geffen Records would become our new residence. So off we rolled into the land of a gazillion records sold, packed sold-out stadiums, private jets, the whole fucking nine yards, right? Not quite. Actually not even fucking close.

After my first two albums—*Pride & Glory* and my solo record *Book of Shadows*, both of which I am still very proud of to this day—didn't go into the charts at number one and stay there selling more records than *Thriller* and *Back in Black* combined, when it came time to do record number three, Geffen bought me out as opposed to me even making another album. As I signed the release contracts with Barbaranne at my side, it was bittersweet. Me and Barb were getting a nice chunk of change for us and the kids to live on for a bit. But I was now viewed as a bust. In the NFL that's a big number one draft pick that can't get over the hump and make the transition from college to the pros, or gets injured before he even enters the NFL. At this point, you could say I was a bit of both. So instead of getting fucking pissed off at anybody or feeling fucking sorry for ourselves because me and Barbaranne couldn't invest in our dream of opening up our own restaurant called Schlongs—which is the opposite of Hooters, where the guys have to be built like brick shithouses with a six- or even an eight-pack of abs, and cocks ten inches and over, where Barbaranne gets to interview them and sleep with each and every one of them, which you'll read more about in my next book, *How to Keep Your High School Sweetheart Happy*—what did we do? We went out and took our record buyout money and got our first Rottweiler. I had always wanted a Rott as a kid because they represented strength to me. So we found this little guy with paws bigger than his body, whose birthday was January 14, the same as mine, and he was born in Freedom, Oklahoma, which represented our being free from the Geffen contract, with the world being ours for the taking.

I named him Dorian after my favorite bodybuilder Dorian Yates, who represented strength not just in his physique and blood-and-guts training style, but in his mentality and mind-set of overcoming injuries and setbacks only to destroy all and everything in his path to conquering six Mr. Olympia titles. So we drove little Dorian home and plotted our next move.

Like I've said, along your musical fucking journey of doom, don't get pissed to the point where you're smashing shit, blaming every fucking thing with or without a pulse for why shit didn't pan out for you—because it does fuck-all. Trust me, I've tried it. Not so much blaming other people for my not achieving my goals. I dump all my excuse-riddled pathetic bullshit on my loving wife, Barbaranne. She could very well thank me exclusively for her conversion to Buddhism—serenity now. By the way . . . you're welcome, Barb.

Anyways, what I recommend is approaching your problems, or whatever fucking dilemma in life the good Lord places upon your shoulders, head-on in pure Black Label/General Patton style. We are stranded in a lifeboat in the middle of the fucking Atlantic. We've got food and water for three days. We can all fucking bitch and moan about it or start fucking paddling—there is no argument. Shut the fuck up, get it fuckin' done, or die. So after that little Black Label/General Patton pep talk, the comedy tour was about to begin.

Now, like I said, after two commercially unsuccessful albums, then being let go by a major record label, in the business I was viewed as a bust, a failure, washed up, damaged goods, a has-been, done, or whatever word you want to use for "Go fuck yourself, douche." And I completely understand it. As a businessman on the outside looking at me, how could you not think that? The way I looked at it was, the *Appetite for Destruction* first-album success didn't happen. The road in front of me was going to be rougher, bumpier, colder, stormier, a flat-out pain in the fucking ass. So fucking what. I've been with Barb for twenty-six years and we have three kids—and you're gonna scare me with this horseshit? Go away and come back when you got something real. Victory is for the fucking brave, not the timid and excuse-riddled weak. And like I've said, a lion is a fucking lion and does not need to be told, or reminded, what it is and what it has to do. So roll up your sleeves, hike up your skirt, and let the balls—or in my case, labia— that the good Lord gave you hang down, and get to fucking work.

Excuse Me, Mr. Wylde, Would You Like to Eat Some Ass?

So NOW THE SUCKING-DICK, EATING-ASS, *"CAN YOU PLEASE GIVE ME A record deal, mister, pretty please?"* bullshit began. It is rather amazing how within a few short years, you could go from golden child to damaged goods—to the point where no chick wants to fuck you because your dick is so covered with herpes, gonorrhea, crabs, and whatever pus is slowly dripping out of the head of your cock (which we will also discuss later; I told you rock 'n' roll was a rather odd religion—these types of things are actually applauded as opposed to frowned upon). In my case, whoever would actually pick up or return a phone call, me and Barbaranne took a meeting with them.

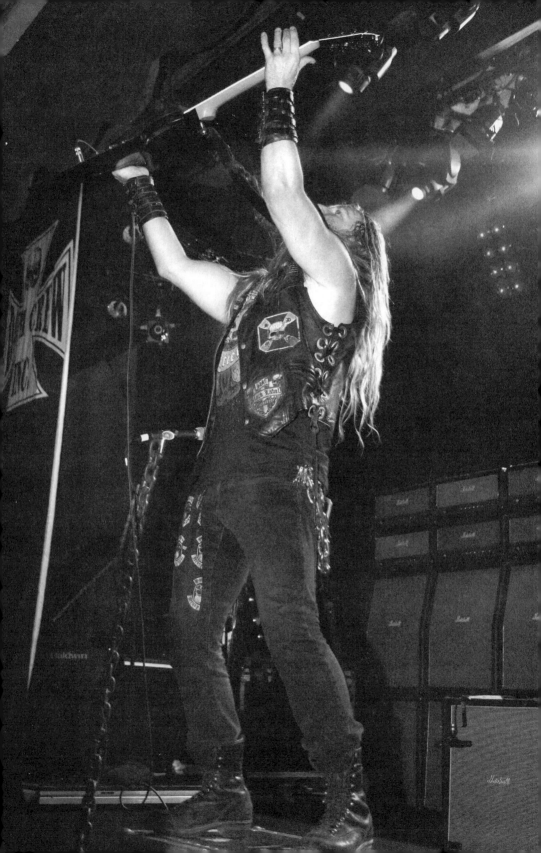

Now, these record companies and promoters—the first thing I tell them is, "Look, I know you don't give one cunting-flying-fucking rat's ass about me. And I don't give a fuck about you. I don't need birthday fucking cards sent to me, the wife, and the kids to show you care. Although I appreciate all the thought that went into the anniversary card you got for me and Barb that folds out into a twelve-inch cock. I will most definitely use it on Barb to create a true Hallmark moment. I know I'm a fucking piece of cattle, and I mean fucking money. I get it. All I ask of you is that you do your end of the fucking deal and I'll do mine. And that's that. This way, if things don't work out, it's just business, nothing personal, and we can still be friends and move on."

Remember how I mentioned *unimportant people making important decisions*? Anyway, I'm at one of these record company fucking meetings, where this fucking Einstein unleashes these words of musical wisdom to enlighten me as, I know, I'm a clueless dumb motherfucker who's never been to the dance before. He says to me, "Zakk, you know this whole Viking-Jesus's-biker-henchman thing you've got going on?"

I said, "Yeah, you forgot to throw in the fact that we bake all the cookies that the fucking Girl Scouts sell. What about it?"

"Well, I was thinking, if you changed the image of the band to maybe more of a Limp Bizkit type of thing, that would definitely help."

I didn't know whether he was making a fucking joke or he wanted me to knock his fucking teeth out, or see if I could cave his fucking skull in with my Wesco mining boots. I was like, "You're fucking joking, right?"

"No, I think it would really help," he said.

"Hold on a minute, you mean to tell me that if I put on a backward fucking baseball cap, throw on some baggy motherfucking clothes, a pair of fucking Vans, and start rapping "Yo yo yo"—that's gonna fucking fix everything? Are you out of your fucking mind? Are we supposed to make believe that I never fucking played with

Ozzy? Instead of being proud of the fact that I stood in the same spot as my hero Randy Rhoads and shared the same stage with my hero and mentor Ozzy, I'm supposed to be embarrassed of where I came from? Fuck you, douche! And fuck Limp Bizkit! I'm in Black motherfucking Label Society!!! Why don't you just take your fucking record company, and Limp Bizkit, and cram it up your fucking cunt sideways."

Needless to say, that meeting didn't pan out as well as expected.

So that's where the Black Label war on Limp Bizkit began. Right then and there I felt like my whole musical existence had been attacked and fired upon. He could have mentioned any other band that was popular and that I should be more like, but he said Limp Bizkit. If they are responsible for the trend that means Black Label won't taste victory, then they must be fucking destroyed!!! I kid you not, this was my complete fucking mind-set, as I felt it was kill or be killed. So during every Black Label mass after this record company meeting, "Limp Bizkit sucks fucking dick!" became the war oath as the Black Label armada rolled on seething strength from one Black Label mass to the next and refused to be denied. That's why I've always said Black Label is not a band, it's a mentality where lions gather and adversity is the fucking air we breathe.

As far as the Limp Bizkit guys go, I've never met them. Guys who have worked with them or roll with them have said to me, "They are all super-cool guys and good people." God bless them. Any band saying they wouldn't want a smidgen of their success is full of shit. I've never wished bad on anyone in my life (except for JD, obviously), as it takes away from your concentrating on getting the fucking job done that's in front of you. And if they are complete fucking cunts, just forget their existence altogether. Instead of wasting my time thinking about some douchebag, I would rather have Barbaranne suck me off and fist me, preparing me for my next prostate exam, to ensure that I have a clean bill of health, so I can continue to play this magickal music—which makes me feel like a giddy little schoolgirl—called rock 'n' roll.

But if Limp Bizkit was in the same position as I was thirteen years ago, during the birth of the almighty Black Label in 1998, I'd expect nothing different from them if some record company know-it-all douche who obviously knew what was best for them and probably isn't in the music business anymore said the same thing to them. Here we are thirteen years later with our Black Label family growing stronger and stronger, and *Order of the Black* entered the *Billboard* charts at number four. Now let's say some record company guy tells the fellas in Limp Bizkit, "Guys, your shtick is getting old. That was thirteen years ago. Maybe if you dressed more like . . . Black Label? They have a number four album!" I'd expect them to say, "Black Label can suck my left fucking ball! We're Limp fucking Bizkit, asshole!"

You think I'm joking but established artists who have sold millions of records have fucking idiots who don't even know who's in the fucking band or anything about their past telling them what kind of music they should be playing or what kind of clothes they should be wearing. Always remember—play what you love and what moves you. And have a set of fucking balls and don't be afraid to stick up for yourself. I've been put in positions where I've felt uncomfortable about doing something, and in the end they pretty much all turned out with me asking myself, "Why the fuck did I listen to that asshole?" If you believe in what you are doing, those beliefs are yours, and not anybody else's, to change.

Weekend at Bernie's

A BUDDY OF MINE TOLD ME WHEN HE WAS WORKING AT SOME RECORD company that they were about to release a new Jimi Hendrix album of lost tapes of Jimi snoring or stubbing his fucking toe, or God knows whatever else they could find recordings of Jimi doing—brushing, flossing, mowing his lawn, eating potato chips, you get the idea. So the record company was having its weekly boardroom meeting discussing the battle plan of how they were

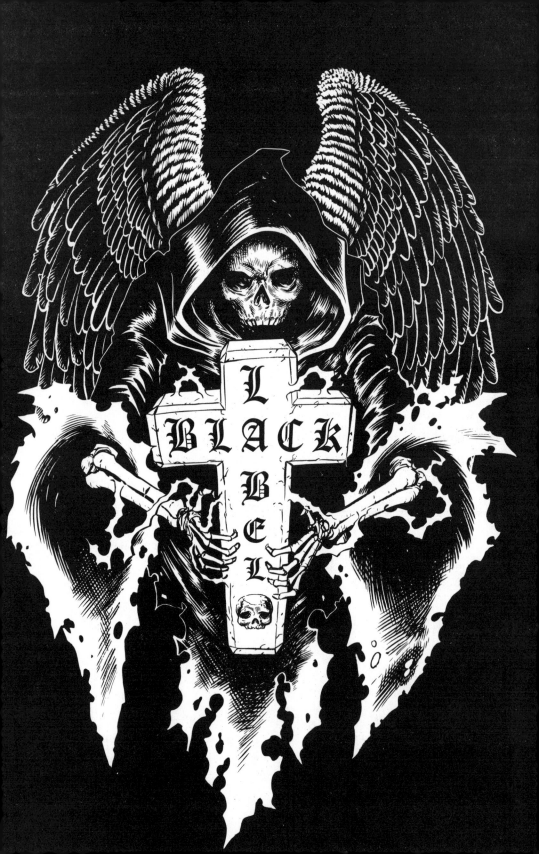

going to promote the new Jimi Hendrix offering. Everybody was firing off ideas, bouncing them off each other, when in walks a twenty-two-year-old girl who works for the label. She says to everybody at the table, "I'm going to book Mr. Hendrix's flights and take care of all of his travel arrangements. Does anybody know where he prefers to stay?"

My buddy said there was dead silence, and then they broke out dying laughing. The girl handling the travel asked, "What the fuck is so funny?" Then she said, "When you find out where he likes to stay, let me fucking know because I have to book this shit."

At least the Dallas Cowboys cheerleaders have to take a test on the history of the Cowboys' players and its franchise history. That's why the music business is so fucking awesome—you don't even have to know the name of the deceased person you're working for! Being involved in this shit truly is a gift that keeps on giving.

At the end of the day, play what you love and what moves you. Plain and simple. GIFD.

Gotta Promote the Record!

OVER THE YEARS, GOING TO RADIO AND PROMOTING WHATEVER ALBUM was out at the time has always been a blast. And I've met some great people who, whether they're still in the business or not, when we run into each other again, we always have a great time catching up, laughing our asses off telling war stories. Now here's another gem of radio fucking comedy.

The record company and their radio staff people are the absolute fucking best when they get all jacked up. Especially the radio people in their market or territory, when we are gonna pay them a visit with our cuddliness, compiled with the sheer adorableness of the fucking grand whatever-the-fuck-it-is that we bring to the table. Anyway, at one particular radio station we visited up in the Pacific Northwest, in walks the radio guy or gal from the label, and my brother-in-law and tour manager, and fearless field general, much akin to General George S. Patton—Father Mark Ferguson—along with the general of the Black Label guitar army, Moby. And then there's the wonderful blond-bomber douchebag—me.

So basically the game plan is that I will tantalize them all with my unbelievable fucking greatness, push the album, and bless them with a Carnegie Hall–worthy performance, and in turn they will be so abso-fucking-lutely blown away that they just have to add the single to their playlist! Right? Oh, you sad, sad, pathetic little man.

Now, get this. I jam about three or four unplugged, un-Blackened fucking tunes on the acoustic guitar and piano, tell them a batch of funny fucking Ozzy and Black Label stories, tell them about how wonderful the new album is and how if you buy it, everything in your life is going to be peachy keen and all the other bullshit that makes life worth living! Mission accomplished, right?

Here's the grand prize, kids.

While Moby was breaking down the gear, and I was taking a piss, Father Fergie was talking with the radio programmer (the guy who decides what does and what *doesn't* get played on their radio station) and some of the gang at the station. The programmer guy told Mark, "We love when you Black Label guys come down to the station. Zakk tells the funniest stories and we love it when he performs for us. It's just so awesome!"

Mark answered, "Yeah, Zakk's a funny fucker. So listen, boss, are you guys going to spin the single?"

The guy looked Mark straight in the fucking eyes, everything went silent, and he said, "Ahhhhh . . . No. But anyway, it was really great seeing you guys. Take care."

The only thing missing was, "Don't let the door hit you in the fucking ass on your way out, you fucking idiots!" Once again, fucking priceless!

You're Fucking Out!

Remember how I was telling you about the record labels that I dealt with and how I told them, "I'll do my end of the deal, you fucking do yours"? Well, here's a perfect example of when you know they're lying to you, and you just wish somehow you could prove it. None other than "Mom"—Sharon Osbourne—conceived this little plot of record label investigation during the release of the *No More Tears* album. Mom wanted to have the Boss get closer to the Ozzy Army so she rounded up a batch of in-stores and smaller gigs for us to play, instead of the enormodomes we were doing up to that point. It was her idea to give all the Ozzy-heads a chance to see the boss in a more intimate setting. As far as the gigs went, they were fucking awesome! Between the fucking energy coming off the stage and the insane asylum in the crowds, it was fucking killer. Thank the good Lord the gigs were a blast because the in-stores were a whole other fucking story.

On paper, it all looked fucking grand—Ozzy and the band would roll into the record store with the new album blasting throughout the fucking place. The Ozzy Army could come in, get the new record and whatever other Ozzy album they wanted, and have them signed by the boss and the band. With about fifteen hundred crazy Ozzy-heads at every in-store, you would figure they would sell fifteen hundred copies of the new record, and plenty of other Ozzy and Sabbath records. Then Ozzy and the band would sign everything and a good time would be had by all. How fucking complicated is that? Keep reading.

If I'm a manager at fucking McDonald's and I realize that we are starting to run low on fucking hamburger patties, I am immediately blowing a phone call in for a massive shipment of patties so that we don't lose out on a ton of burger sales. The music business is no different. If you're a record company, your bands' CDs and product are your burgers for sale. You don't sell fucking burgers, you don't pay the bills and you don't eat. Common sense, right?

The boss and the rest of the band showed up at one particular record store and there was a massive line around the fucking building. As soon as we stepped foot in the store there was a Black Sabbath video cranked up on all of the TVs—STRIKE ONE!

Ozzy looked around and said, "Do these fucking assholes realize that I've been out of Sabbath longer than I was in it? Tell someone to put the new fucking record on!"

Once they got that sorted, we sat down at the signing tables. The doors opened and in came the Ozzy Army—all super-cool people, all super-pumped to meet the Boss. After Ozzy signed about five CDs the store completely ran out of the new record. The shelves were pillaged to find every last CD with Ozzy's name on it— one copy of *Blizzard of Oz*, two copies of *Diary of a Madman*, one copy of *Bark at the Moon*, one copy of *Master of Reality*, and two copies of *Paranoid*—and that's all, folks! They had booked a living legend to appear in their store, the Prince of fucking Darkness, and had a total of twelve fucking copies of any music with Ozzy on it—twelve fucking copies to span his entire career of music! The only problem is, we had fifteen hundred fucking people wanting to buy a record and have Ozzy sign it. If the store manager had pulled this horseshit at any other job he would have been fucking fired, killed by a death squad in some countries—STRIKE TWO!

It gets better.

Instead of signing flyers or posters or whatever promotional items might have been brought into the store to promote the fucking album (which, by the way, are supposed to be supplied by the fucking record company), the Boss and the band were signing fucking paper towels from the fucking bathrooms. Oz, being the super-cool guy that he is, just signed anything handed to him. He greeted everybody, right up to the last person waiting in line to meet him and the store employees as well. After we left, on the way back to the hotel, that's when he laid it down.

"Fucking napkins? How many years have I been doing this shit and I'm signing fucking napkins from the bathroom at a record in-store? Are you fucking kidding me?"

After Mom got word of this fucking fiasco of doom, each day

we rolled into any town to do a show, she had the assistant to the band (which really meant best friend and drinking partner)—Will "the Chill"—go out to every fucking store and take an inventory of every last Ozzy record in the place, the name of the store, the manager, contact numbers, addresses. That way when Mom called the record company as we were headed out to bring the doom, she could say, "We were in Miami yesterday and there were no fucking Ozzy records in the stores, assholes!"

The record company would fire back, "Yes there are! There are tons of Ozzy records out there!"

Mom would reply, "Listen, cocksuckers, don't you fucking lie to me! I've got my assistant going out to every big chain and mom-and-pop record store out there! I've got a list of names, dates and times, contacts, which records and how many at each and every store. You're busted fucking cold!"

To this day it never ceases to amaze me that this shit still goes on. If we own a Burger King, and somebody pulls up and orders a burger, we don't tell him, "Sorry, we are out of burgers, but would you like a grilled chicken sandwich?" For fuck's sake, the name of the restaurant is called Burger fucking King, not Grilled Chicken Sandwich King! No fucking burgers? STRIKE THREE, MOTHERFUCKER—YOU'RE FUCKIN' OUT!

It would just be easier to have them give us twenty thousand records, bring them to the in-store, and whatever we don't sell, we have for the next in-store. What the fuck is so fucking hard about that? It's the record company's job to make sure they sell fucking records. Do we not want to sell records? Maybe we should go into the bathroom-paper-towel business, because there were plenty of those fucking things to go around for Ozzy and the band to sign. Better yet, if they could find a way to make a living by coming up with bullshit excuses, they would. Since that's what the majority of their job consists of—weak-willed, excuse-riddled shit. The whole thing is you're supposed to work as a fucking team, not us against you.

Somewhere in the middle of the *No More Tears* tour, the

record company held this dinner in some fancy banquet room and presented Oz and the rest of us with double-platinum discs. They also presented Ozzy with this gigantic frame with all of the platinum albums that he had sold—from Saint Rhoads to Father Lee to when my dumb ass joined the band. It was massive. I felt so happy for Oz—he's one of the coolest guys on the planet and we were all there to celebrate with him.

One of the big guys at the label got up and gave a speech about how awesome Oz was and about all his years of hard work and success, how proud they were to be his record company. Then he said, "We'd like to congratulate Ozzy and his band for *No More Tears* going double platinum!"

Everyone began to clap and cheer, when all of a sudden Mom's voice overpowered everything with, "It could have done fucking better!"

There was dead silence, then uncomfortable laughing, and then clapping again. And then again at the top of her lungs, Mom shouted, "It could have done fucking better!"

Needless to say it was fucking awesome.

Thank you, Mom.

Hair of the Gods: The Metal Beard

One of my favorite nicknames for Zakk is "Hangtime," because he's always got food or something stuck in that filthy thing that he calls his beard.
—RITA HANEY, DIMEBAG'S HAG

WHEN I WAS A CHILD, I DID CHILDISH THINGS, LIKE MASTURBATE HEAVILY, drink my father's liquor, and play the recorder. Now that I am a man I have put away those childish things—and now I masturbate heavily, drink my father's liquor, and play the recorder. What

I'm driving at is that to truly establish yourself in the Great Halls of Metal, nay, in music, it is necessary to grow up and become a man. This means a lot of different things. Some of them you will discover as you continue reading this holy parchment, which will transform the fantasy portion of your life into a reality. There is no higher honor in life than to proudly display the fact that you have evolved into manhood, and the best way to do this is to grow yourself a true Metal beard. And if you truly want to test your manliness you could also try running into your local marine recruiting center hollering, "God bless the terrorists!" However, for your safety and everyone else's involved, let's just stick with the beard.

Everyone from Kerry King, to Scott Ian, to Rob Zombie, and of course, Brother Dimebag Darrell himself all cultivated the sacred emblem upon his iron chin. It is a rite of passage for a band to grow beards. It's a sign that they have moved on from a silly bullshit act into an undeniable wrecking ball of musical alchemy—or possibly that they're too fucking lazy to pick up a razor. I've got to be honest with you, that's why I've got one. But we'll stick with the sacred rite of the Viking for its awesomeness. Beards have been associated with the warrior mentality and dominance for thousands of years, and things are no different in the world of Metal—or in the gay community.

If you're too young and can't physically grow a beard yet, don't worry. Someday you will be able to, and when you actually can, then the time will come to test your manhood against the mothers, girlfriends, and clean-cut pussyfucks who glare snobbily down their shit-brown noses at you. For these people will entice, tempt, and taunt you to shave your beard and relinquish your power—kind of like what my family does to me. Do not give in, my friends, the OdinForce will always be with you. And once you do cultivate your hairy manhood and you lose your job, and you can't pay the rent, and Mommy and Dada won't let you live with them anymore—when you've got nothing left—that's when it's time to reconsider running into your local marine recruiting center hollering, "God bless the terrorists!" For the minute the marines hear this load of shit, it will be the last words muttered out of your pathetic little mouth—you pathetic little man.

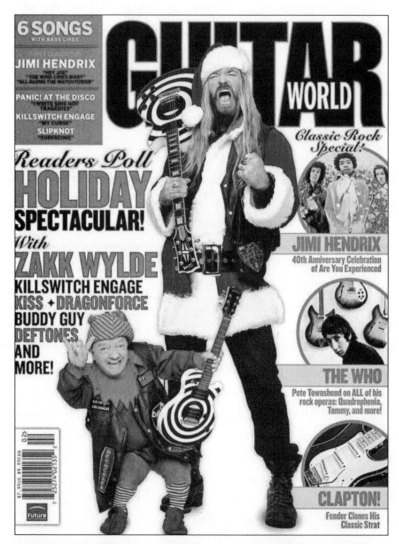

Note from Zakk: This is the only magazine cover that I ever did where—because of the holiday season and me being in a giving spirit—I included JD in the photo shoot.

World Tour Survival Technique: Farming Your Chin Spinach

JUST LIKE THE STORY OF SAMSON AND DELILAH, MY BEARD HOLDS THE power of the OdinForce in its shaggy, dreadlocked twists and turns. It's come in handy in all areas of my life.

- An Irish tickler for when I'm in the sack with my wife.
- A pointer when I'm directing JD to leave the room.
- A stirrer for my coffee, when I'm not using my schlong.
- Sometimes I like to wrap it around my own neck and restrict the blood flow while I jerk off. Okay, maybe more than sometimes.
- A flavor-saver of love for when I want to be reminded of my Immortal Beloved whilst out bleeding on the battlefields of the great Black Label crusades.
- Preparation for my backup career as Drunk Santa at the mall.
- A stunt double for John Holmes's cock in his biographical movie.

The Talk Box
BY THE BEARD OF ZAKK

YO, YOU MOTHERFUCKERS! YOU MAY NOT KNOW ME PERSONALLY, but I'm Zakk's beard.

Now, ole Zakky boy may have gone all tutti-frutti in Beverly Hills, but I'm still keepin' it real, a Jersey beard through and fuckin' through. But just 'cause Little Lord *Fancy Boy* has gone all Hollywood on us, don't think that *I'm* gonna sit here all trimmed and pointy-like and smelling of coconuts. I'm not fluffy, I'm not soft, I'm a hard-core Metal beard and just so you know, yes, if I had a stomach, it would make me sick to live this close to the Dodgers.

So anyways, nice to meet you.

Think of me as the pepperoni on the pizza, the extra cheese if you will. When Zakk makes all his crazy faces at the crowd, I'm the one that kicks that shit into gear! Truly freakin' scary! Imagine if he just puckered up and scowled at you without me! Forget about it—I make this man! And if you think different, I'm gonna have to come out there and pluck out your eyeballs and stick 'em up your ass so you can get a closer look at reality!

Apologies, I'm a slightly angry beard.

You see, I've been in places that only Jersey beards have been and lived to talk about, and believe you me, it's not all glitz and glamour being Zakk's beard. You try it! Have you seen this guy onstage? He's a fuckin' slob! He spits all the time. And only about half of that makes it into the sky; I end up with a fuckin' bath every time he decides to do that. Yo, buddy! I asked for the news, not the weather, asshole!

A lotta times I'm forced to survive off chunks of everything he eats. And more days than not, I end up smelling like that spot between a woman's pussy and her butthole. And let me tell you—*taint* nothin' pretty about that!

I live in constant danger, my friends. But I'm a fuckin' survivor, sharing my stories of survival. The closest I ever came to death was during a video shoot Zakky boy did with Ozzy for a song called "Dreamer." Sharon Osbourne put a fuckin' hit on me and told Zakk that he had to shave me off! Thankfully, Rob Zombie, the director of the video, came to my rescue. I heard Sharon say, "Doesn't he look silly with that thing? He needs to shave it off right now."

"No, I think it looks cool," Rob said, defending me. "What's wrong with having a beard?"

That was a close one. Sharon was looking for backup to take me out, but she got the opposite reaction from my brother Zombie. Actually, it's me and Rob's beard who are the greatest of pals. We've been catching our boys' whiskey drool for years now, and we back each other up.

Soon after, Zakk trimmed me into a much more Metal beard than before. I lived on to fight another day, my friends, standing proud as the most Metal of all facial hair.

By the way, I'm also good friends with Kerry King's beard. Don't try any funny shit! You don't want the two of us comin' round, ya hear me!

So remember, beards are for growin' and *furginas* are for mowin'! Good night, motherfuckers, and all hail the almighty Metal beard!

Note from Zakk: Father Eric wrote this. I had no fucking part of it at all. He thought it was funny. I really don't see any humor in it, but we left it anyway. I mean really—who gives a fuck about my stupid beard? You know when you go to the movies and there's a part in the movie that really sucks and you wonder why they left that part in the movie? This is that part. Hey, Father Eric, maybe you can show this little ditty to your imaginary girlfriend while you're showing her your vintage Star Wars dolls—you truly are a fucking idiot. Hopefully we can rebound from this horrendous part of the book. Remember, this was *your* idea. By the way, you're not funny and neither is this section.

True Rocker Test

THIS RIDICULOUS BIT OF BULLSHIT CAME ABOUT ONE DAY WHEN MY buddy told me, "Oh, you'll spot my friend, he's a *true* rocker."

True as opposed to *false* rocker?

Okay.

Whatever the fuck that means.

So we got to talking about what really constitutes being a true rocker. I love listening to my Sabbath and Zeppelin albums while throwing back a couple of cold beverages. You know, while cramming an empty beer bottle up my ass and sitting on my washing machine during a spin cycle—my cock in one hand and a beer in the other. Which begs the question: Does this classify me as a true rocker or just a guy who loves having bottles stuffed up his ass?

This is where we test your instincts to see if the blood of the Berzerker flows freely through your veins or if you need a little work in the Department of Heavy Metal.

Your answers will determine whether or not you are truly Berzerk and should keep reading, or if you are merely a Viking infant in need of a dipey change. Those of you whose scores reach into the clouds where Odin himself resides can refer to yourself around the house as a true Berzerker and command thy family to address you only with your Berzerker name. Around my house, I won't even speak to my family unless they first address me as Godred Crovan, Victor of Sky-Hill and Ruler of Man and the Isles. And now that I think about it, that's probably why nobody speaks to me unless it's time to feed the dogs or take out the garbage.

In pure Black Label fashion, we'll use the honor system here—so keep your own score and be honorable, motherfuckers. We'll start with an easy question first so you can get the hang of it.

1. Who is the lowest bloodthirsty, money-grubbing vulture in the music business?

a. My manager.

b. My agent.

c. My promoter.

d. My loving wife.

Answers:

a. 10 points. Bingo.

b. 10 points. You are correct.

c. 10 points. Nailed it.

d. 0 points. I'm God-fearing and *wife*-fearing as well. You gotta be out of your fucking mind if you guessed "d." Remember, you lay down to rest each night next to your wife . . . and at some point you're going to fall asleep. This leaves two things not in your favor: a pissed-off wife and sharp objects in the home. Always remember something a priest actually told me when we exchanged our vows— "Son, the girls don't like to be disappointed."

2. How often should one brush their teeth on the road?

a. Twice a day.

b. Once a day.

c. Usually every day, but if I'm on the road, I don't mind skipping a few days. Just suck off a guy who's been on a healthy diet of broccoli and cauliflower.

d. What the fuck is brushing your teeth? You gonna ask me if I shower too?

Answers:

a. -10 points. Have you been paying attention? (It's simple: I write, you read.) This book is about Metal Viking debauchery, not overzealous ways to manage good hygiene!

b. -5 points. You're probably taking this test with your girlfriend, and she's answering the questions for you and helping you keep score. You pussy.

c. 10 points. Now we're talking. People will back away from you either because of your smelly breath or because you're out sucking guys off.

d. 10 points. Pure Black Label fashion, brother. On one tour I went seventy-seven days without a shower or brushing my teeth. Of course, when my wife caught up with me, she hosed my ass down before laying a finger on me. True story—I recall one time when my cock and balls got to the point of smelling like a rotten fish market. I dropped my trousers, Barb was about to go to work on me, and she actually gagged from the stench of rotten tuna and salmon and said, "I'm not going near that fucking thing until you shower."

And I explained, "But I'm a hardworking man."

She calmly replied, "No, you're a fucking idiot."

Then I said, "But now we both smell like Chicken of the Sea."

She said, "I'm done here. Now you can go back to sucking off guys who are on a healthy diet of broccoli and cauliflower, asshole."

Then I said, "First of all, I never stopped sucking guys off. Just lock the door so the kids don't come in. I'm gonna jerk off by myself. I love you, my little Chicken of the Sea!"

3. **What do you do when you're onstage and you need to take a shit?**

a. Have the band cover for you while you take a bathroom break.

b. Hold it in until after the gig.

c. Wait until the drummer's solo and then run out to the bus and shit in his bed.

d. Dimebag Darrell's tried-and-true "bucket technique."

Answers:

a. 10 points. Although you did just hit the brakes on the show, I'm awarding you a ten-spot for being so bold as to have a thousand people wait while you go blow a fucking toilet up. You fucking septic, you.

b. 5 points. Problem solved. Just don't shit yourself before you walk offstage.

c. -10 points. We've got two problems here: (1) No one shits on the bus. (2) What sick fuck shits in someone else's bed? This is some fucked-up, GG Allin shit that should have ended when they dropped the last nail in his coffin. God bless GG. That motherfucker literally gave his all when he walked out onto the stage. Nobody ever left a GG Allin show sayin', "Wow, he really *half-assed* it tonight."

d. 20 points. After a sleepless night of drinking his favorite Black Tooth Grins, my brother Dime could be in the middle of a fucking guitar solo, walk to the side of the stage, drop trou, and take a shit into a bucket without missing a motherfuckin' note. And you only thought Dime could come up with brilliant riffs and blistering solos. How's that for talent? You score 10 points for knowing about Dime's bucket technique here and another 10 points for knowing that the show must always go on. Nice job, Berzerker. In fact, if you chose "d" and just started reading this goddamn book, then you're on the List.

4. **You're in a band and you really want to make it in the music business. You are introduced to a guy, who knows a guy, whose guy knows a guy, who can help your band become successful. In order for him to help you out, he informs you that you have to make out with his three-hundred-pound sister in the backseat of a car. How do you respond?**

a. Simply tell him, "No, thanks, I love cock and balls. And I like it rough and unshaven."

b. Pound your beer, and then another, and then another, and then another, and then suck it up and make out with this big fat wildebeest mongoloid troll. The bigger the waistband, the deeper the quicksand. You know what I mean.

c. Strike him in the throat with the blade of your hand, yelling out something that sounds Japanese but is actually not of any language at all.

d. Tell him you have herpes, but your bass player will do it. You should also thank him for the wonderful sex with his mother. And ask him to thank her for the salad-tossing during the hand job; she really went the extra mile to make it a pleasant evening.

Answers:

a. 5 points. I find that claiming gayness gets me out of a lot of situations these days—like instead of telling my wife that I'm not in the mood for sex, I just tell her I'm gay.

b. 5 points. This is exactly what I did. I took one for the band. Back when we were kids, this chick mounted me in the back of some beat-up car in the parking lot. If your back and ribs get crushed as much as mine did, give yourself another 5 points, since that's all you're gonna get is points. This in no way helped my career, nor my overall self-esteem or physical condition. As this chick sat on me trying to graze upon my face, I knew I had made a mistake, and that mistake resonated through every vertebra in my spine. To this day I still attribute the majority of my back pain not to power-lifting in the Doom Crew Iron Dungeon, but to this very unholy disaster of *Titanic* proportions. I should have just said I was gay.

c. 0 points. This is a break-even, because while hitting anyone for offering you their own bloodline is fucked-up, the fact that you used old-school kung fu is awesome. So no points, but because you invoked the spirit of Bruce Lee I'm not going to fault you either. May the spirit of Saint Lee and jeet kune do always be with you.

d. 10 points. This would have been the correct choice. It's not what I chose, but I wish I had, just to have the nightmares in JD's head and not in mine. Oh, the horror. But be sure to thank him for the wonderful sex with his mother.

5. What is a Black Tooth Grin?

a. After you go down on someone, it's the smile you make when your teeth are full of pubes.

b. A crackhead's smirk.

c. A cocktail.

d. Any smile in Louisiana or that belongs to a Doom Crew member.

Answers:

a. -5 points. That's disgusting. And how dare you talk about my wife like that.

b. -5 points. That's disgusting. And how dare you talk about my wife like that.

c. 5 points. Nailed it. My Black Label brother Dime's favorite drink was the Black Tooth Grin . . . A shot of Crown Royal topped off with a splash of Coke.

d. -5 points. If you were thinking hillbilly here, you actually lose points. Go back to your *Deliverance* thoughts.

6. You find yourself in the middle of a Black Label Society mosh pit. As you look around, you realize that there is no escape from the circling chaos that surrounds you. You decide to . . .

a. Find the biggest, scariest motherfucker in the pit and punch him square in the face.

b. Cry, panic, and scream.

c. Stay in the mayhem and see how well you do.

d. Pull out your cock and spin it around like a windmill until people clear out of your way.

Answers:

a. 10 points. This is exactly how I met and fell in love with my loving wife, Barbaranne. Now the only time I punch her square in the face is with my cock.

b. -15 points. Stop acting like JD. He does enough of that for all of us.

c. 20 points. There ya go! You're in the pit and you haven't done anything stupid. You may still get your ass kicked, but that's okay, because you're not afraid to take a few lumps of sugar with your tea.

d. 0 points. I have no idea how to assign a score to what you've just done. I don't know if I'm impressed or terrified.

If you do want to see your scores up on the board, here ya go, from lowest to highest:

-40 to 0 points . . . Level: JD—In other words, you're worthless and weak.

5 to 20 points . . . Level: Order of the Idiots

25 to 45 points . . . Level: Black Label Brethren

50 to 70 points . . . Level: Berzerker

75 points . . . Level: Bea Arthur—Order of the Black Label Illuminati

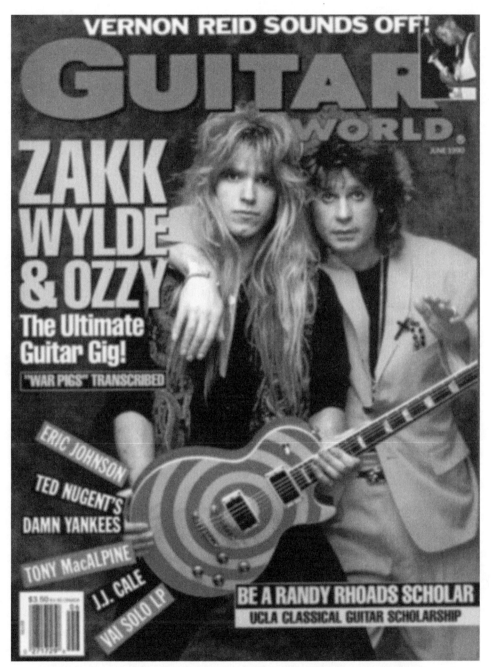

I didn't realize Ozzy had a chick in his band. She's not bad. She kind of looks like Pamela Anderson but not quite as breasty. Although I'm a tit guy, I'd still fuck this chick.

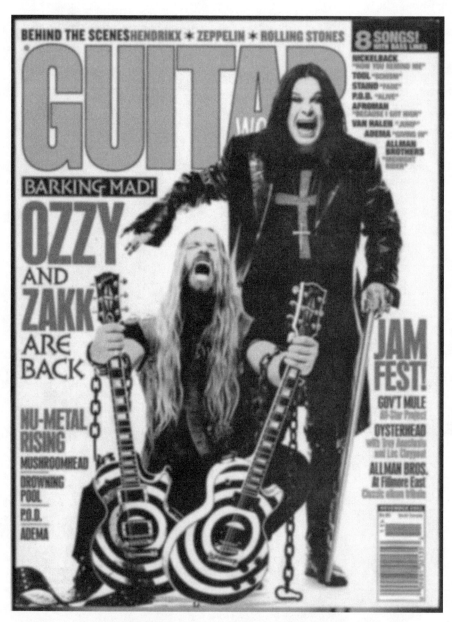

Whenever Ozzy and I would do these photo shoots and the photographers would ask us to make screaming faces, the Boss would always say, "Look at this stupid shit. People must think we fucking sleep like this."

"You mean, you don't?" I asked Oz. "I thought all married guys sleep like this."

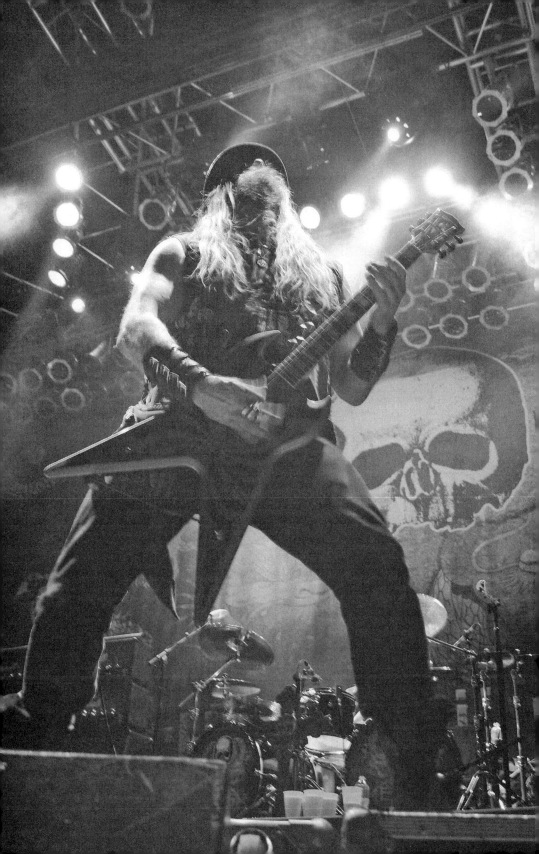

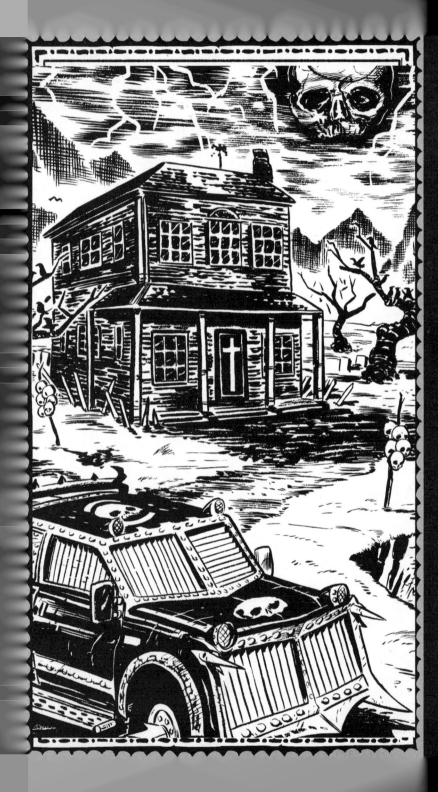

CHAPTER TWO

The Black Vatican

And then Odin descended from the skies and showed himself to me. Armored on his black steed, he bade me go forth and conjure from the wells of the damned a mighty fortress to reach into skies shared only by Asgard. Within the walls of this fortress I should set open the Hellfires of the Underworld, whose flames and molten heat I employ to forge the blades for conquest and make ready for battle!

Deep within the bowels of this formidable stronghold would move fantastical creatures, good spirits and demons alike, all protected by hallowed grounds beneath. Among them, hordes of drunken warriors would congregate in this most holy of battlements and stand witness to the creation of the secret songs of Valhalla itself! Rise, my brethren, rise! For the Gods have called upon us to beseech the heart of Valhalla and set forth a new order. An Order of the Black!

And in his counsel, Odin spoke of those who would seek to defile the sanctity of this sanctum sanctorum. Of a small and shrewd beast with cloven feet that would soil these holy grounds in fits of shameless rage with its unclean hands. This clever foe would guise itself as an associate of the Order and call itself JD. And I should withal forbear conference with this simple and plain villain, for mine call of duty is lucid. I shall press on with lion heart and emerge from thy sanctuary victorious, bringing unto mankind the glorious and pleasant sounds of Metal!

Note from Zakk: "Deep within the bowels of this formidable stronghold"? The only thing that's got a strong hold on Father Eric is that I'm his number one biggest fan because of the fact that he keeps pulling this ridiculous shit out of his ass, or God only knows where from, and I'm still his friend. This is all coming from a guy whose Viking heritage can basically be traced back to his upbringing in Orange County, California. That's even worse than my coming from New Jersey. At least we get winters and snow. Un-fuckin'-real. Between me and Eric, we come from the musical Viking lands of No Doubt and the almighty Jon Bon—as in Jon Bon motherfuckin' Jovi.

No More Tears: This Album Is the Shit!!! (I Mean Really, THE SHIT!)

DURING THE MAKING OF THE *NO MORE TEARS* ALBUM, OZZY HAD THESE stink bombs—those little rotten-egg-smelling glass stink bombs. When we first got into the recording for the album we were working in Bearsville, New York, with Steve Thompson and Mike Barbiero, who were known at the time for their work with Guns N' Roses and Tesla. They picked up Ozzy in this town car and, on the way to the hotel, were telling Oz how excited they were to work on the record, how they were gonna record it, and all that stuff. You gotta understand that Ozzy really doesn't give a fuck how any album is recorded or any of the details. He's more of a "Let me do my part and get the fuck out of here" type of guy. Oz doesn't know, or care, about the brand of mics or the type of recording console the engineers are using.

The guys were telling him how great the studio was and all the "shop" stuff that Ozzy didn't give a shit about. As far as Ozzy was concerned, they could have been speaking Chinese to him—he didn't know what the fuck they were talking about. So Oz started busting these fucking stink bombs in the back of the car. These guys were getting gassed out and Oz was telling them he had been having really terrible gas because of his nerves and fear of flying. The whole ride back to the hotel stank to high hell and they didn't say anything because they felt sorry for Oz and his "medical" condition. This became an ongoing gag for Oz throughout the entire production.

The next day we were in the studio sitting at this SSL Neve mixing console and these guys were telling Oz that the Who's legendary *Tommy* album had been recorded off that very console. Oz leaned toward them and asked in his classic Oz voice, "Who? Tommy who?"

One of the guys answered back, "You know, Oz, *Tommy*."

More confused than before Ozzy asked, "Tommy who? Who's Tommy?"

Again the producer said, "You know, *Tommy*."

Oz became impatient. "Who in the fuck is fucking Tommy?"

Finally, one of the guys said, "Ozzy, the Who's *Tommy*. The Who recorded on this board."

That's when Ozzy leaned back over to me and said, "Hey, Zakk, I think you're gonna need to start shoveling coal into this motherfucker to keep it going!"

As soon as Ozzy left the room to go use the bathroom, Mike and Steve leaned over to me and said, "Dude, Zakk, can we ask you something, man? Is Ozzy always like that? Fucking ripping farts all the time? It's pretty bad, man." So I said, "Yeah, it's 'cause of his nerves, he actually goes to see a doctor for that, because he can't help it." They went on to tell me how horrendous it was coming back from the airport. These poor guys ended up just dealing with it because they thought Ozzy had a medical problem. And of course the Boss was having a blast with that one—firing off his stink bombs all over the fuckin' place when the guys weren't watching.

Me, Mike Inez, and Randy Castillo were roommates during those sessions, and then Ozzy and his right-hand guy, Tony Dennis, who has been with Oz since the very beginning of his solo career with Saint Rhoads, were in the suite next door. In our kitchen we had all these empty beer trophies from all the beer we were drinking, up on a shelf that wrapped around the room. There were literally hundreds upon hundreds of beer bottles up on the wall—we weren't fucking around.

Our typical routine was to jam all day, then stop by our room for a couple of beers, and then at night we would go over to this place called the Tinker Street Café. One day, Ozzy had snuck into our room and put some of those stink bombs in the beer bottles. There were so many of these fucking bottles, God only knew where the stinky ones were—there was no fuckin' way we were gonna find them. That motherfucker. All we could do was laugh. The Boss fucking gassed us out. Once we got out of the room, we saw Ozzy and told him it was pretty fuckin' funny how bad our room smelled and how he got us good. He played dumb and said, "What? I don't know what you're fucking talking about." Sure he didn't.

"That's cool, man," I said. But in my head I was saying, "Payback is gonna be fucking brutal."

Ozzy typically spent most of the day watching VCR tapes of World War II documentaries, since he is a huge war history buff, so while we were jamming, he wouldn't have to be bombarded by our volume of doom all day and could just come in later to check everything out and sing a bit. He had moved the couch over to where he could stretch out and watch TV. One day Ozzy and Tony had to go into the city to do some interviews. As soon as they left for the interview, I took a shit into a brown paper bag and slid it under Ozzy's couch, right below where his head would be. The couch had tassels hanging from the bottom so you couldn't see what was underneath. Then Randy took a shit in a Tupperware container and stuck it in the back of their refrigerator behind a bunch of stuff so they wouldn't find it right away.

My shit must have stayed under the couch for five days. Oz said the whole time he smelled something that reeked like rotten fucking ass and couldn't figure out what the fuck it was. Well, he finally figured it out. And the games continued.

The next day we finished jamming and went back to the room. Randy took a shower, and then we got ready to split for the night—headed to a couple of bars in town. The entrance to our side of the house we were staying in was this hallway where you opened one door, stepped into a corridor, and then opened another door to get inside. We all followed Randy out the door and into the hallway. He made it through the first door and then stopped dead in his tracks. He flipped the light switch and it didn't work.

"Hold on a second. It smells like shit. That motherfucker did something in here," he said. Randy lit his lighter and waved it around, and he discovered that the door handle had been completely smothered with shit. Obviously Ozzy had taken a spoon or something and smeared shit on anything that we might grab or touch in the hallway. We looked through the hallway window into his fuckin' room, and there he was, peeking out from behind a curtain like Mrs. Kravitz, smiling, laughing, and waiting to see if we were gonna grab the shit handle. These kinds of pranks ran rampant until we all headed back home. For several days after I got back home I was double-checking everything at my own house to make sure it didn't have shit on it. It was like when war vets come home and get those fuckin' nightmares and flashbacks. As always, it was nothing but laughing our balls off and having good fucking times with the Boss.

Eventually, Ozzy had a recording studio built into his home. While we were in there recording the tracks for the *Black Rain*

album, Oz and I got to talking about how much money went to studio costs over the years. For me, it was seven Black Label studio albums, some live records and DVDs, and a couple of solo albums. That's a decent chunk of change right there. But for Ozzy? It was millions upon millions of dollars. It cost a few hundred thousand dollars to make each record and his career spans back to 1968. Obviously the first records were low budget, but if you added all of them up, you could take all that money and build twenty studios.

Fast-forward to 2009, when Barb and I converted our guest-house into a recording studio, or as it came to be known, the Black Vatican.

Back when the Warden and I first bought the mountain we live on, the guesthouse was where we lived with the kids. Sometimes, it would be us, the kids, the tour manager, band members, guitar techs, the whole fucking cast and crew in all its glory. Yeah it was tight, but we always had a great time with all of our Black Label brethren—barbecuing, drinking, shooting steroids, taking Viagra, starting a religious cult, starting our own brokerage hedge fund, buying bulk Girl Scout cookies and reselling them at a higher price so we could afford the barbecue, booze, and steroids. All the while Barb designed the main house that we live in now.

When we used to go into the recording studio it would take

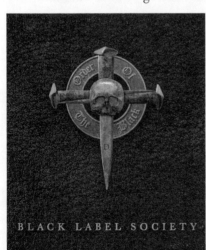

BLACK LABEL SOCIETY

me an hour or two to get to the studio and an hour or two to get back home. Add up all the hours driving back and forth, combined with the money spent on the studio, and it only made sense to have my own place to record. You know, why rent when you can own?

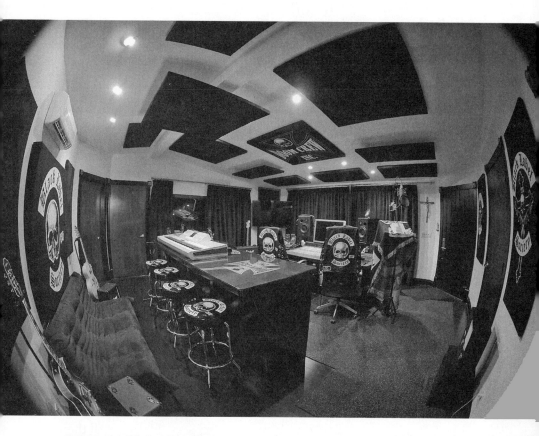

Order of the Black

WE RECORDED THE ENTIRE *ORDER OF THE BLACK* ALBUM IN THE BLACK Vatican. Pretty much like every other Black Label album, it took us ninety-four days, including writing, recording, mixing, mastering (with George Marino), and artwork, to get it fucking done.

The great thing about the Black Vatican is, not only can I record, but I can mix there as well. So basically, we can make the doughnuts, box them up, and ship them all out of the same place.

Here's where all the magick happens—where the performances go down. You know, where we run our Black Label racketeering, prostitution, money laundering, and gambling. We just don't dabble with illegal narcotics. We only bootleg alcohol. It's because we're nice people. For fuck's sake, you've got to draw the line somewhere. If we got into illegal narcotics, I don't know how I'd sleep at night.

Anyway, the control room is kind of like the bridge on the legendary USS *Starship Enterprise*. Except for on our ship, we can't save you. Because everyone on board this ship is a complete fucking idiot. You can see the drum room off to the side, behind glass, so that we can all see each other and the joy upon our faces as we head into the musical train wreck that is the almighty Order. You can also see where I record my vocals and spew my literary masterpieces of poetry that become Black Label lyrics of wisdom, wit, charm, and adorableness that could only come from something as precious as the taint between my balls and my ass.

Here is the piano room. If you look up to the left of the piano you'll see a video screen and camera that allows me to see the rest of my Black Label brethren at the console and in the drum room, where they can also see me and tell their friends they were lucky enough to share breathing space with me. Remember, I'm the lead singer, so I can pull out this douchebag shit any time I fucking

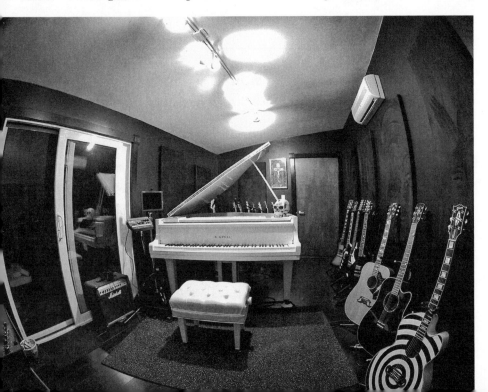

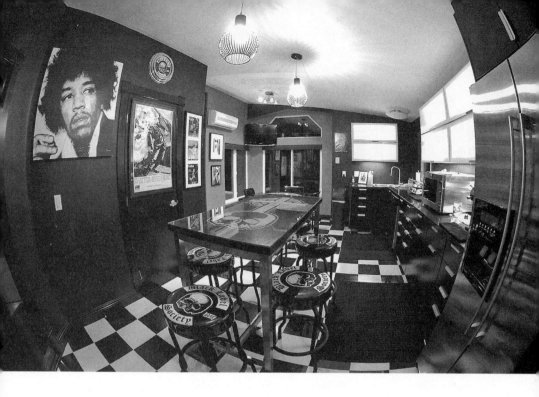

want. Sue me. Go ahead. I've actually sued myself several times for defamatory remarks made to me, by myself.

This allows me to keep a close eye on JD, wherever he may be lurking around the studio—you know, when he's not pillaging the kitchen. Oh, and if it seems like I'm picking on JD a lot—that's because I am. But in all fairness, I've given him a platform to defend himself, directly proportional to the level of his importance in the band—he gets two words at the end of this book.

The Black Vatican kitchen. JD's favorite place in the studio, where he can receive a *free* meal, wash it down with a *free* beverage, get *free* Internet access (where he can hook up with scantily clad women on Facebook), and watch pay-per-view (for *free*). Have you noticed how many times I've mentioned the word *free* here? Now you know why it's JD's favorite room in our sonic Black Label cathedral.

The Black Vatican lounge. For inspiration, the walls are covered with huge posters of Father Van Halen, Saint Rhoads, Pope Page, Father Di Meola, Father McLaughlin, Father Trower, and other guitar gods. Basically, it looks just like my bedroom when I

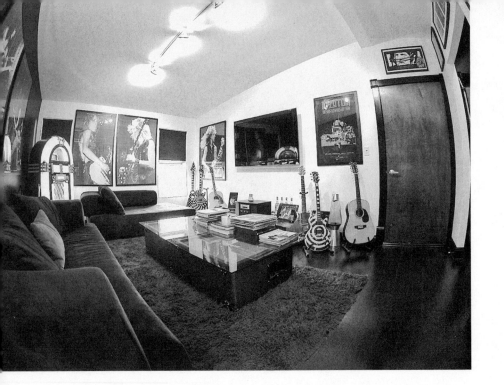

was fourteen except now the pictures are in frames instead of just duct-taped to the wall. Thank you, God—you rule!

Zack Fagan (of Under the Wire) was the guy who put Ozzy's bunker together. He did such an awesome job with that studio that I had him come out and build mine as well.

It's great having the studio, but I picked a terrible time to stop sniffing glue and drinking booze. Back in the day when I would be out at a studio making an album, we would buy these blocks of studio time from noon until midnight every day to record. By the end of each recording day, I'd be too tired or too wasted to drive home, so I'd lie on the couch and pass out. At that point I figured there was no sense going home anyway, since as soon as I got up in the morning it would be time to get my ass back down there and do it all over again. But the deal is, they charge you an extra thousand dollars if you spend the night. I can't tell you how many thousand-dollar nights I spent doing that.

Now, with the studio right next to the main house on the grounds of our compound, if I was still drinking, I could get

BRINGING **Metal** TO THE CHILDREN

blasted to all hell and then just float, or roll down the hill, until I landed at the house. But I'm high on life now. Yay! Go team! Frank Sinatra once said, "I feel sorry for people who don't drink. When they wake up in the morning that's as good as they are going to feel all day." I do have to disagree with Mr. Sinatra. After Barb fingers my asshole and sucks me off, I feel as if I'm brimming with "country freshness" and ready to take on the day!

But when I get up, that's not the worst I'm gonna feel all day. I'm gonna see JD's mug and want to ram my car straight into a fucking telephone pole. The best I'm gonna feel? That would be the magickal moment in my day when the Mongoose leaves the room.

Under the Wire
BY ZACK FAGAN

HAVING WORKED WITH BOTH OZZY AND ZAKK IN THE STUDIO, I was honored when Zakk asked me to design, engineer, and construct the Black Vatican. No two studios are built, or sound, the same. And Ozzy's and Zakk's studios are no different. In fact, while Ozzy and Zakk are linked forever in friendship and music, their studios have totally different vibes and couldn't be more unalike.

I utilized a more traditional approach when I picked equipment for Zakk's place. My philosophy is that the Classic Neve and API mic preamps are *must-have* pieces of equipment in any modern studio, regardless of your recording medium. Everything starts at the mic preamp. And when you want to capture the pure essence of hard rock and Heavy Metal guitars, Neves and APIs do it the best. Ozzy has some Neves also, but no APIs.

Zakk also had some Eventide Ultra Harmonizers in storage that we added to the equipment rack. They take a while to warm up and sometimes they lose their settings but nothing sounds like the original. Of course the plug-ins are cool, but it's nice to patch into a piece of history every once in a while too!

As far as the equipment list goes, I chose everything in the racks except for the Eventides. I knew what Zakk needed and put the studio together like it was my own. He always wanted vintage gear, which I agreed was the way to go. And while we didn't put in any hardware Pultecs, we did get the plug-ins to satisfy Zakk's need for the vintage EQ.

Ozzy's studio is an underground "cave" with no windows or natural light, whereas the Black Vatican is flush with windows offering natural light and beautiful views of the mountains. Glass is challenging to work with because it reflects sound around the room, causing echoes and false interpretations during playback. To resolve this, we installed acoustic treatments on the walls and ceilings and heavy sound-absorbing curtains for the windows.

One day on the job, I was out on the porch and was startled by a sudden thunderous noise. It was Zakk playing his guitar in the driveway with his Marshalls cranked full blast. He played like that for over an hour, with no worries because his neighbors are so far away, there's no one to bother.

I'm sure Zakk will tell you about the Pazuzu Loo, the studio's bathroom designed to literally scare the shit out of you. That's one of Zakk's passions, scaring people. During the construction of the Black Vatican, he made it his personal mission to scare the bejesus out of anyone he could. I'd be bent over measuring something and he'd quietly push the door open, creep up on me, and then yell at the top of his lungs, "Whattaaayaaaaaaa doooooooooin'!!!!!!" while slamming something heavy onto the floor for the added boom!

Note from Zakk: Father Fagan, awesome job on the Black Vatican, my Black Label brother!

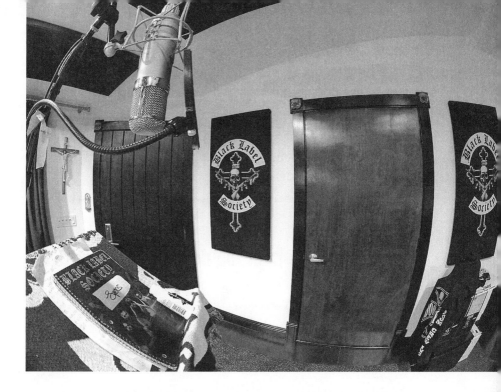

This is where the gospel of the Black Label Order religion is spoken. A religion of confusion for the confused, by the confused, who not only enjoy being confused but have no other option yet to be completely and utterly—confused. Mind you, we're all happy.

Now, when it came to painting the outside of the recording studio, Barbaranne picked out some nice brown colors that matched our house, and JD's underwear. But when the painters arrived, I was there to intercept and send them back to the store to exchange all the brown paint for flat black. That's right. I made the executive decision that the entire exterior of the Black Vatican *should* be black. I thought it came out great, but the Warden fucking hates it, and that's putting it lightly. She said it looks ridiculous and then asked me if I was Anton LaVey or twelve years old. But I dig it and if Jimi Hendrix had a home studio he'd probably have painted it purple and it would have looked cool as hell. I'm the Black Label Society guy, not Brown Label Society, so the Vatican is *BLACK* . . . end of story.

Right after the killer paint job was done, I sent some photos of it to Father Eric to show him that I actually did change the color. Eric loved the color and agreed it was the perfect choice. So then I told the Warden, "Look, you love Eric, and Eric loves the black paint job, so by default, you love the black paint job." How do you like that philosophy, Barb?

Barb replied, "You're not a philosopher. You're an asshole."

"Get That Shit out of the House"—The Warden

As you can probably tell by now, the whole studio is mainly black and white, from the checkered tile floor in the kitchen to the black walls throughout the interior. We did use red for one wall in the kitchen and also for the entire bathroom, which I've designed as a tribute to the 1973 film *The Exorcist*. The Pazuzu Loo, as we now call it, is decorated with original images and oddities from the movie, some signed by Linda Blair. At one point we were trying to get a small statue of Pazuzu for the Pazuzu Loo.

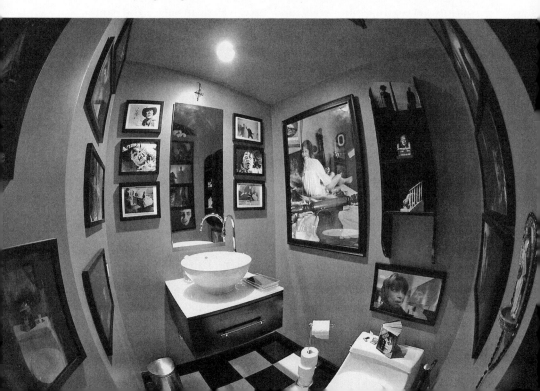

That's where the Warden put her foot down. She said it would bring bad spirits onto the property. I think that regardless, if JD is using the Pazuzu Loo, there's gonna be some serious bad spirits in that toilet anyway. What would you expect from a guy whose nickname is Meatball Lasagna?

To give you a quick crash course in Babylonian demonology, Pazuzu is the king of the demons, ruler of the wind, and bearer of storms and drought. He has the body of a man, the head of a dog, eagle-clawed feet, two pairs of wings, a scorpion tail (which I think is to scale, otherwise it would be pretty ineffective), and a snake for a penis. And while he's known for bringing famine during dry seasons and locusts during rainy seasons, I think he's not all that bad as far as demons go.

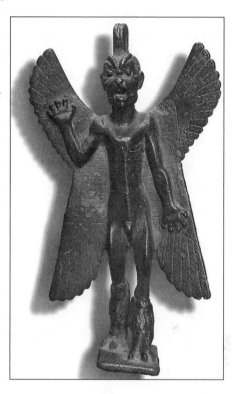

Pazuzu drives away other evil spirits and protects humans from plagues and other misfortunes. It sounds like he got a bad reputation after his appearance in the movie if you ask me. But the way he dragged Linda Blair's character Regan around the ceilings also hints that he might have some anger issues or maybe didn't get enough hugs from his Babylonian mommy.

In *The Exorcist*, Pazuzu is responsible for the demonic possession of twelve-year-old Regan MacNeil, played by Linda Blair. Regan undergoes some seriously disturbing psychological and physical changes when she is possessed. It's hard to forget those images of her scarred and bleeding face and now no one has to forget them, because I've practically wallpapered the studio's bathroom with them to frighten the guys while they're taking a piss. When I'm working in the studio, my eight-year-old son Hendrix loves to hang out in the lounge and play video games. But the poor little guy covers his eyes when he goes into the Pazuzu Loo because it's "too scary" and he winds up pissing all over the place. You can be sure of one thing: I'm not gonna catch any of my friends whacking off in *this* bathroom. That's what I thought at least. After recording the *Order of the Black* album, JD broke the news to me. He said initially he would bless himself with the holy water that we keep at the door every time he entered and exited the bathroom, but Pazuzu couldn't deter him from exploding in there a few times. Now I'm wondering which pictures did it for him. Was it the shot of Regan foaming at the mouth or the shot of her with her head spinning around?

Pazuzu has become the practical joker of the Black Label Society. It seems like when something goes mysteriously wrong, he's always behind it. The other night I was going over the final artwork for the *Order of the Black* album, reviewing all of the lyrics to make sure everything was written exactly how the songs were recorded. I went over it with a fine-toothed comb and got everything perfect. A couple of days later, after everything had gone to print and it was too late to make any changes, I was reading the lyrics to "Godspeed Hellbound" and found that the lyrics are flip-flopped in some places. Sure enough, in the CD insert, that is the song with a picture of Pazuzu on the same page. It's like Pazuzu is sitting at a pub in the sky with a couple of his buddies, laughing at us and saying, "Suck it, Trebek!"

Actually I had a dream about Pazuzu and asked him if he was behind the misprint on the lyrics. He said to me, "Don't blame me for that shit. It had to be some fucking moron working in the printing department of your record company."

My "Run-In" with Satanism

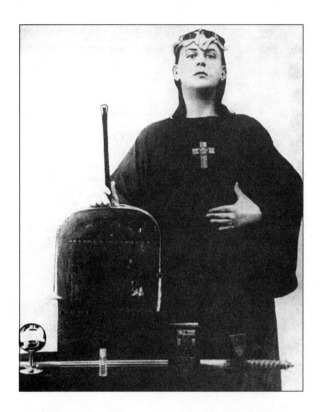

SATANISM. IT'S FUNNY HOW STUFF LIKE THIS GOT BLOWN UP IN THE media and people started using the "S" word. How anyone could ever think of Oz as a Satanist is beyond me. Within the Ozzy band, our running joke was that if you didn't know anything about Catholicism or Christianity, you would be converted by the time you left the show because he says "God bless you" about ninety thousand times during any given night. I've never understood the whole Sabbath-and-Ozzy-Satanism thing. He's always got the crucifix on the stage and on his clothes, and one around his neck made by his father. In fact, Ozzy's father made the crosses that all the guys in Black Sabbath wear, with their names engraved on them. So yeah, it always puzzled me why anyone would think of him as satanic. The funniest and coolest guy on the planet? Definitely. Satanic? I don't know what the fuck they're talking about.

When we were working on the *Ozzmosis* record, we stayed at a hotel on Lexington Avenue in New York City. I would go into the studio with the guys and track music all day and then head out to the pubs at night. I also had an interest in reading up about all the occult stuff that Jimmy Page was interested in. I would go into this occult bookstore called the Magickal Childe—this place was absolutely amazing. It had books on everything from Christianity to Wicca to Judaism to Buddhism to Hinduism to Luciferianism to Satanism. I bought some books about and by Aleister Crowley to find out what the big deal was—you know, why Page was so into him. I picked up books on all the occult players—Anton LaVey's *Satanic Bible, The Golden Dawn,* and stuff like that, just to check it all out.

It was also during those New York sessions that I wrote most of the songs that were on my *Book of Shadows* album. I would go over to this bar on Thirty-fourth and Lexington and drink until six or seven o'clock in the morning. The guys in the pub were cool, and I'd bring my guitar in there and jam cool songs all night—Neil Young and stuff like that.

Back in the hotel, Barbaranne didn't like seeing all these books lying around. She said they were dark and evil and that we didn't need that kind of shit around us. I would explain to her, "Barb, they're only fucking books, just paper with words like any other book. It's not a big deal."

I told her, "If these guys were the enemy, then maybe it would actually be good to know what the fuck the enemy does—you know, as a soldier of Christ, shouldn't I know what the opposition is up to?" That philosophy didn't fly well with the Warden—we weren't getting any laughter out of that one.

One afternoon I was looking for my books, *The Satanic Bible* and the Crowley books. I knew I had them in the hotel room because I was reading them that same morning before I left for the studio. But I couldn't fuckin' find them. When Barb got back to the room from cruising around the city all day, I asked her if she had seen my *Satanic Bible* and the Crowley books.

That's when she told me, "Yeah, I fuckin' heaved them out the goddamn window earlier, because we don't need any bad, dark shit in our lives."

Being the good Catholic and wonderful Samaritan that I am, it suddenly raised another concern. Our room was on the twenty-first floor. You wanna know fucking evil? Take a hit in the head from a *Satanic Bible* that dropped twenty-one fucking floors before colliding into your skull.

"Are you fucking kidding me?" I said. "You know what evil shit you should have heaved out the window? Those *Cosmopolitan* magazines that give advice on how to know if your man is cheating on you and whatever other bullshit they cram in there to ruin a hardworking guy's day. Not even Anton LaVey would want to take credit for the evil manipulative shit in that rag."

I could just imagine some guy down there sitting on a bench near the hotel—had a terrible day, his wife just left him, he lost the house, has nothing left, just lost his job. He's just sitting there thinking to himself, "Please, God, give me some kind of sign. What do I do?" Then *The Satanic Bible* comes plunging down from the sky and plops right into his lap. Contradictory to Barb's belief that she was doing good, she could have actually been converting people to Satanism, one book at a time.

The next morning I was out in front of the hotel getting a cup of coffee and talking to Tony, a hotel employee. I told him what happened to my books and that we were lucky that Barb didn't kill anyone when she tossed them out the fuckin' window. Tony told me he saw the books out on the sidewalk the day before. They were gone by then. So once again, Barb was indirectly spreading Satanism rather than preventing it—out there recruiting for the dark lord. I swear to fuck I see a *Seinfeld* episode in here somewhere.

Back at the Magickal Childe, they had a poster of Aleister

Crowley that was actually priced at six dollars and sixty-six cents. I had to ask the guy working there, "Excuse me, how much is that poster there?"

Without cracking a smile the employee said, "That would be six dollars and sixty-six cents."

I had to buy this thing because of the price alone so I said, "Here's seven dollars. Keep the fuckin' change," and headed out with my new poster.

Over the first few days in the studio I put up a bunch of cool posters on the walls to give the place some character while we were recording. You know, so it would look like my bedroom as a kid. It looked killer when I was done, with posters of Led Zeppelin, Crowley, Hendrix, and stuff like that.

Ozzy came into the studio one day while I was tracking guitars to see how things were going and hear some of the new tracks. He was checking out all the posters, telling me stories about his experiences partying with John Bonham and how he was the nicest, sweetest guy on the planet and loads of fun to be around. Then Ozzy asked, "Hey, Zakk, who's the bald-headed cunt on the fuckin' wall?"

And I asked, "What?"

"That fuckin' bald-headed fuck. Who is it?" he asked me again.

"You don't know who that is?" I asked him.

"Who the fuck is it?" he asked.

I said, "Oz, you've been singing about him for the last twenty years, man."

Oz gave the man in the poster a long stare and then asked, "Who the fuck is this fuckin' guy, Zakk?"

"Who else could it be, Oz?" I asked him.

"Who the fuck is this fuckin' cunt on the fuckin wall?!" His patience was gone.

I said, "Oz, that's fuckin' Aleister Crowley, man."

He looked at him again and then said, "Oh, is that what he fuckin' looks like?"

We must have been on the fucking floor crying for about

twenty minutes after that one—absolutely pure Ozzy pricelessness!

Back in the Sabbath days, it was Geezer Butler who was well-read on religion and the occult. And he had a memory like a fuckin' library. You could ask Geezer about anything regarding the occult or anything else mysterious and he'd lay it out for you as if he was a history professor.

One day Ozzy took my *Satanic Bible* and was looking at it. You know, before Barb chucked it out the fucking hotel window. He thumbed through it for a few minutes and then came to me saying, "You know, Zakk, if you're reading this stuff, you're practicing it." So I said, "Really, Oz? Because I saw Geezer thumbing through my *Flex* magazine the other day, so I take it Geezer's gonna be taking a shot at the fuckin' Mr. Olympia competition this year! I guess he's gonna be benching four hundred and fifty pounds this week after all that practice!"

Oz kept thumbing through the book and then said to Geezer, "Anton LaVey. Now, where do I know that name from?"

Geezer told him, "Remember when we did the record release for the first Sabbath album in San Francisco? Warner Bros. threw a big party for us. It was on California Street. The Church of Satan headed the parade."

Oz responded, "Oh, so that's the guy. No wonder the record didn't do as well as it could have."

Captain Kirk Visits the Black Vatican

HAVING THE BLACK VATICAN HAS NOT ONLY BEEN PERFECT FOR RE-cording my own music, but it's also proven itself a noteworthy mecca for other great artists.

Recently, we beamed up Father William Shatner to the Black Vatican to collaborate with me on a version of Black Sabbath's "Iron Man," an adaptation we did for Father Shatner's record *Seeking Major Tom*. It was an honor having him in the studio. I've loved *Star Trek* since I was a kid—the toys, the whole nine yards.

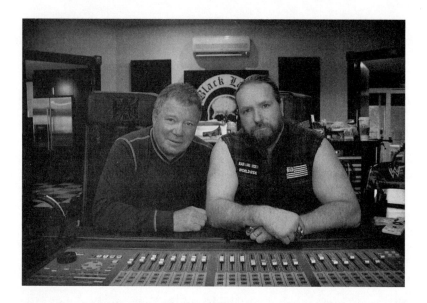

My father even took me to a *Star Trek* convention once. So to actually have Captain Kirk in the Black Vatican was slightly illogical yet truly amazing.

Note from First Officer Commander Hendrikx: I was at the Black Vatican that day to collect data of this encounter with Captain Kirk and Captain Wylde. (You can find the video from this day on YouTube.) When Captain Kirk and his lovely wife Elizabeth arrived, I asked him how he managed to find the place so effortlessly—it's not an easy location to find—and he leaned toward me and replied, "Well, son, I just used my Global Positioning System. There was no need for the cloaking device, as Federation law does not allow Klingons anywhere near the Interstate 5 highway."

Impressed with his strategy, I replied, "Brilliant, sir. Welcome to the Black Vatican, captain. Please follow me up to the studio. Captain Wylde is expecting you."

We were all settled in the studio except for his officers, Chief Tactical Officer Adam Hamilton and Chief Engineer John Lappen, who were lost somewhere in the dismal abyss that surrounds the almighty Black Vatican Mountain. While on his com-link with

Officer Hamilton, Captain Kirk announced that they were somewhere near a cosmic wormhole. "Does anyone know where the black hole is located in this system?" he asked.

"I know exactly where it is. Tell them to stay calm. I can be there in a matter of nanoseconds once I reach light speed," I said.

"Remain at your current location!" the captain commanded his officers. "Do not enter the wormhole! Help is on the way!"

The captain then turned his attention back to me. "Commander Hendrikx, make haste! They are stranded on the cusp of space and time. If they enter the wormhole, we may never find them!"

"I'm on my way, captain!" I said as I raced to my craft and took flight toward the supergalactic phenomenon.

As I closed in on the gigantic wormhole, I detected their spaceship parked near its perimeter. I pulled up next to their vessel and asked, "Do I have permission to board?"

"Yes!" they exclaimed. "But before you do, I noticed that there's an It's a Grind coffeehouse in this supergalactic parking lot. Would you mind if we paused for a cappuccino?" I quickly boarded and reset their coordinates for the Black Vatican.

"Cool, follow me," I said, and off we went. Had I shown up a moment later, the two officers and their ship would have been reduced to subatomic particles and slurped into the spiraling wormhole.

After leading them up the Black Vatican Mountain at warp speed, I brought them to the studio, where we landed our fleet in the driveway. I escorted our visitors to the Black Vatican, where I turned to Captain Kirk with pride in my accomplishment and had the opportunity to utter something I've always wanted to say: "Captain Kirk . . . mission accomplished."

Note from Zakk: Yep, that actually happened. Father Eric was, is, and always will be, a complete douche. No matter what planet, galaxy, or universe, there seems to be no sign of intelligent life anywhere . . . when Eric is around.

Weapons for War

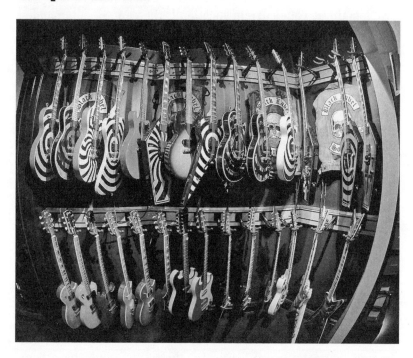

Guitars. What more can I say? More proof God exists. Although I'm known as a Les Paul custom guy, I love them all. I haven't run into a guitar I haven't liked. If they're a little banged up, give them a little TLC, and they'll give you a lifetime of it back. To this day, I'll look on eBay or go around to music stores while on the road, and if I see a really cool guitar, I'll bring her home.

I just find them so fascinating. Each one has its own personality and charm. It really is amazing that no two guitars are alike. No doubt the true sound of a guitar player is from his hands, from his soul, and from the good Lord. But what makes a Les Paul unique is its fat, thick tone, and what makes a Strat unique is its liquidy single-coil tones. And what makes me unique is that I'm a

Bringing Metal to the Children

warm, fuzzy, swell kind of guy with a fourteen-inch cock—stacked with the fact that my wife is all of five foot two, which makes it look that much bigger as it's splitting her in half. What makes JD unique? Nothing. He is an utter waste of flesh. Sorry, I take that back. The guys who supply him with his medical marijuana consider him the greatest guy on the planet. Rightfully so; he's been keeping them in business all of these years.

Long-Distance Drinking
by Rita Haney, Dimebag's Hag

My relationship with Darrell allowed me to have some of the most amazing people and friendships in my life, and Zakk is one of those people.

I remember one particular day Zakk and Darrell were on the phone for seven or eight hours. I kept havin' to bring Darrell a different phone because they kept going dead. These two guys were doing shots all day . . . long-distance drinking! Zakk was in California in the recording studio, playing songs like "Whiter Shade of Pale" on the piano. Darrell was at our place in Texas, out by the pool. The two of them just spent the whole day drinking together, doing shots, all by phone. I think to myself now, if only Darrell was here today, he would so appreciate Skype and iPhones, and the boys would enjoy things like that.

They both understood what it meant to be *that* guitar player and have that kind of weight on your shoulders, which nobody else could understand. Those two could always relate on that level. I think that's one of the reasons why they had such an amazing bond and friendship. And thank God those two didn't grow up. I love the fact that they were always like kids.

Darrell used it to do odds 'n' ends around the house.

Dave was over at our house one night when our friend Outlaw showed up in this beat-up, mangled old pickup. This truck was so trashed, I didn't think anyone would pay a hundred dollars for it—but that is exactly how much Darrell paid Outlaw for it! Unfortunately, the truck wasn't Dave's for long. He left for tour on Ozzfest that summer and never came back. He passed away from heart disease.

After Dave passed, the truck stayed at our place and Darrell often used it to do odds 'n' ends around the house. One day, Zakk was in town for another one of their infamous all-nighters, and he and Darrell ended up jumping into the truck and proceeding to create one of the original *redneck landscapings* in our front yard. They tore all around the studio destroying every plant and tree in sight, and then came back around the front where there *used* to be this apple-blossom tree. They took a drag strip start at this thing and knocked it clear into the neighbor's yard. I had to run down and close the gate so they couldn't leave the property.

When the taxicab van finally showed up to take Zakk to the airport, he picked up one of the branches that had come off the apple-blossom tree and stuffed it up on top of the van. It was completely hilarious watching the cab driver freakin' out and Zakk yelling at him, "Just drive!" as these guys headed down the road with this giant tree branch hanging off the roof of the van. He and Darrell always tore up some stuff, but the way I look at it, you can put that stuff back, but you can never replace the memories. As Darrell would say, "You roll with it or get rolled over."

During that stay, Zakk went down to the studio with Darrell and recorded the answer-back vocals on the Damageplan song "Soul Bleed." What jump-started the recording was that we had pulled the cars out of the garage prior to

Zakk's being there and had it set up for a photo shoot that Darrell had been doing for a guitar catalog. Zakk was sitting in a chair in the middle of our garage with an acoustic guitar, playing songs for us. It was so amazing and the acoustics in the garage were incredible. I have at least an hour of video footage of that, where Zakk was like our own personal jukebox, just a wonderful time. In fact, we started calling him the Jukebox, because he can play absolutely any song you want to hear and it always sounds amazing.

Zakk's many talents always amazed Darrell and me. He started out being known as a guitar player and then let the world hear him sing and then play the piano. A few years ago, I was staying at the Wylde compound during preproduction for the Mafia tour. One particular morning, Barbaranne had taken their daughter Hayley Rae down to Mrs. Rhoads for her piano lessons, and their son Jesse and I were in the kitchen deciding what we were going to do that day. Zakk sat down at his grand piano in the entry room and played "Tiny Dancer." It sounded so amazing, listening to his performance echo around the house. I know if Darrell had been there, we would have crawled underneath that piano and listened to him play all morning, like we used to lie on the floor and listen to the Jukebox back at our house. It's mind-blowing what that big, burly, scary-looking guy can play and the feelings that come out in his music—really magical.

Note from Zakk: Thanks, Weety! Awesome times for sure. But let me tell you something that's truly magickal—Saint Dime's workout routine.

Now, this is coming from Father Chris Kinsey, who worked security and took care of Dime. Chris is a big boy himself—works out regularly, eats clean, does bodybuilding and power-lifting, which was what me and Chris used to shoot the shit about when we'd all roll together.

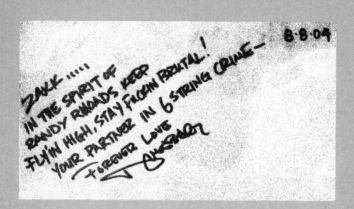

ZAKK......
IN THE SPIRIT OF
RANDY RHOADS KEEP
FLYIN HIGH, STAY FUCKIN BRUTAL!
YOUR PARTNER IN 6 STRING CRIME—
FOREVER LOVE
8·8·04

When Dime was getting ready to roll on the road with Damageplan, I had been talking to Father Chris, asking how my brother Dime was doing. Chris said, "Actually, Zakk, I got him working out now, getting ready for the tour."

"No shit," I said. "Don't fucking tell me he's hitting the fucking iron. Like benching, curling, working back and legs, the whole nine yards?"

Chris says, "Wait, slow the fuck down. I'm not entering him into a power-lifting or bench-press competition just yet. I got him doing push-ups, sit-ups, curls with dumbbells. Baby steps for now. And I'm gonna get him to start up some cardio soon as well."

"Are you showing him what to eat too?" I asked.

"Yeah, I'm trying to clean up his diet."

I then asked Chris, "Yeah, but he's still pounding the sauce like it's nobody's fucking business, right?"

He says, "Well, some things never change, Zakk. But he is making an effort, though."

"What do you mean?" I asked.

"Now he's putting Diet Coke into his Black Tooths instead of normal Coke."

So I told Chris, "You mean to tell me that crazy motherfucker thinks by still drinking a gallon and a half of Crown Royal a day, but replacing the Coke with Diet Coke, that

A few years back I got a call from Rich "The Duke" Ward (of Fozzy) inviting me to come down, hang out, and check out the guitar parts for a Kiss tribute album that he was tracking with his singer, and my good buddy, Father Chris Jericho. Bruce Kulick was also in on the project. Bruce was lead guitarist in Kiss from 1984 to 1996 and is a super-cool guy.

After they wrapped up their session we started just hanging out and playing songs, something BLS, something Fozzy, a Stuck Mojo song, Ozzy songs, the whole spread. It seemed like we were getting drunker with each song. We kept turning up the volume on the studio speakers. And Bruce was getting nervous, saying shit like, "Guys, you can't turn the speakers up, it will damage the

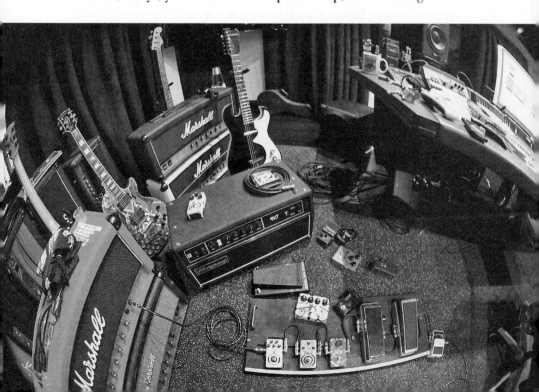

speakers." Father Jericho insisted the opposite, explaining to him that we simply had to have it louder. Chris rightfully said rock and Metal should be turned way the fuck up to sound their best. So we cranked that shit louder and louder until the speakers finally did blow and smoke was literally coming out of them.

"Oh my God, the speakers are blown! The speakers are blown!" Bruce was swearing. And we're singing back at him, "We blew your speakers in the name of rock 'n' roll!" We continued to play the music through those speakers, regardless of the shitty sound and smoke; yet another fantastic night of debauchery and destruction.

World Tour Survival Technique: Meditation for Tranquility of Mind and Spirit—Serenity Now

WITH ALL THE EXCITEMENT OF GOING INTO THE STUDIO TO MAKE YOUR album, it is a good idea to find a way to keep your mind clear and focused on the task at hand and not let the process get you too stressed out to be creative. Fundamental to making good music is being in the right mental place.

Here is what I want you to do right now:

Imagine, if you will, that you are relaxing in a beautiful mossy meadow. You are listening to a brisk stream as it gurgles and playfully tosses pebbles about in its childlike grasp. A light summer wind bends the branches of willow trees overhead. Their leaves rustle like the sound of angels laughing. You feel the warm sun baking the small of your naked back. Your belly lies flat along the coolness of a large stone that sits adjacent to the giggling brook. You are completely peaceful and at one with nature. Suddenly, you feel your inner guts separating as a large moose crams his dry, leathery cock straight up your ass. Your eyes widen and bulge out of their sockets, your shoulders crumble, and your fingertips bleed as you grate them into the stone before you. It takes only a second to realize what is happening, as your tear-filled eyes spot a massive hoof braced against the stone you are being crushed against, and shadows of the moose's giant antlers dance on the rock face before you.

If being raped by a gigantic moose doesn't shock you into focus, I don't know what the fuck will. Stop being a baby and handle your shit. There's no fucking meditation in Get It Fucking Done.

Note from Zakk: This meditation is an actual excerpt taken from a romance novel that I found stashed in JD's bunk after our last tour.

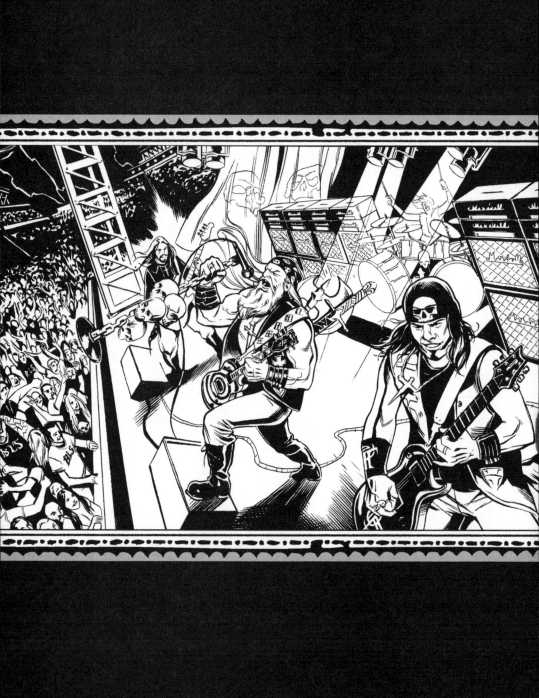

Chapter Three

GIFD

Once the fires of mine forgings were set ablaze and mine halberd shined with edges of sonic cries, the time would near for an assemblage of battle-ready brethren to prepare to lay siege to unsuspecting villages across the land and seas. Our dreams of glory and the Spoils of War shall dance within the heads of the horde, for the weight of the expedition's success lay firm upon the shoulders of the Berzerkers. Make haste we shall, for there is no time to tarry!

With our force of marauders set to task, we trained in skillship and strategy for war. And on the first eve, as I lay face to the moon, Odin camest to me once more and spoke of faraway lands and of peoples of foreign tongues. And he employed me to command the Berzerkers to take the entirety of the known world, by rugged trail or by treacherous sea, building allies as we could, for soon cometh the winter of discontent. A fleet I assembled, and set charge the armor of the tribe to be fashioned, our crests to be emblazoned upon our shields and upon our banners for all to witness, for all in this battalion shall fly these brave colors with honor! Soon our brows shall be bound with victorious wreaths.

And by the end of the cycle of the third moon, they were battle-ready, armed to the teeth, and hungry for the blood of the innocent. All hath been forged in the likeness of mine leadership. And if we fail not in our deep intent, our foes shall be packed posthaste up to the heavens. For we bear the emblem of the Berzerkers, and none shall pass without the judgment of mine battle-axe!

Note from Zakk: "Emblem of the Berzerkers"? It's quite obvious after you've read this garbage that Father Eric bears the emblem of a fucking idiot. Yes, I've said this in the last chapter and the chapter before that. But it clearly needs to be told again and again and again and again. "No time to tarry"? WTF does that mean? Whatever it is, ignore it. But do keep this in mind—the farther you get through reading Father Eric's literary antics, the lower your IQ will actually become, until there's actually nothing left—just like him.

First . . . a Few Words About Feelings

AT THIS JUNCTURE OF YOUR QUEST FOR GLOBAL DOMINATION I FEEL obligated to take a moment and discuss the importance of feelings. I'm not talking about *feeling* as in "Man, that guitarist plays with some serious feeling. As in David Gilmour throwing down on the solo in 'Comfortably Numb.'" What we're addressing here is *feelings*, as in, "I didn't get put on the guest list for the show and it hurt my feelings." Well, in the immortal words of our fearless tour manager and field general Father Ferguson, "Feelings? I don't have time for fucking feelings. I'm eyeballs-deep in shit right now. Sort it out your fucking self."

Next.

The Secret Recipe for Black Label Chinese Chicken Salad

HERE IS WHERE I WILL TELL YOU, THE READER, THE SECRET THAT I AND the rest of the successful music community have kept hidden for so long. I shall impart to you the secret of my Metal-maniacal success, of how I got the gig for Ozzy, why Black Label Society is on a path of global domination, and how I'm able to continue to bathe my Immortal Beloved wife in my conquest on a nightly basis and keep her begging for more. Here is where I will let the pussy out of the knapsack. And since you paid the twenty-some-odd bucks for this book and I truly appreciate the extra dough, with my kids coming up on college and all, I'm gonna spell it out for you right here! But I warn you . . . this secret is so powerful, so magnificently perfect, that it just may drive you insane. I am putting my life on the line at the risk of offending the Shaolin monks of the Metal World, who may indeed track me down and assassinate me as the Bruce Lee of our times, except that I have none of the skills that Father Lee possessed, and none of the moves. But I have applied Father Lee's teachings of jeet kune do in the sack with my wife, Barbaranne—she is truly a formidable foe. So for all you have done for me, I am about to pay you back tenfold . . . and here it is:

WORK YOUR FUCKING ASS OFF, YOU LAZY PIECE OF SHIT!!!

You may be familiar with other similar (but different) phrases: Rust Never Sleeps, I Get Knocked Down and I Get Up Again, Never Surrender, Fight the Good Fight, Persistence and Failure Cannot Occupy the Same Space, If at First You Don't Succeed Try Try Again, Don't Be a Quitter 'Til You Hit Her in the Shitter. To tell it true, I'll quote one of the wisest sages to ever grace God's green earth—No Rest for the Wicked.

I realize that the concept of hard work is a startling and unforeseen illumination, but I'm not sure you completely get what I'm talking about here. I'm saying that practicing with your band twice a week and playing a local show a month isn't going to ever cut it. You literally need to bleed for it, pounding the fucking pavement like you're going to end up in hell itself if you fail. Then again, what the fuck am I talking about? I must have failed because I'm already in hell—I'm stuck with JDesus in my life. Moving on.

Just recently, I ran into some kid with his dad who was out in Los Angeles studying guitar at the Musicians Institute. His father asked me, "Is it a good place for my son to be?" Setting aside the hookers, all the crack cocaine, people dressing up like transvestites, the medical marijuana, and all the cool bars, I said, "Yeah, your son couldn't be in a better place as an aspiring musician."

All joking aside, he said they came from Oklahoma. And while there have been some great Okies who have come along in the music world, such as the amazing picker of doom Steve Gaines of Lynyrd Skynyrd and the one and only Father Cantrell of Alice in Chains, the fact is that being in Los Angeles at MI, not only are you going to run into other great musicians who share the same passion as you do, but you're right in the heart of the music business. And also, if you're into transvestites, crack cocaine, booze, strippers, medical marijuana, and having a fruity cocktail at my manager's Malibu mansion's wet bar, you couldn't be in a better place as an aspiring musician.

In my twenty-five-year career in music I've recorded six records with Ozzy, eight Black Label Society records, one Pride & Glory album, an acoustic album called *Book of Shadows*, and several live-show DVDs. That's about twenty albums, live recordings, and DVDs in twenty-five years, an atrovious span. Mind you, this alleged word *atrovious* that I just hit you with, I have no fucking idea what it means. I don't even think it *is* a word. [Note from the editor: Not a word as far as I can find.] Father Eric just explained to me that it means "grand" or "spanning great distance." Kids, I apologize. Father Eric feels the need to put these big words in here so when he's at a bar picking up a chick, he can really impress her with his vocabulary and his GI Joe doll collection.

My recording routine is to get into the studio for a few weeks, get the record done, and get it out for people to hear. Get It Fucking Done has been our mantra over all the years we've been hitting it. Guns N' Roses is one of my all-time favorite bands, the guys are all good friends, and I even played with the band back in '95. I love Axl, but I can't fuckin' understand how some bands take a dozen fuckin' years to make an album. The problem is that when you spend fourteen years getting the next Guns N' Roses record in the stores, all the fans have grown up and you have a completely new generation who don't know who the fuck you are. I know Axl was being a perfectionist. And in the end, having that much of a perfectionist mentality is also responsible for dozens of amazing hit songs and over a hundred million albums sold worldwide.

For me personally, an album is like a high school yearbook photo—a snapshot in time of where you were and what you were doing. When you look back at the album artwork and listen to the songs you wrote and recorded, you can look back and remember exactly where you were and what was going on at that time in your life. This is aside from the fact that I just like to keep working. I can't stand sitting at a fucking beach, hanging out exposing my pasty-white Mick-Kraut skin to the scorching sun, with sand finding its way up my asshole, and doing fuck-all. I always find myself telling the Immortal Beloved the same thing: "How the fuck is this having a good time? And how much money is this setting me back? I could have bought another Marshall head or another Les Paul instead of a couple of flights to the Bahamas." That's not a vacation to me. That's a fucking prison sentence.

A vacation to me is doing what I love. And that's creating. Although a lot of people have asked me to please find something else to create—such as empty garbage cans, which I could place myself inside. I ignore those chuckles and continue on with my annoyance.

I go into the studio most of the time without any songs written. Of course there are ideas. I play guitar and piano every day, so I'm always working on new material. But when I get into recording mode, that's when the ideas really come together into songs with themes and lyrics.

World Tour Survival Technique: Get It Fucking Done

ONCE YOU GET IN THE STUDIO, YOU JUST HAVE TO GET IT FUCKING Done, knock it out. We don't demo anything, because I've always found that when you demo songs, you end up just chasing the demos. Like when we worked on the *No More Tears* album, we were so excited when we first recorded "Mama, I'm Coming Home." Between Ozzy's vocal performance and the rest of the band's excitement, when we did the recording for real, we found ourselves constantly going back and referencing the demo tape, where the performances were amazing, yet the sound quality wasn't. Once again, it's kind of like when you get your first blow job. That feeling you get is incredible. And when I *gave* my first blow job to earn enough money to fuel up the van and get us that extra case of beer, that feeling was incredible as well. Not quite as satisfying as getting one, but incredible nonetheless. And you ask, "Nonetheless?" Well yes, the fact that I was sucking somebody off for beer money was incredible. Though the thought, "Why the fuck am *I* doing this?" ran rampant through my head—I thought as a lead singer I wouldn't have to be doing this kind of bullshit. Guitarist? Maybe. But lead singer and lead guitarist? Get the fuck out of here. Today we leave that part of our business to JD. We don't have him coming out of the PA half the time anyway.

Therein lies the problem with doing a demo. Just go in with

good mics and good equipment and record it for real. If you're getting married, you don't do a trial run at getting married. You have sex with her first. And then you go, "Okay, now let's get married for real." That's how I did it.

If you know what you're doing, just Get It Fucking Done, right there, the first time.

How *Not* to Get It Fucking Done

BUT BEFORE ENLIGHTENING YOU BASTARDS AS TO *HOW* TO GET IT FUCKing Done, I want to first tell you how *not* to Get It Fucking Done. Believe me, there are more than a few things over the years that didn't pan out as well as I had hoped. One of those is the idea that making an epic demo and constructing the perfect cover letter, and then shotgun-blasting that package to every A & R rep, record label executive, booking agent, management company, and promoter will do anything more for your band than give you a moment of hope while you sit around waiting for the inevitable rejection letters that you'll be getting in the mail. I actually still have the letters Warner Bros. and several other major record labels sent in response to the letters that my mother sent out on our behalf. Back then, just the fact that we got a response from a major record company was epic.

Back when I was a young clueless douche, I jammed in a few different rock bands. I remember it like it was yesterday. We had a fucking blast—learning cover songs from our favorite bands, always listening to music, talking about our musical heroes and how much they rule, and dreaming about being in the same position someday.

One of those early bands I played in was called Stonehenge. We hadn't even seen *This Is Spinal Tap* at that point and our name was Stonehenge. Obviously we had already tapped into Valhalla at an early age. We were a three-piece band. I was the singer and guitar player. Tommy Karrick was the drummer and John Kern played bass. But it seemed like every time we had a gig we'd be in some kind of argument and John wouldn't play, so our buddy Rich Diaz, who was actually a guitarist, would wind up playing bass at the gigs.

I had an Electra guitar and a pink Fernandes Stratocaster with Eddie Van Halen stripes. I played through a Yamaha practice amplifier, and later a Marshall combo that I had wired into a self-made cabinet. It was all *Sanford and Son* rigs back then for sure. For my effects I had a distortion pedal, a chorus pedal, and a wah pedal.

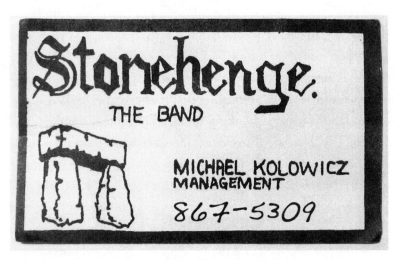

The best thing about that band was our buddy Mike Kolowicz, who was our manager. He had this briefcase that he carried around with a one-page performance contract that my mother helped him write—you know, in case our gear got smashed or anything like that. Then he had this fuckin' hatchet he kept in there—a fuckin' tomahawk—along with a ham sandwich and an apple. Mike was the true Peter Grant of Stonehenge.

We had jerry-rigged our own light show made from six coffee cans hanging from a stand, something we made in our electrical trades class at school. I actually still have the switchboard we made to control the lights, with switches and all. We had used our light show at a couple of parties before our friend Frank's dad, an electrician, checked it out and told us how dangerous it was and that someone could get killed just touching it. I guess all the wires were live or something like that. But with how loaded and beyond fucked-up everybody was at these gigs, I doubt anyone would even have felt the electrocution. They were all too busy feeling the electric shock musical therapy that was . . . STONEHENGE.

Our first big gig was at Ketchum's Kitchen, which really meant that we were playing at a keg party in someone's kitchen with the last name of Ketchum—Kevin Ketchum, to be exact. We asked for forty bucks to play—our big guarantee to play the kitchen gig. When we got there, Mike hit Kevin up for the forty dollars and showed him the contract. He explained to Kevin that if any of the equipment got damaged or ruined, he would be responsible. Kevin signed this thing and then up came the matter of the money, which he didn't have. He figured he would just toss around a hat during the party and collect the cash. Well, Mike, being the Peter Grant of Stonehenge, was *not* cool with this idea and told him, "That's too bad, man, because you know what, Kevin?"

"What's that?" Kevin asked.

"You ain't got a motherfuckin' band," Mike told him, matter-of-fact.

He took back the contract, tossed it in his briefcase next to the hatchet and ham sandwich, slammed it shut, and walked out the front door.

We were really bummed out because we wanted to play, and went whining to Mike about it, sounding like a bunch of Kansas City faggots—as Taggart from *Blazing Saddles* would have put it. He turned to all of us and said, "Listen, motherfuckers, you're never gonna make any money in this fuckin' business if you're acting like that." Next thing you know, sure as shit, Kevin came running out to the front lawn with the forty bucks, saying, "Mike, I got the cash, bring back the band."

And so it started right there at fifteen years old and it's never ended—it's the same exact horseshit game you get all the time from every promoter. Just when I thought I had graduated fuckin' high school in 1985—yeah, we've all gotten older, but it's the same king-and-queen prom bullshit going on all the time. But I digress. Let's get back to the legendary performance that forged my career—Madison Square Ketchum's Kitchen.

We opened up the gig with "Bark at the Moon" and right away Rich's bass cabinet blew the fuckin' window above the kitchen sink right out of the house, as he had his bass cabinet placed up on the kitchen counter. Tommy was wailing away on the fucking drums, his back pinned up against the refrigerator. And I was blasting away through my Marshall combo amplifier, just over near the pantry. They sure did stock some delightful treats in the Ketchum household. Later on in my career this would be known as catering.

By the end of the gig, doors were kicked in, windows were smashed, cigarettes and booze littered the floor—and no one had been electrocuted, as I could still see Father Mike alive and well, standing behind our light console of doom. It was a golden moment in rock 'n' roll and a snapshot of what lay ahead for my later years. It was definitely one unruly show, but the most riotous show during Stonehenge's illustrious and legendary career was when we played at Bobbie Bush's house—a gig that would be forever forged into history as the Bobbie Bush Demolition Derby.

Bobbie asked us to play at her house party just after her parents had sold their home. Her family was out in the Pocono Mountains for the weekend or something like that. Since the house was sold already, she had this bright idea that she was gonna invite half of our high school over as a going-away party. It was the perfect situation—the kind of fucking story that they make movies about, where the parents have left town and the entire high school, and God only knows who else, shows up at the front door. The house was clear of any furniture, stocked with ice-cold kegs of beer, blow, weed, speed, and every type of hard liquor imaginable. You know, kind of like every other rock show. And our band was billed as the live entertainment for this exodus of doom.

The night of the gig it was pissing down rain to the point that if you walked out on the lawn, you'd be sinking into it like it was fucking quicksand. All the gear was set up in the dining room. The house was bilevel, so when you went into the entrance some people would go down stairs, others would go upstairs. From the band's perspective it felt like we were playing at a fucking coliseum with people in front of us and also watching from up in the top balcony. We were playing songs from Jimi Hendrix, Black Sabbath, Rush, Ozzy, Cream, and a bunch of other cool artists and everybody was having a great time. The damage to this place though—my God. Now, being a parent and the motherfucker that's got to pay all the bills, if I came home to a disaster like this, I don't know where I'd fucking start—the mud that got tracked into this place from the rain completely demolished the carpets and made it look like a muddy football field by the time our gig was done. All of the sliding closet doors had been caved in, there were fist holes in the walls, cigarettes stomped out in the carpeting, empty and spilled bottles everywhere, garbage all over the fucking place—the house was completely annihilated. Some asshole had even written STONEHENGE WAS HERE on one of the walls in the living room. At that point, there was nothing living in the fucking living room! Fortunately for the band, none of our gear was damaged, just the venue—I mean, house—what was left of it.

After the big gig, we needed to get all the gear out of there and it was still pouring rain. My buddy Tommy brought his truck up on the lawn, so we could come straight out of the house and into the truck and avoid getting all the gear soaked. Tommy had one of those monster trucks with all the lifted shit, and it was a beast getting all the gear in the back. This was back when you had to get out of the truck to engage the four-wheel drive by locking it manually on the wheels. We got this thing into four-wheel drive, and then me and Tommy started throwing all the gear into the back of the truck bed. It had a cab over the bed so everything was protected once inside the truck—speaker cabinets, drums, fuckin' everything. That's when we noticed that the wheels were sinking into the front lawn. We ended up spraying mud all over the fucking place and getting nowhere.

I had to go back into the house to get the last of the gear while Tommy was digging up mud and shoving planks under the tires to see if he could get his truck out of the mud. When I tried to get back inside, our buddy Big Dave was making out with one of the chicks from the party and holding the door closed, keeping me out in the rain. I was yelling at him to let me in, but he was fucking around and thought it was funny keeping me out in the fucking rain. I could hear that motherfucker laughing with his cock-gobbling whore. So I went around to the back of the house, got inside, grabbed the last of my gear, and loaded it into the truck. A few minutes later, there was another pounding at the front door and Big Dave thought it was me again. He was holding the door shut again and yelling "Fuck off!" But this time it wasn't me—it was Bobbie's parents. As soon as I heard them yelling, "Let us in!" I didn't even want to see the look on their faces, so I ran out the fucking back door and headed straight to Tommy's truck.

I tossed my cables in the truck and jumped in. The truck was running and mud was firing all the fuck over the place, spraying back at the house, leaving it looking like King Kong had diarrhea and just shit all over the fucking house. We slid across the front lawn sideways and then literally caught air as we bounced off the sidewalk and ran the SOLD sign right the fuck over and took off. God only knows what Bobbie's parents said when they saw the straight-up, absolute fucking demolition of atrocity that had been exercised on their beloved home. When they saw the writing on the wall, STONEHENGE WAS HERE, they must have thought, "That's wonderful. Now go the fuck away and never come back!"

Pretty much all of the gigs that we did back then was just one fucking roller coaster of comedy. Nothing but good times. Actually, amazing-and-beyond-fucking-hysterical awesome times.

Looking back on the days when we started getting serious writing original music and had hopes of getting a record deal, we would send out demo tapes and letters to record labels, thinking that we were going to get a deal, with that drop-dead seriousness we had. I mean it's just fuckin' crazy to think about now—our music flat-out absolutely sucked. It was some of the worst and cheesiest "music" you've ever heard in your life. And remember what I say, because this is the flat-out God's honest truth: Play what you love and what moves you.

We were the epitome of the complete opposite of that. And the crazy thing is, I love Black Sabbath, Led Zeppelin, Jimi Hendrix, and Randy Rhoads. Yet our music sounded nothing like that. Our sound was so nutless that it made Bon Jovi sound like the heaviest Black Death Metal band you've ever heard in your life! Next to us, you would have thought Bon Jovi was Varg Vikernes—the Black Metal guy who ran around burning down churches! Looking back, I am glad we went through it. It made it clear to me that if I loved all those bands, then my musical styling needed to be at least somewhere in the fuckin' ballpark. The point is that if you're diggin' Metallica and Pantera, then your band should be able to open up for them and not get booed off the fucking goddamn stage.

Certain things just don't go out of style. Like with Guns N' Roses. Sure they were a bunch of nobodies at one point, playing clubs in front of ten people, but it didn't take long for that ten to become one hundred, two hundred, one thousand, tens of thousands. There was no *"Dear Record Label . . . blah fucking blah . . . we are so passionate . . . blah blah"* letter necessary for them to make it. They just did their thing and it was incredible. That's what got them signed. End of story.

Who the fuck actually sits around listening to shitty demos all day, hoping to discover the next Rolling Stones that no one else has heard about? It doesn't happen. If there is a band that is amazing and they are out playing shows, the crowds will continue to grow, the word will spread, and then there will be some greedy motherfuckers who will go, "We can make some money off these fucking clowns!" It's just the God's honest truth. And there's nothing wrong with that. If you really look at it, these guys actually believe there is a chance that money can be made off of your fucking band.

Take my manager, for example; the second he lent his ears to the musical stylings of the almighty Black Label Society, he didn't see musical notes. He saw dollar signs. And the music he heard? It was the sound of a fleet of Brink's trucks backing up the driveway of his Malibu mansion. And this is exactly why I hired him: to rape, pillage, violate, and plunder all evils as he strolls through the satanic scumbag underworld known as the music business—a world that is almost as frightening as marriage.

Just keep doing what you are doing, which is working your ass off so that you can do what you love full-time. If you ran a hamburger stand, and that was your only source of income, you would put everything you had into it to make it a successful franchise. You start off with a little stand and work your fucking way up until you become McDonald's. You have to treat your band as your job. And since it's what you love doing, it never seems like work. In Black Label, before my feet hit the fucking floor in the morning, I look forward to seeing my Black Label Shit To Do list for the day. And when I go to bed each night, right after I thank the good Lord for everything he has given me, I look at my colors and my guitar, thinking about what I can do to push the almighty Black Label Order forward. Actually, I got that from Les Paul, as I read that is exactly how he would go to bed each night, looking at his guitar. It was the last thing he saw before going to sleep and the first thing he saw upon waking up.

With our shit back then, we actually sent our demos and letters from my parents' house. I remember we were so excited one day when we actually got a response letter. It said something like, "Dear Douchebags, thank you for submitting your demo tape. We enjoyed listening to it and encourage you to continue in your pursuit and follow your passion. We wish you the best of luck on your way." We were so excited thinking that people in the record industry acknowledged us and actually knew who we were. The reality of it was that someone probably tossed our garbage demo tape in the trash without listening to it and then sent us the same boilerplate "Thanks, but no thanks" letter that went out to all the other pathetic bands across the country that did the same shit as we did.

If you've ever read any of those over-the-counter piece-of-shit textbooks on how to make it in music, then you've probably been injected with the same idea that a demo, along with a proper cover letter, will be the key to getting discovered. I would suggest wiping your ass with this advice, along with the cover letter if you've already started writing it. This shit advice is all written by some numb-nutted douche who never made it in music and decided to write a book as if they had been responsible for the Beatles' White Album. In case you're not familiar with this poor recommendation, here is an example of the type of letter you would be encouraged to write. I know this to be true, because I routinely receive letters like this asking me to notice a band I've never heard of or take someone out on tour with me. And mind you, their band might shake Valhalla itself, but a letter like this probably isn't going to get their demo a visit into my CD player. Just ask yourself this: As you are busting your fucking balls trying to get out of your shitty job and get your band to the mecca, Madison Square Garden, do you have fucking time to listen to other people's shitty demo tapes? No, you don't. You're too busy trying to get your own music heard. Making connections is far greater than sending out a stupid fucking demo tape.

Case in point:

There I was, Jeffrey Phillip Wielandt, from New Jersey, playing in a shithole in my home state. One night, a guy by the name of Dave "Face" Feld saw me play and asked me after our set, "Did you ever think about auditioning for Ozzy?"

I kindly asked Dave, "Do you know the guys in Led Zeppelin too?"

Dave told me, "I'm buddies with Mark Weiss [legendary rock photographer]. He's actually shooting with Ozzy this weekend. If you get me a tape of you playing, and some Polaroids, I can get it to Mark, who can give it to Sharon. I can't promise you anything, but I can make sure that Mark will get it to Mrs. Osbourne."

Without my walking into the club that night and meeting Father Feld, and us having that conversation, there would have been no Ozzy gig, no Black Label, no Pride & Glory, no *Book of Shadows*. Who knows? I probably wouldn't have even changed my fucking name to Zakk Wylde. So yeah, connections, some luck, and people you know definitely help. But then again, I can help you get an opportunity, but you have to be ready. Luck can't help you if you ain't ready. That's just life in fucking general. The sooner you fucking realize that, the sooner you'll stop having any of that woe-is-me shit.

Now here's a typical bullshit letter that a struggling band sends out in desperation and in hopes of getting their band noticed. Don't embarrass yourself like this:

> DEAR MR. WYLDE,
>
> I am the vice president of Dipshit Records, a newly formed record label with offices in Milwaukee and Baton Rouge, as well as the manager of the metal band Satan's Left Ball.
>
> Enclosed is a copy of their debut album, Satanic Placenta, released in February on Dipshit Records. Also enclosed is a copy of a recent review of that album, as a testimony to the band's most excellent sound.
>
> I am writing to see if you would consider having

*Satan's Left Ball open for Black Label Society either
on the Berzerkus tour or in the future, in the U.S. or
overseas. Satan's Left Ball plays all of their shows
with the same passion and fury that I have witnessed
from BLS.*

*Satan's Left Ball is in preproduction for their
follow-up album, which will also be released on
Dipshit Records. We are currently in negotiations for
a major-label distribution deal that would put this
album in Best Buy, Wal-Mart, and Target stores among
others as well as all digital outlets including iTunes
and Xbox Live (Rock Band video game download!).*

*I hope you like what you hear, Zakk, and if we can
tour with Black Label Society please have someone
contact me. I would like to send a limousine for you
when Ozzfest comes to Baton Rouge to have you come
by our studio to meet the band.*

Regards,
Mike Hunt
Senior VP of Douchebaggery
Dipshit Records
Baton Rouge, LA

It just doesn't fucking work this way. Your letter should describe how great your band is, how the Rolling Stones actually opened for you, how your music will save people's marriages, reseed their balding heads, and gain them passage to all fruitful things to come in the afterlife. I mean, if they don't know who the fuck you are, at least they'll have a good time reading a bullshit promotional letter instead of lumping you in with every other asswipe in the mix. If you go the route of the letter above, you might as well be selling carpet shampoo or a better scooper for getting cat shit out of the litter box.

To help you out, because I appreciate the dough you spent on this book, I've taken the time to devise a letter for you that I, if I were nineteen and in a band trying to make it in the music biz, would send out. Remember, show your enthusiasm and don't hold back.

Dear Mr. Record Company,

I hope this letter reaches you with urgency, as it is about to save your life. At this time I recommend that you completely isolate yourself from anything else that may distract you and then sit your ass down, fucker, and finish this letter.

If you haven't heard of the band I manage and front, Black Label Society, you probably spend most of your time practicing flexibility so that you can learn to blow yourself like Ron Jeremy, rather than keeping your ear close to the Metal scene. And for that I commend you. There are only two achievements in this life that will elevate your soul to the highest level: being able to blow yourself (thus eliminating any reason for dealing with a nagging girlfriend or wife) and signing my Metal band, Black Label Society. And since you probably don't have the yoga skills to make the first happen, you better check out my band—we are fucking awesome.

Black Label Society has sold more singles and albums than the Rolling Stones and the Beatles combined. Our band has sold out arenas in dozens of countries that we've never even been to or even heard of. Who gives a fuck where Kuala Lumpur is, as long as the ticket sales are through the roof, right? Our band is literally top-shelf, annihilating all other bands, and the potential of this Metal Machine is so powerful that if you sign us, it will save your marriage, raise your IQ by fifty points, give you superhuman strength, and basically make you more powerful than you could possibly imagine. The moment we ink the deal, God himself will send down a choir of angels to celebrate the occasion. Once again, we are fucking awesome.

I thought I knew excitement when my wife gave birth to our first child, but it paled in comparison to when I first heard our demo. We are fucking awesome. Becoming a born-again Christian was also a powerful day in my life, but again, by no means did it deliver the excitement and energy I received after first hearing our full-length debut album. We are fucking awesome. I mentioned earlier our record sales. Well, that offering was produced on a four-track recorder in our garage. As you can imagine, only great things will come if you invest in the future of this band, which you should sign to your label, because we are fucking awesome.

I'm including a CD for your listening pleasure. You may want to be in a private room when you listen. Why? Because we are fucking awesome.

Don't blow it like the idiots who passed on the Rolling Stones and the Beatles. This band is going to be the next big thing and if you don't realize it now and sign us, your life is going to be a miserable sack of shit. For all of the dipshits who missed out on signing Led Zeppelin and Black Sabbath: Well, here is your one chance for redemption . . . possibly even salvation.

If you decide not to sign us, you have no business being in the music industry; you don't know what you're doing or how to run a record company. At this point you really ought to start thinking about stepping off the top of a skyscraper or tying a side of beef to your back and sleeping with my wife.

Don't fuck it up. Don't make a decision that will
end up with our knocking your fucking teeth out.
By the way—we are fucking awesome.

You're welcome.

Zakk Wylde

Black Label Society

SDMF

I doubt any letters ever went out from Guns N' Roses or Van Halen before they got signed. Trust me, when the A & R reps went out to the clubs in Hollywood to see Guns for the first time, they were blown away by the band and the energy of the show. It was a lot like the first time I slept with Barb—she said to me, "My God, you are amazing!"

"I know," I told her, "Julie, Jessica, Susan, and Mr. Sinatra all said the same thing." Not the real Sinatra, my next-door neighbor Steve Sinatra—he couldn't hold a tune to save his life, but he gave a hell of a blow job.

Back to Guns N' Roses.

Their band was undeniable, and the record labels were scrambling to sign them. Trust me, GNR wasn't auditioning for anybody. They were amazing before they were signed. Same went for Van Halen; those guys were killing it on the Sunset Strip and had their pick of labels. If anything, there was a bidding war to sign them. When you've got great songs, are successfully building a following, and are packing the clubs, you're good to go. Keep doing what you're doing. Once again, all you should be worried about is promoting and pushing the band forward. Get your gigs, your merch, a van, a U-Haul, some friends as Doom Crew guys—and off you roll. With me, it's not Black Label 24/7—it's 25/8, 366 days a year, and fuck taking weekends off. God's day isn't just Sunday—it's *every* day.

From One Record Label to the Next
BY BARBARANNE WYLDE

IT'S SO AMAZING HOW THE MUSIC INDUSTRY IS PERCEIVED before you make it and how it actually operates. You would think of this massive company of savvy music listeners who know all the players, bands, and everything else there is to know in order to make their acts successful. For years, Zakk and I had these preconceived notions about which record labels would be the best for Zakk, and later just watched as their disappointing realities unfolded. When we signed with "Record Label X," we thought we had actually reached Valhalla.

Many years prior, when Zakk was doing Pride & Glory, we were with Geffen Records, whom we had been so excited about. We ended up getting kicked off that label in a short amount of time. After that, we went down a long, winding road of the most independent of independent record labels and back again. So by the time we got to "Record Label X" we were completely excited and felt that they were a killer label for Zakk's music and had an A & R guy who was really into what we were doing. It was a great situation all around, or so we thought.

One day during those recording sessions, Zakk was in the studio playing back some of the recorded tracks for the record label executives who had flown in from the East Coast to hear the new material. In walked this A & R girl, a totally cute rocker chick who looked the part and gave off the vibe that she knew what was up. She zipped right over to Zakk and said, "Oh my God, this is so cool! I'm so excited! I have loved you since you were in Black Sabbath."

Zakk, mostly preoccupied by the music being played back through the mixing console, reached over the board and lowered the volume. Then he turned to me and asked, "Did she just say that I was in Black Sabbath? Whatever, Black Sabbath, Black Label Society, maybe she just slipped up," returning his attention to the music.

I walked over to the not-so-savvy rocker chick and said, "You know, Zakk was in diapers when Black Sabbath was formed. Zakk played with Ozzy Osbourne. But we love Black Sabbath too," trying to lighten the mood. The other A & R guy was looking at me like he couldn't believe what she had just said. He and I both knew that if you catch Zakk in the wrong moment, he's not always that funny person we all know and love, if you know what I mean. Things could get heated and ugly in a heartbeat.

Once again, she opened her mouth and said, "Zakk, I gotta tell you, I fucking love 'Crazy Train'! That fucking guitar solo you do in that song is so mind-blowing, it's one of my favorite songs and also a really great pop song." This time Zakk turned the volume down and looked over at her.

"That would happen to be Randy Rhoads," he replied in a silly and sarcastic voice, fucking with her because she obviously didn't know what the fuck she was talking about. He turned back to the speaker monitors and rolled the volume up even louder than before.

I looked at our manager, Bob Ringe, and the label manager and said, "Is one of you guys gonna take this girl off the project or am I going to? Which one of us is going to tell her to get the fuck away from us? Because in about two minutes I'm gonna kick this chick to the curb!"

Zakk leaned over to me and said, "Sweetie, she would be perfect for our threesome."

I just looked at him and thought to myself, "Why would I want to share her with you?" and then kneed him in the balls, fisted his prostate, and went right back to my managerial duties.

The A & R guy looked at me and said, "Barbaranne, I have to apologize for her. She is really good at what she does. However, I was told that when she worked at another record label, they were repackaging the Jimi Hendrix collection and she literally asked what hotels Jimi preferred to stay at so she could book his travel arrangements."

When we got back home, Zakk said, "Barb, this record isn't gonna make it anywhere with these guys." And off we went to yet another label. It's always the same in this business—one step forward, ten steps backward, and it never ends.

Note from Zakk: Don't let Barb fool you. She went for the threesome. And it was more of a palming, caressing, and fondling of my balls than a knee. Her fist in my prostate? Yeah, that happened. Twice.

Remember—don't waste your time on frills and creative packaging that will make an impression. I highly doubt the Beatles sent out their demo tapes with a strip-o-gram or that Led Zeppelin packaged their demo in a sugar-cube castle with jujubes and gumdrops. Sure, sending your demo around the neck of a grizzly bear will make a lasting impression, but probably not the one you'll want to be known for, as the bear will devour the bloody entrails of the record executive who you were hoping would notice your band.

This brings us back to the question of "Who has the time to sit around listening to crappy demos all day?" No one I've ever come across in this business. Trust me. I've done what doesn't work. I've sent the demos and the letters and everything, and it's a complete waste of time, and I'm sure you'll agree that your girlfriend could be using her tongue in a lot better ways than licking postage stamps and envelopes. Instead of spending your energy killing trees and clogging up the postal system, the best thing to do is get your band together, write great music, promote the hell outta your band using the Internet and word of mouth, and get out there on the road and play for as many people as possible. It speaks volumes when people come to see your show and you kick the living shit out of their ears and blow their fucking minds. Of course this is all hard work, and not every musician has the intestinal fortitude to hit things that hard, but if you're going to succeed, you've got to man up, or as I like to say, Black Label/Patton up. Just look at it this way: For every guy who says, "My girlfriend/wife told me it's either her or the music," or who sells his guitar and goes for a shitty day job he fucking hates to get a steady paycheck—fuck them. Don't feel any sympathy for those motherfuckers. They ain't lions. And it just leaves more room for you and your band to rule the fucking world. In the immortal words of Saint Bon Scott:

> *Playin' rock 'n' roll . . .*
> *Gettin' robbed, gettin' stoned, gettin' beat up,*
> *broken boned*
> *Gettin' had, gettin' took, I tell you, folks . . .*
> *It's harder than it looks*

Life is tough. That's a good thing. It weeds out all the weak-willed motherfuckers. In Black Label, our motto is: Life is tough. Start eating nails for fucking breakfast. And right after a nice healthy bowl of nails, I lie down for a nappy while Barb rubs my tum tum. Then I take a shit and she glues my ass back together.

General Patton—Born in 1885 and passed away in 1945, General George S. Patton Jr. fought in World War I and later commanded corps and armies in North Africa and Europe during World War II. He played a major part in saving a boatload of American and Allied soldiers at the Battle of the Bulge. His nickname was Old Blood and Guts. How much more Berzerker can you get than that?

Another general and good friend of Patton's was asked what he remembered most about George. He replied, "He'd rather fight than eat."

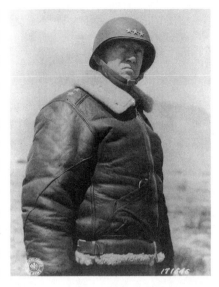

Basically, the complaint department was eternally closed and Patton expected everyone to live, breathe, eat, and bleed for the cause, just as he did. He didn't just walk the walk, he backed up all and everything that he said, and even more. General George S. Patton is a huge fan favorite within the Black Label Order and an inspiration to how we run our musical military operations. Black Label is much more than a band—it's a mentality. Life is war. Face your fears and accept your war. Black Label/ Patton up and destroy life's mountains of adversity. Remember, life and victory are for the brave and the strong, not the timid and excuse-riddled weak—JD.

State of the Black Label Nation

I'VE BEEN SAYING FOR A WHILE NOW THAT I'M NOT IN THE BUSINESS OF making records anymore. Nowadays for bands, it's about their live performances and selling T-shirts. On one hand, the days of *Appetite for Destruction* are over. But at the same time, it gives the bands and artists so much more control than ever before. Today, bands are literally their own bosses, which is pretty cool. You don't have to worry about not getting signed to Atlantic Records if you're twenty-nine years old and conceding to the fact that the dream is over. Fuck that.

You can make your own records, put them on the Internet along with your T-shirts and whatever other cool stuff you come up with, and sell it all from the garage of your house—or your mom and dad's for that matter. So there are no excuses as to why you didn't get signed to Interscope Records or whatever. Today, you can make a good living playing your music, with your vision, through live shows and the Internet. I have friends who couldn't stand their miserable jobs and now make a living selling stuff on the Internet, and love doing it. They're now their own bosses.

Your success is dependent on your own work ethic. There's no blaming anyone at the record company for fucking up your vision or not promoting your record right.

As far as all that shit that went down with Napster, their saying fuck Metallica for being greedy multimillionaires and that music should be free: Hey, douchebags, there was a point in Metallica's career when they were all eating out of fucking garbage cans, with twelve of them piling into one van and playing in front of maybe eight people. Why are they millionaires? Because they worked their fuckin' balls off for every goddamn penny they earned back then. These guys underwent a multitude of ass reamings before they became the gigantic machine of today. They weren't being fucking greedy. They were actually sticking up for the entire world of baby bands so that they don't get ripped the fuck off! In fact, it would have been easier for them to say, "We're fine. We're making millions." Instead, they stuck up for all the little guys and the rest of the industry so that they wouldn't get screwed.

World Tour Survival Technique: Making the Doughnuts

ONCE THE RECORD COMES OUT, IT IS TIME TO HIT THE ROAD AND GET the word out. I love hanging at Black Label family meet 'n' greets. Me and the rest of my Black Label brethren get to chill with our entire extended family—all the Berzerkers and Berzerkerettes. It's one big Black Label dysfunctional but loving family gathering.

The advice I always give bands that are starting out is to change their birth names to something more rockeresque, spend all their money on the tightest designer jeans they can find, and invest in a few cases of Aqua Net professional hair spray. And if there's any change left in the piggy bank after the new threads—eye shadow and condoms. It's solid decision-making skills like these that will keep your Metal machine moving forward.

Once you've handled your business, then focus on building a following doing live shows, and then handle all your own merchandise. These are the two areas where bands can make the money they need to record more songs and help pay for the costs of touring, whether it be going out on weekends in a van with all the guys or taking a road trip to play some shows. It's completely hands-on and whoever works the hardest will succeed. Everyone has got to start somewhere. Jimi Hendrix, Jimmy Page, Eddie Van Halen, and Randy Rhoads didn't wake up and become the gods that we've all come to love today. They each picked the guitar up, practiced, and got better and better and better. When your band starts out, you may be playing in front of eight people, and then there are ten, then twenty, then fifty, then a hundred. What I'm saying is that just like a plant, if you keep watering it, it keeps growing. And I say the same thing with my cock—the more Viagra I throw into it, the bigger it gets, and the more Barb moans and tells me, "It feels like child-birthing when you pound me into realms of pleasuredom that I've never experienced before. Give it to me *balls deep.*" Okay, you get the idea—just do the same thing, but with your band.

When we first started Black Label Society in 1998, our drummer Phil Ondich, or as I labeled him, "the Philthy One," was not only a great drummer and drinking partner, he was also a killer artist. Philth handled all of the artwork for the band. I would scribble down my ideas for T-shirts, beanies, and caps. Then after

Philth got done laughing his balls off at my Salvador Dalí-of-patheticness artwork, he would design them and bring them to life. Then we'd have them printed up ourselves and store them in our garage at the house. Barbaranne would take the orders off our website and print them all up. Then we'd pull the orders from the garage, stuff them into packages, and take them down to the post office ourselves. I even thought about hiring JD to help out but I would have ended up firing him at some point because he is useless. This is really a shame because with his little hands it would have been so much easier for him to stuff the envelopes. And nothing has changed since then—he's got the hands to get the job done, just not the work ethic.

Everything was hands-on back then and if anything went wrong we had nobody to blame but ourselves. I would always rather be as self-reliant as possible. Even today we carry all our own gear, merchandise, and anything else we can handle on our own. And all of this happened before the band had any merchandise deals or anything like that. It's how we started out and I really enjoyed doing it. When I was a kid I would have loved to have received a package actually sent by Jimmy Page, Eddie Van Halen, or Randy Rhoads.

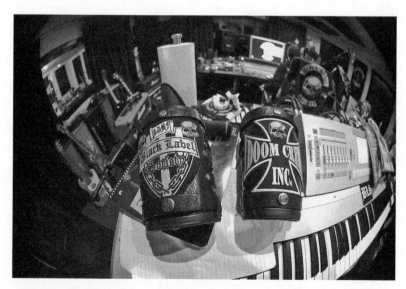

World Tour Survival Technique: The Great Crusade

So now your band has a strong identity and you've got your album recorded. And if you've paid attention up to this point you've come up with some cool merch and have stocked up on all of the cocaine and strippers you'll need to entice the radio programmers to play your mind-blowing record. It's clear to the Nordic gods that you've made the decision to grab your sac and be a true fuckin' Viking warrior. With all of these weapons now in your arsenal, it's time to embark on your magnificent campaign toward world dominance. Well done, my battle-ready brethren. Now it's time to tell your parents to keep your room clean and not to mess with any of your *Star Wars* toys while you're away on tour. Also, remind your wife to keep the kids quiet after nine P.M. each night so that your parents can get a good night's rest before they leave for work in the morning—somebody's gotta pay for all the diapers and the baby formula.

In order to get your band out on the road, you can either get out there on your own or get on a bigger tour as a supporting act for a more established band. As with anything, there are pros and cons to both, but if you want to play music for a living, you'll probably want to do it all. If I were a young Metal bodybuilder starting out and looking to carve my name into the bowels of Heavy Metal, I would van it. I'd get all my bandmates to pitch in and buy a van and book as many gigs as we could get to with a tank of gas. We'd hit the road night after night to get the songs out there. This is exactly what Black Label has been doing on a larger scale since day one. Sure, there was a little more cash in the bank to start off with, but the concept is exactly the same, just scaled up.

You've got to be cool with people and make friends out there, not just hit the stage and leave. You want to make friends everywhere you go so those people will want to come back next time you're in town, because you and your band are cool guys to hang out with. And if that means you have to pork someone's obese sister or friend in order to keep them coming to the show, so be it. Remember that story I told you earlier about when I got talked into making out with that heifer so that her brother would help out my band, you know, with all his "big connections" in the biz? I let that three-hundred-pound titanic love machine jump aboard, crushing my ribs and lungs as she tried to eat my entire face in the back of the car. Remember—MERCILESS. It really was my first attempt at making a big-time career move and as mentioned earlier, it didn't work at all. I'm still suffering back problems from this little incident. So maybe this paragraph doesn't really offer the best advice. The more I think about it, the more I think we better pretend like this part of the conversation, and this part of my life, never happened.

To get your band on tours nowadays you usually have to pay to play. It only makes sense; just like Coke and Pepsi duke it out for product placement in movies, you may actually have to buy your way onto a tour to be able to play in front of massive amounts of people. You're paying for the crowd, since your own band couldn't draw more than a few friends and family members to come see you. This way you're killing two birds with one stone, crushing it onstage in front of thousands of people every night instead of playing in front of a few dozen, plus you're on a major tour, which will beef up your Metal status, leading you to more opportunities. It will also keep you away from whoring yourself out like I did. Trust me, you're gonna be taking enough ass-reaming while in the music business—choose yours wisely. I didn't and my lower back will never forgive me.

With all the players involved in Black Label, I refer to running the whole thing as a military operation. My management team, the Warden and Bob Ringe, stay at the "White House," back home. I don't need management out on the road with me to hold up my balls, wipe my ass, and tell me how adorable and wonderful I am. I already know that. In fact, as part of my therapy, a therapy

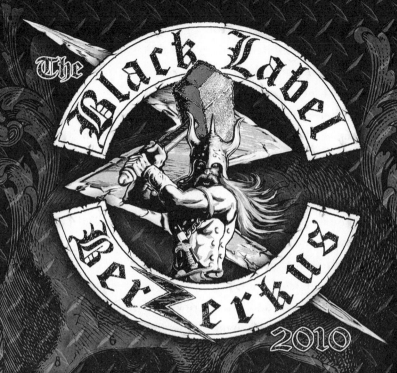

The **BLACK LABEL BERZERKUS**
2010

Black Label Society
Children Of Bodom
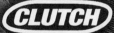

zakkwylde.com   **blacklabelsociety.com**
zakkorderoftheblack@gmail.com

that I developed, I stare at myself in the mirror and repeat this mantra to myself over and over—while wiping my ass. Actually, I don't really need the mirror. I just need the constant reminder that I'm wonderful and fucking adorable.

The president and his staff aren't running around out there in the battlefield where the bullets are flying; they stay at the White House making executive decisions while their soldiers fight the war. And if your manager happens to be Bob Ringe of the almighty Black Label Order, then there are massive split-second, make-or-break decisions that need to be made. This includes decisions about what kind of furniture is going to match the Italian stone floors and handcrafted shutters in his Malibu mansion, which wheels will look best on his new Mercedes Benz SL65 AMG, and whether he should go with the king palms around the pool or just more imported, high-priced European furniture.

When the band and Doom Crew are flying, I refer to our plane as Air Force One. If we're on the road in the tour bus, then we're all part of the Black Label Navy Team traveling in the Black Label nuclear submarine. I call it this because the bus, since it really is just a big metal tube, seems more like a submarine (Yes, I realize that the bus is on the road and not underwater. But mind you, back in the day, our liver, kidneys, and pancreases were constantly submerged in liquid.) And when we take to the water, like with the boats and ferries, it's also the Navy Team. Yes, it is very exciting. And I wonder sometimes, because it is a submarine, why couldn't JD's submarine sink to the grubby bottom, just sink like his self-esteem, his work ethic, and . . . should we even bring up his erectile dysfunction? Probably not—because all of the guys that he's slept with say that everything works just fine in that department. Now his dysfunction as a human being is a whole other story. You know how the U.S. military's motto is Be All That You Can Be? Obviously JDesus never got that memo.

Sex and Religion

BY PHIL CIULO, SERGEANT AT ARMS

ONE THING A LOT OF PEOPLE DON'T KNOW ABOUT ZAKK IS THAT he's a faithful Catholic who prays all the time, at home and on tour. Zakk's one of the most religious guys I know. One time in Winnipeg, Canada, we checked into our hotel and had just finished a couple rounds of drinks in the hotel bar. Zakk decided it was time to go pray. "Wake up the guys, we're all going to church right now," he said.

"Zakk, it's ten o' clock at night, brother. We aren't gonna find a church right now."

"Get the guys, we're going," he said.

So we all end up in a cab running around town looking for an open church, and all of them are closed. Finally, Zakk got out at one of these stops and knelt in front of this church, out in the frozen fucking tundra. It was thirty degrees below that night and Zakk stayed out there praying for twenty minutes. I thought he was gonna freeze to death. JD actually suggested that if we left Zakky out there long enough, maybe he would actually freeze to death, therefore giving the band a chance to "upgrade" their front man. Unfortunately for JD, Zakk was so sauced up on the booze that his blood was not capable of freezing.

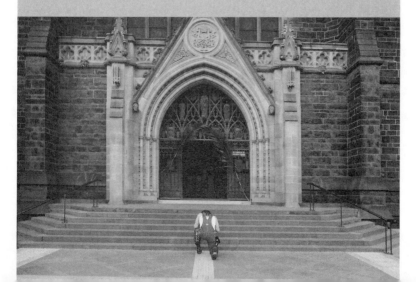

Another time in Winnipeg, we went into this fuck store and Zakk bought a batch of dildos and sex tricks. Barb was out on the road, and he was planning on harassing her later with his porn-shop shenanigans. He paid for the stuff and handed the bag to me to carry. Five minutes later, Zakk decided we're going to church, and there I was carrying a black bag full of dildos. We ended up in this Catholic church, during the hymns and sermon, and I was sweating whether or not this heavy bag of dildos was going to break open. How would I explain that one? An hour later, Zakk had his communion and we were out of there. God forgive us.

Note from Zakk: Actually, in that photo above, I'm not only giving thanks to the Good Lord, but I am also asking, no, begging my savior Jesus Christ, his holy spirit, and almighty God above to grant me strength and surround me with his white light as I battle the forces of darkness and pure evil that emanate out of one Meatball Lasagna—John "JDesus" DeServio.

Here's a shot from my birthday party in 2010 that Barb threw for me at a Moroccan place in Hollywood. Not shown here—my Black Label brother Nick Catanese, Father Cantrell, Father Jericho, and Father Blasko, among many other friends who came and celebrated. Unfortunately, the list of guests also included my brothers Father Eric and Father Phil—and again I use the term *brother* in the loosest sense, as in "Oh brother, they were invited too?"

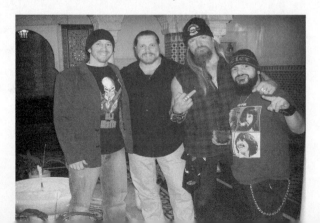

Scraps from the Lion's Table

WHEN YOU HAVE A FAMILY AND YOU'RE ON THE ROAD, THINGS ARE NATurally a little different than when you're single. If I were single I'd be out reaping the spoils of my grandiose celebrity and bathing women across the globe in my conquest each night, before, after, and possibly during every show. Now, mind you, the chicks that actually like me have humps on the back of them instead of in front of them, have more hair on their genitals than I have, and can bench-press, deadlift, and squat more than the entire Doom Crew combined—no wonder why I have so much time to practice. I think I'm gonna get my name changed again—to Eunuch Boy.

To be honest, this is the only reason I ever picked up a guitar and is the only reason any guy with the right frame of mind should consider playing a musical instrument. Not for the love of music. Not for the creative freedom. Not to follow your passions. You should do it in the sheer hopes that you might one day find yourself lathered up in a motel shower with two chicks at the same time. And all the better if you wind up in one of those showers with all the handicapped grab bars. God bless the Americans with Disabilities Act of 1990.

Note from Zakk: I didn't put in that shit about the disabled. Eric did. Sick fuckin' asshole.

Alas, as a married man, I've been told that now it's gonna be boring as I get the same thing every night for the rest of my life. So that's why I mix it up. You know, throw the gorilla suit on the wife while I fuck the living shit out of her. I love the feeling that I'm conquering not only her but wildlife at the same time. Whenever I buy these fucking costumes for her, people ask if they are costumes for my kids for Halloween. I just say, "Yeah, of course," right before I cut out holes for the vagina and tits and ass.

For the Love of God, Do *Not* Pick Up the Phone!

ONCE AGAIN, AS THIS BOOK OFFERS TIDBITS OF ROCK 'N' ROLL WISDOM, here's another story of stupidity and brilliance coming together, fusing into one hard lesson learned by one blond bomber douche—which would happen to be me.

Back in my high school days, or even earlier, all the chicks I was ever into dropped me like a bad habit, sack of shit, flat-out douche, or whatever other word they might use for someone they want to get the fuck away from them. I'd always get them flowers, candy, the whole nine yards. They'd just leave me with the bill and a set of fucking blue balls. So when me and Barbaranne hooked up, and she actually appeared to like me, I knew she was a keeper. And here we are, twenty-six years later, with three kids. But before I put that wedding band on her finger and locked her up in the basement of our house, I had to fulfill my fantasies of being *Bond*—that is, James Bond.

Now, like I said, being the Mr. Intercontinental that I am, with chicks lining up for herpes before spending a single date with me, there I was, nineteen years old, playing arenas and stadiums around the world with my hero, the legendary Ozzy Osbourne. Between the poofy hair, looking like some chick I'd want to fuck, and the fact that I was playing with the Boss, for some weird reason, I experienced something I never had before in my life— girls were actually coming up to me.

Enter *Bond*, James Bond—Mr. Intercontinental.

I remember we did this gig in Texas. I brought back some hot-looking mama-jama with massive jugs, curves of doom, and a full-on gorilla coat of hair on her back, just the way I like my women. Mind you, she was missing a few teeth and her hands were more callused than those of any bricklayer I've ever met. Basically, she was nothing like Barbaranne, except for the back fur.

So after a hot rocking show with the Boss, back to the hotel bar we went, where we were firing back cocktails like it was going

BRINGING 𝕸etal TO THE CHILDREN

out of style. Not long after, it was me and Mighty Joe Young getting it on in my hotel room.

Guys who had been out on the road for years told me, "Whatever the fuck you do, you fucking idiot, if you've got a chick in your room and an old lady at home, tell that chick not to even think about answering that fucking phone if it rings."

Of course. No problem. Right? Wrong.

Let the comedy fucking begin.

So after me and King Kong fought like Kong vs. Godzilla in Tokyo all night long, we both crashed out in the bed.

The phone rang.

In my head, between being so tired and having a decent bombo on still, I didn't know whether I was dreaming or what the fuck was going on. Next thing I knew, I felt these massive jugs rolling across my chest as Mighty Joe Young picked up the phone.

"Hello. Yes, this is a girl."

At this point I still thought I was dreaming. Well, whatever dream I was having was about to turn into a terrifying fucking nightmare.

Tits McGee then said, "Yeah, he's right here. Hold on a second. Zakk, it's your sister, Amy. She says it's a family emergency."

Now, mind you, my sister, Amy, is eighteen months younger than me, but there couldn't be two more completely different people on the fucking planet. Put it this way: She once went to an Eric Clapton concert and complained that it was too loud and too heavy. You know those Yanni concerts on pay-per-view? And you ask yourself who the fuck watches this shit? Well, that would happen to be my sister, Amy.

My sister would never call me out on the road unless it was something serious. The first thought I was thinking was that maybe something terrible happened to our dad, being that dad was an older guy and a World War II vet. I woke right the fuck up and sobered right the fuck up immediately as I grabbed the phone out of her hand.

"Amy, what's up?"

There was first silence on the other end of the line.

Then:

"Who the fuck is that whore in your room?"

I didn't say a fucking thing. I was fumbling in my mind about how the fuck I was going to get out of this one.

"I said, who the *fuck* is that whore in your bedroom? You tell that fucking bitch," she said, "to get the fuck out of your fucking room right now!"

If you haven't guessed by now, it wasn't Amy on the other line. It was Barbaranne—the Immortal Beloved. It's a pure Black Label stupid-yet-brilliant story, where I had stupid covered and Barbaranne handled the brilliance. She knew that I would never have picked up the phone if she said it was her. So in a split second, she knew to say it was my fucking sister and that it was a family emergency! So devious, so diabolical—yet so brilliant.

Again Barb said, "I want to hear you say it. Tell her to get the fuck out of your room. Say it!"

So I sheepishly mustered up my most pathetic, candy-assed douchebag voice and said, "You're gonna have to leave now."

That wasn't good enough for the Warden. Barbaranne told me, "I want to hear you fucking say it. Tell her to get the fuck out of your room."

Finally I told Milk Jugs, "Just get the fuck out of my room! Now!"

I got back on the phone with Barbaranne and said, "Are you fucking happy now?"

Barbaranne answered, "You're not in a position to talk to me like that. I'll deal with you later."

So, kids, the moral of this story is, if you've got an old lady, and you get an opportunity to fuck a chick who has man-hands and a furry back, just keep the visual in your head. Go back to your room solo, shove one fist up your ass, and tickle your prostate, leaving the other hand free to drink your beer and hammer your cock. That's about all the advice Uncle Zakk can give ya. Don't end up like me or Tiger Woods. You don't want that.

One night after a show, the guys brought this really filthy skank on the bus. This girl was just fucking salivating at the chance to be a star on the tour bus porn set. While we were drinking beers in the front lounge and laughing, she started blowing one of the guys, then another, and then another. I watched while this chick made her rounds with several of the guys and crew. Then she wanted to get fucked by everyone, and at one point she asked our sound man Dave his name and started screaming, "Fuck me, sound man Dave!" Being the class act that she was, she obviously wasn't interested in last names. Before Dave was finished with her, she yelled out, "Enough of you, I want to fuck the little guy," pointing at JD.

JD explained, "I'm sorry, I'm gay." See, kids, claiming homosexuality *can* get you out of a bind here and there.

The next day at sound check I walked into the venue and JD, who has a baritone voice and does an amazing Jim Morrison, was up on the stage with the band playing "Riders on the Storm," only he had changed the lyrics to "Fuck me, sound man Dave, your throbbing cock I crave."

Thick-Stick Nick

WE ALL USED TO LIVE VICARIOUSLY THROUGH THICK-STICK NICK CATanese and his stories, because he was single during the bulk of his time out with the band. He's settled down now, but he was a road dog for quite some time, and good for him. That's one of the reasons I called him my evil twin.

One particular summer we were on the road for Ozzfest, and all of us were on the same tour bus. I had my wife and the kids, Hayley Rae and Jesse John Michael, out with us; they were six and seven years old. This definitely put a cramp in the guys' style. The back lounge, which was usually used for many *other* things besides video games and listening to tunes, was now being occupied by the little ones.

One day, while in Pennsylvania, we were getting ready for a show at a club and this one girl was all hot on Nick. I think the guys had gone out to a strip club the night before and she was someone he had put on the guest list or whatever. She was hanging around all day and they were definitely looking for their moment to hook up, but Hayley Rae and my niece, who had come to the show, were absolutely obsessed with Nick. These two little girls just loved him. They used to fight over who was gonna marry him, who loved him more, and so on. These two girls were up his ass all day and the poor guy couldn't get five minutes alone with his new *friend*.

Hayley Rae was really jealous and whenever this stripper got close to Nick, she threw things, like pretzels, at her and told her, "He's mine." Barb and I just died laughing as this whole thing developed. Not long before, Nick had given Hayley this little promise ring, so he really dug his own grave on that one. From the time she was like six years old, she thought Nick was her boyfriend and God help any girl who got close to him. And this particular time, he really needed to get away from her to catch some groupie time. As it turned out, he didn't catch his break until *during* the show!

Everything ended up *going down* during my guitar solo. Nick took his stripper off the side of the stage and she took a knee and blew him right there. The whole time I was playing my guitar solo, Nick was praying that this was one of those nights when I'd decide to play a long one; I guess he was almost there. I think we both had our peaks during that solo. He wrapped it up, got back onstage, and we finished the show like a well-oiled machine.

The next afternoon, Barbaranne, Nick, and I were at catering when my son Jesse John Michael came up to Nick and straight up said, "Nick, I need to ask you a question. Everybody keeps saying that you had sex last night while Daddy was onstage, and I don't understand how you can take all your clothes off before Daddy is done with his guitar solo." I fuckin' spit my food out laughing while Nick turned sixty-five shades of red.

Back then, little Jesse John Michael thought sex was *kissing naked.* So Nick answered, "No, bud, I don't know where you would hear such a thing; how could I do all that while your dad is playing his guitar solo?" Satisfied, Jesse said, "That's what I thought. How could you get all your clothes off and kiss her and then put all your clothes back on before my dad is done? Everybody is telling lies." Then I explained to Jesse John Michael, "Son, you oughtta see what I do to your mother. Those aren't lies."

World Tour Survival Technique: To the Victors Go the Spoils!

WHEN YOU'RE STARTING OUT, DON'T COUNT ON GETTING A TOUR RIDER. In fact, count your blessings if you can squeak a few free drinks out of the bar and have a fun night. But it is good to dream that one day you will reach the Berzerker band level where you will be able to draw up contracts that cover all the lighting, staging, and sound requirements that a venue is to provide you when you show up to perform. The tour rider also covers all of the artists' wish-list items, like dressing room accommodations, transportation, and meals. As an artist you can ask for whatever you want. And how badly the promoter wants to have you play at their venue dictates how much they're willing to provide. Van Halen used their rider to get tubes of K-Y Jelly, booze, and cigarettes, and the legendary bowl of M&M's with "absolutely no brown ones." Marilyn Manson used his to get bottles of absinthe—that fuckin' shit Vincent van Gogh used to drink before he cut his own ear off and brought it to a prostitute. And aside from the obvious massive quantities of alcohol and smokes, Guns N' Roses abused their tour rider for guacamole and porn.

There aren't too many bands out there that would have the fucking set of steel balls to hand a promoter something like this, but it would be cool if they did . . .

Rock 'n' Roll Deity Tour Rider

UPON ARRIVAL: HOTEL REQUIREMENTS

Upon arrival to each city, Promoter to organize a ticker-tape parade to welcome artists. There must be a minimum of five thousand (5,000) people in attendance with banners, shirts, and face and body painting in the colors and décor of the band. Police escorts are to be called upon to bring artists through the parade, followed by a marching band and minimum ten (10) floral decorated floats.

Promoter will ensure that the Venue will provide for one (1) penthouse suite for each member of the band, with cinnamon candles burning and the Jacuzzi heated to 104 degrees. Ice buckets filled with bottles of Dom Pérignon champagne are to be placed within arm's reach of the Jacuzzi. (NOTE: If the artist has to get out of the Jacuzzi to reach the champagne, punishment will be a payment in the form of one rare 1937 three-legged-buffalo nickel.)

In advance of show, Promoter to submit minimum of twelve (12) photos with statistics of local stripper escorts to the attention of each member of the band. The artists will select three (3) or four (4) top choices, which are to be in the room upon arrival. These girls are not to wear more than a kimono and should bring with them a basket of scented oils and a copy of the **Kama Sutra** written in Sanskrit.

Married artists in the band are to be provided with around-the-clock security guards stationed outside of their doors. Guards are to be given photographs of the artists' wives and will be instructed to eradicate them should they show up unannounced.

Promoter to provide limousine service from the hotel to the venue. Each artist is to receive his own private limousine and have the option to bring the stripper escorts with him to the venue.

Large walk-in closets are to include sex swings, various toys for foreplay, and several male and female costume pairs, including cave people, Mexican banditos, and a Mr. and Mrs. Easter Bunny. All costumes should be dry-cleaned immediately upon departure and at the promoter's expense.

DRESSING ROOM REQUIREMENTS (SET UP AND READY BY 10:00 A.M.)

Purchaser will ensure that the Venue will provide one (1) private dressing room for each member of the band, equipped with king-sized bed, minimum sixty-inch flat-screen television, PlayStation, and small petting zoo. Animals are to include a pair of barely legal panda bears, baby white tigers, komodo dragons, and one (1) small dehorned mountain goat. Animal handlers to be provided and available at all times in case one of the animals bites a guest or takes a shit.

One entire wall of each dressing room is to be outfitted with a shark tank. Sharks should be in good health, have amazing patterns and markings, and be from exotic places around the world like Tavarua (*no* shitty Pacific blue sharks!)

Each room is to have a complete kitchen installed and have a private chef on standby to cook for up to twenty-five (25) people at once. Menus to be provided in advance, as well as one (1) special menu for a lactose-intolerant vegan, with allergies to all green vegetables and hyper-allergies to any fruits that remotely resemble sexual organs.

Each room to be equipped with a portable pool, at least five (5) feet deep, and equipped with a seventeen (17)–foot high dive and a fully stocked swim-up bar. All bartenders are to be female and should remain topless until after the artists leave the venue.

DEPARTURE

Band should be given the key to the city prior to departure, with emotional and impactful speeches made by at least two (2) recognized leaders of the community.

A large monument is to be erected and unveiled at the band's departure celebration, representing the community's appreciation of the artists' visit. Monument to remain for ten (10) years minimum, and is to be made of valuable material such as brass or iron (ABSOLUTELY NO CEMENT OR ADOBE BRICKS!).

Within a week of the group's departure, local schoolchildren are to be instructed to write thank-you letters to the artists, describing how their lives have improved from listening to their music and simply knowing that they were in the same town. Letters should be proofread and, if need be, rewritten so that the artists don't have to spend too much time looking through them. Poorly handwritten letters and letters that do not show outstanding merit are to be discarded as they are an insult to the eyes of the artist.

Note from Zakk: Now, mind you, this is Father Eric's little fantasy tour rider. As for me, I really couldn't give a shit what's in the rider. I would always prefer to be self-sufficient and buy my own shit, whether it's food, booze, water, or whatever the Black Label necessities might be. On tour, we usually just pull the submarine into a supermarket or liquor store and grab whatever we need. This way we always get exactly what we want. You rarely get exactly what you want when you're renting equipment or relying on others to go get things. This brings me to a great rider story.

I remember Oz telling me about the early Sabbath days when they were getting all the weed, cocaine, chicks, and booze provided to them in *Titanic*-sized boatloads. What they didn't realize was that they were the idiots who were paying for all that shit! Oz was saying, "Yeah, the whole time we thought it was because the promoters really liked us."

When they saw the rider bill at the end of the tour and realized that they actually lost money on that tour, they shit their pants. Word to the wise—nothing in life is free, my friends. You pay for everything. If you don't need it, get rid of it.

Of Mayonnaise and Manliness

THE BAND AND I HAVE ADAPTED THE NATIONAL PASTIME TO A CONdensed format that we can take out with us and that utilizes items found in most of the roadside diners and various eateries we encounter along the way, as well as from our backstage catering services—condiment baseball. This is one of our favorite games to play on tour.

It came about while hanging with Father Mike Inez on Ozzfest. Out of sheer Black Label mischief and comedy we decided to sneak off and grab all the condiments from the backstage buffet—you know, those massive jars of mustard, ketchup, mayonnaise, relish, and half-and-half—and anything else we could get our mitts on. We set up a small baseball diamond out back and slow-pitched the ginormous jugs of shit to the batter, who would hack away with wild swings, but when they connected, holy shit, what an explosion! Mustard and ketchup and all sorts of crap flying through the air and splattering all over the fucking place! Of course we'd run the bases, but that was more out of respect for the integrity of the game; it was really all about being able to smash stuff and justify making a huge mess. There are only two things in life that legally allow you to have this much fun and toss this much goo— condiment baseball, and when your wife allows you to go anal while choking the life out of her until she reaches orgasm. Okay, not the choking part, but definitely the ass-gaping.

But remember, these reindeer games are reserved for the battle-tested warriors of the horde; if you're a rookie on the road, expect nothing and consider yourself content if you score a meal and some drinks here and there. If you slap a promoter with a rider that looks like the one Guns N' Roses handed out, he'll probably just slap you right back and find someone else to play the gig. Be reasonable and when you grow up into a big rock star you can start asking for all the cocaine and dildos you can imagine. Always remember what Ozzy said about the Black Sabbath rider—if you're getting paid a hundred dollars to play somewhere, and all the bullshit on your rider costs ninety dollars, you're only gonna get paid ten. Don't forget, you pay for everything.

That's right, children; it all comes full circle, back to being a fuckin' man! Just because a guy is grown doesn't mean that he's necessarily a man. And if you want to enjoy the spoils of war, you've got to step to the task with a big, man-sized set of swingin' balls! And while we're on one of my favorite subjects—manliness—I decided to bring in a current expert on the subject. Who knows about manliness more than the self-proclaimed manliness expert Forrest Griffin?

Allow me to tell you a little bit about his expertise. This is a guy who was raised in the South by his mom. Now, on the surface, this may sound like a fertile breeding ground for a mama's boy, but that's not the case here. Forrest's mom gave birth to him while shopping at the grocery store and didn't miss an item on her list that day. She's beaten the piss out of Rottweilers to save his ass, wore the pants in the Griffin household, and instilled in Forrest the mental toughness necessary to become one of the greatest UFC fighters to enter the cage.

Now, I've seen Forrest fight in the cage several times. Did he show the stylistic boxing skills of the great Muhammad Ali? Not at all. Did he bring with him generations of traditional grappling reminiscent of the Gracie family? Nope. Did he even show that he could formulate a complete sentence in his post-fight interview? Negative. In fact, the only thing that comes to mind when I reflect on his fighting style is a chick fight I witnessed back in high school. Tons of wild swings, shrieks and scratching, and hopes that somebody's luscious tits would come flopping out, and whoever pulled on the other's hair the most came out the winner. But what Forrest lacked in skill, talent, and familiarity with the English language, he more than made up in heart—the heart of a fuckin' lion. When Forrest gets into the ring, yes he fights like a woman, but he handles himself like a true Berzerker, ready to die for his cause. Well, maybe not die, but at least have his nose moved to another location on his face.

Without further ado, I'd like to introduce the former UFC light heavyweight champion of the world—Forresssssst Grrrrriffiiiiiiiiiin! (I've always wanted to hear my name announced like they do before a big boxing or MMA match. I actually have my wife announce me like that before I invade her womb with my man-plow. You know, as in "Here CUMS ZZZZZaaaakkkkkk WWWyyyyyyylllllddee! Vagina Stretcher, Nine-time Champion of the Labia Octagon!!!" In case you aren't familiar with a man-plow, it's a penis. Although in some medical books it's known as a womb polluter.

Note from Zakk: Forrest, seriously . . . put that thing down. You're freaking people out at the PTA meetings. It's bad enough that they watch you beat the shit out of people for a living. Just be nice—say hello to people, make friendly conversation, and don't punch anyone. Thanks, buddy.

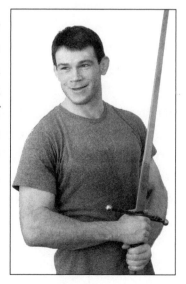

Forrest Griffin's Testament of Manliness

HEY THERE, I'M FORREST GRIFFIN. YOU'VE PROBABLY HEARD OF ME—well, of course you have heard of me. I'm not only a superstar athlete and a man of the world, but I'm also a self-appointed expert on manliness. Believe it or not, I hold a bachelor's degree in the study of manliness. And when I look at Zakk Wylde, the first thing that comes to mind is that he is some sort of Viking who was spit out of Valhalla due to his excessive amount of manliness. Even when I look back at photos of Zakk during his early years with Ozzy, where he looks like a cross between Farrah Fawcett and Lita Ford, I still see pure manliness—it takes a set of Godzilla balls to walk around looking that much like a chick. And the fact that he took that look and transformed it into the current Viking thing he's got going on now just reeks of machismo. Every time I see the guy, I want to ask, "Dude, where is your funny-shaped ship? You know, the one decorated with the heads of your enemies?" At the very least, the guy should carry a large broadsword wherever he goes, like into Starbucks or the Coffee Bean. But Zakk probably doesn't visit coffee shops like the rest of us squirrels, he just rips the coffee tree straight out of the side of a mountain and gnaws on its trunk and branches for his daily caffeine fix. He's just that much of a man.

Due to the massive sac of manliness he hauls around, I thought Zakk would be the perfect guy to contribute to my new *New York Times* bestseller, *Be Ready When the Sh*t Goes Down* (hopefully you bought fifty copies). He did a phenomenal job designing the Deathcore Warmachine—a vehicle designed for postapocalyptic survival based on his F-350 Super Duty truck—and, in all fairness, I thought I would reciprocate (in case you don't know what *reciprocate* means, it's kinda like when you promise your girlfriend you will go down on her if she gives you a blowee—except it's where you actually follow through with your promise). So, let me tell you why Zakk Wylde is a purebred Rottweiler of manliness:

● He has a wife who is way too hot for him. Considering that his beard looks like something a plumber would pull out of a clogged drain in a whorehouse and the fact that he smells like something a plumber would pull out of a clogged drain in a whorehouse, that is a massive accomplishment of manliness.

● He drinks like a thirsty fish. Well, he doesn't drink anymore, but it is important to remember that Zakk didn't quit drinking, his body did. And when he kicked the sauce, did he do what all Hollywood types do and go join an AA group or try to get on some schmuck-ass celebrity rehab show? Fuck no, he just quit. You could say he just *got it fucking done*. I like his acronym *GIFD*. Personally, I would have made it Get It Fucking Done, Motherfucker, but eventually you gotta stop with the letters. Get It Fucking Done, You Goddamn Motherfucking Douchebag-Riddled Cock-Cuddling Goat Fucker would also be neat, but in the end I guess GIFDYGMDRCCGF is probably less effective and memorable than GIFD.

● He uses no pussy hair-care products to tame his bestial mane. As a matter of fact, it appears as though the only products he has ever used are sweat, grease, and the Anal Eaze he uses to help him endure the ass-pounding he receives while trying to get radio programmers to play the latest Black Label Society bona fide smash-hit single. I'm telling you, it would literally break my heart if I found out he actually got stuff done to his hair. I would have to tear up my manliness manifesto. [Editor's Note: We reserved the right not to inform Forrest that Zakk actually triple-washes with Gee, Your Hair Smells Terrific and goes to José Eber's hair salon in Beverly Hills.] However, if I discovered that he has a harem of twenty virgin women follow him around on tour and stroke his hair with a silver brush with a bone-tooth handle, I could accept that— seriously, how long does it take to grow that much hair? He doesn't just dazzle his audience with blistering-speed guitar shredding, he also literally beats and pounds his chest while onstage like he's some kind of silverback gorilla, upholding his stage territory and challenging anyone to try to take his banana. Don't take his banana. It won't be pretty. We've all heard about his opting to put his wife in a gorilla suit instead of a French maid outfit when having "relations," so I don't think we really need to go any further into this punching-yourself-in-the-chest thing.

● The guy can bench-press over three hundred pounds. Over the past few years, he's suffered like twenty-seven injuries. He's had three pulmonary embolisms, throat surgery, hernia operations, and a broken back. Not to mention the gaping ass he has after the barrage of pummeling he's taken during his time spent in the music business. But none of that shit matters to him because he can bench over three hundo. Basing your overall health on how much you can bench instead of the actual physical state of your body is ultra-manly. Zakk is so manly, in fact, that when he breaks a leg or gets the flu, instead of going to the doctor, he goes to the gym. As long as he can still press three hundred pounds, the world is as right as rain. It all comes down to the bench, my friend.

● Like Batman, Zakk is a master of every martial art. He is so manly he can even make finger-painting cool. I'm not insinuating that he does finger-painting, be-cause I'm pretty sure he doesn't want me exposing that side of himself. But still, if he did in fact finger-paint (again, not saying that I've seen his finger paintings or anything, especially not that portrait he did of a nude male model during his Thursday-evening art class), it would be manly.

● Although Zakk will probably get mad at me for telling you this, I feel it is an important ingredient in his manliness. That guitar he always plays—yes, it turns into a battle-axe (imagine the battle-axe He-Man used to wield, and you're right on the money). If he plays a secret note, his musical instrument suddenly transforms into an instrument of death. No one knows this because anyone around to see this transformation instantly loses his or her head.

As you can see from the list above, Zakk Wylde is all man. (Possibly some kind of super-evolved man-gorilla-Viking, much more masculine than just man or gorilla alone. He has told me that his wife has an affinity for zoo animals and dated several different species of them while they were in high school.) However, no one is perfect. Below I have included a list of things that actually take a little away from his manliness points:

● An article about Zakk in *Revolver* magazine mentioned that he has a tremendously hyperreactive gag reflex. He says he discovered this while undergoing treatment for a polyp on his vocal cords, but it makes you wonder if perhaps he discovered this a lot earlier. Perhaps on some lonely night while on tour.

● I understand why a short guy would wear lifted boots, but Zakk is a tall guy. I mean, how tall do you want to be? I justify his boots by telling myself that it's his way of scaring away the annoying kids. I'm not saying he's out to kill children, but he definitely wants to scare them. And it works, for the most part. I know if he gave my son candy, I would not let him eat it.

● For the longest time I thought Zakk actually wore a kilt, but recently I discovered it is actually a flannel shirt tied around his waist. You know, the kind of shirt that dykes like to wear. I don't know why he would even own a shirt like that because everyone on the planet knows that he has never in his life worn a shirt with sleeves. The guy even has a sleeveless leather jacket. On one side, the flannel tied around his waist makes him look like a fat chick trying to hide her ass, which is not that manly. However, on the other side it resembles some *Mad Max* homoerotic-type leather attire, which is definitely manly.

● While it is certainly manly to be a rock god, the fine-motor coordination it takes to play the guitar bothers me a little bit. But at least he is not a singer. That would have really cost him some manliness points. [Note from the editor: Forrest still doesn't realize that Zakk is in fact the singer of Black Label Society. We try not to feed Forrest too much information at once or he may turn into a gremlin and start destroying everything in sight.]

There are very few people who I would want by my side when the apocalypse comes (and trust me, it is coming sooner than you think), but Zakk Wylde is definitely one of them—especially if he brings his guitar battle-axe and cuts off the head of anyone who is not a proud member of the almighty Black Label Order. So, in closing, don't fuck with this guy. I'm a professional fighter and get paid to punch people in the face, but I would not fuck with this cat in a million years. Seriously, heed my words and you may live to see another day.

Note from Zakk: Father Forrest, thanks for the dyke comment, my Black Label brother. I figured somebody was gonna pick up on that sooner or later. But it's actually not to hide my fat ass. It's to proudly proclaim my dyke-ness. Wait . . . so I am gay! Just a gay chick. I was confused up until right now—I'm cool with that.

And thanks for the comment warning people that you wouldn't fuck with me in a million years. Maybe if people read it coming from you, they will listen. As it stands, everybody is always picking on me and hurting my Black Label feelings.

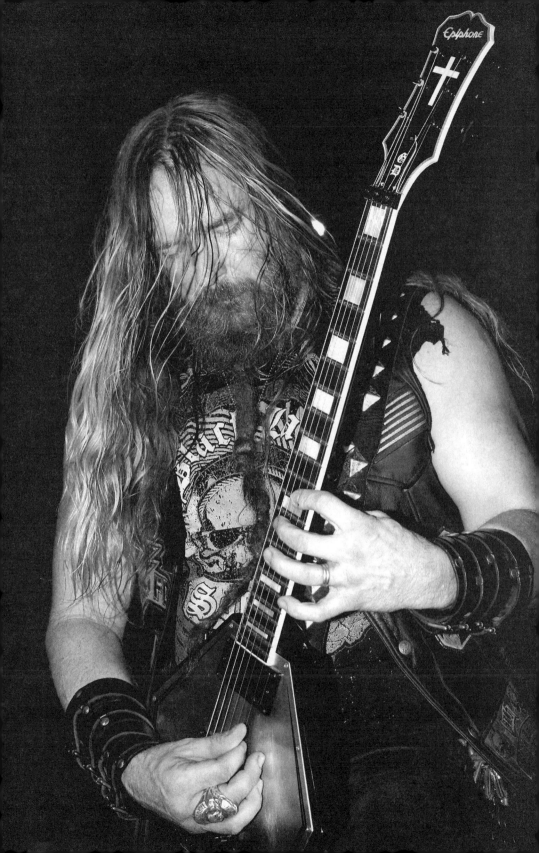

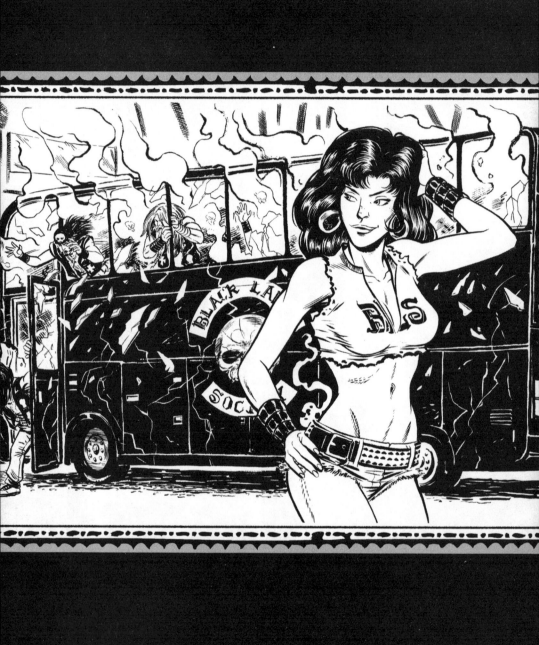

CHAPTER FOUR

𝔑o 𝔖hitting on the 𝔅us

Stern alarums set forth dreadful marches. The Battle
cries of the Berzerkers resonated through the very Halls
of Valhalla, and from above the sounds of steel and
iron clashed with conflict. The wails of willful women
echoed through the ether as our horde crushed the
countryside on its quest. Neither the enemy nor the
excrement of our own reckoning soiled the progress of
this divine undertaking. Many times the fiend of the
bowels would, without warning, raise its mighty brown
turtle-like head to wreak havoc upon the Berzerkers
and sabotage their efforts to bring forth the Metal! But
our hearts could not accept failure and with each debauchery our legend swelled like the engorged Mjöllnir
of the Narwhal.

And on this adventure of conquest we rode in caravan with other, like-minded crews of warriors, and these
allies joined us in battle, in song, and in drink. And so
strengthened our Metal brotherhood with the roars of
ten thousand lions. And the armies came together and
grew into the OdinForce of reckoning. For it was Odin's
behest we awake remembrance of the valiant dead,
and with our puissant arms renew their feats! For the
blood and courage that brought our mighty ancestors
renown swelters through our veins!

And the Berzerkers rode their barbed steeds to fright
the souls of our fearful adversaries. O, belike his worship we shall ride to Victory! Our plan is one of strength,
determination, merciless and forever! With true preparation, our longevity shall be eternally known.

Note from Zakk: "For the blood and courage that brought our mighty ancestors renown swelters through our veins!" For fuck's sake . . . Reading this horseshit makes me want to take a blunt butter knife and slice my fucking veins, as it would be less painful than reading this horrendous fucking drivel that pours out of Father Eric's horrendous dribbling fucking brain that resides in the empty cavity that is known as Eric's cranium. C'mon, man. Enough already. Let me ask you this—how much time did you spend writing this peanut-brained crap instead of going out looking for a girlfriend?

Rules of the Road

As you can probably imagine, there aren't a whole lot of rules when you're out forging the metal of Valhalla. Vikings will be Vikings, but we do have a few laws to keep the order of things, day in and day out. I'm talking about the Black Label rules of the road here, with Rule No. 1 being: *No shitting on the bus.*

Every touring band knows this one. There is absolutely no shitting on the tour bus whatsoever. Even with the fancy new buses that have the grinder in the toilet so you can safely take a shit—I don't trust those fucking things either. Unless you're willing to Black Label up after you've committed the Unholy and shove your fucking hand down there to clean your own shit up, don't do it. That's how it works on these buses. You can't just pour some magic powder down there and disintegrate the shit you just unloaded. The driver has to go in there and literally clean the shit out by hand. Not only that, but it stinks the entire bus up to holy hell, and there's no escaping it. It's like you're in a submarine loaded with shit stink—a rolling port-o-john. In the immortal words of one Arthur Fonzarelli, "That ain't cool, Cunningham."

When we were out on the road for *No More Tears*, Randy Castillo brought a girl on the bus. This chick was drop-dead gorgeous, with a smoking-hot power-ass of doom, the whole nine yards. The only thing she actually lacked was knowledge of the cardinal rule for any touring band's bus. Actually, she probably lacked any knowledge whatsoever. Fuck, she probably didn't even know her own fucking name. God bless her—she looked amazing.

I was sitting in the front lounge when she came on, and several of us were there bullshitting and noodling on guitars. She asked to use the bathroom in her cute squeaky little mouse voice, and of course, none of us thought anything of it. Within about two minutes, this smell creeps up through the bus. It's the kind of unforgettable smell that has the effect of freezing time, sound, and space. It was as if my life flashed before me during a near-death experience. And actually, something really did die that day on that very bus—our hopes, our spirits, and all we've lived to believe in. Right after receiving that devastating right-cross of shit-stink, we were all looking around at each other silently, but our eyes were clearly saying "No, she didn't just shit, did she?" thinking that chicks just don't do that—girls don't go to the bathroom!

A lot of traumatic things happened in that exact moment in time: Santa Claus no longer existed, the Easter Bunny had just been shot, and this smokin' hot-ass chick just dropped the kill bomb of all nuclear kill bombs in the Ozzy band bus bathroom. She painted that porcelain throne deep brown with kernels of corn clinging to the sides of the gaping mouth as the bowl devoured her entrails. She obviously thought it wouldn't stink and it would work like a normal bathroom. But her ass stench invaded every air space on the bus. There was no escaping it. Just like whenever I take a double dose of Viagra and hunt Barbaranne down with my rod of doom and force anal sex upon her innocent yet soon-to-be-plowed-and-gaped heart-shaped ass, there is no escape. And just like the astronauts in *Planet of the Apes* before me, who crossed over into the forbidden zone, I too shall enter the forbidden zone, woman—your succulent ass.

I digress.

When this hot rockin' mama-jama came out of the bus bathroom it was completely awkward because we all knew she just shit and it was obvious to her that we all knew. I couldn't even look at her, I felt so bad. No longer did she seem to be that magical, Farrah Fawcett–back-in-the-day-looking babe who had strutted onto the bus with her overly short skirt and stripper heels. Now she looked like my three-hundred-and-fifty-pound tub-of-shit buddy Joe, after he blasted a smelly fucking taco meal out of his grimy butthole. Her once-so-sexy, mouthwatering, apple-ass—an ass only rivaled by Clint Eastwood's—now looked like a beef delivery system.

To make things worse, one of the guys came from out of the back of the bus yelling, "All right, who the fuck just shit?" This girl was just beyond mortified, man—red-faced and busted. She bolted out of there before it got ridiculously stupid, and we never saw her again. The bus driver was so pissed off because he had to clean that "bitch's shit," as he kindly put it. We all take it for granted that everyone knows there's no shitting allowed on the vehicles, but obviously they don't. Make sure you post a sign, big and bold, that simply states, NO SHITTING ON THE BUS!

Of course, squeezing your ass cheeks shut for five hours isn't realistic, and there are many long stretches of highway and lonely country roads where indoor plumbing will be a tough find. This is when it becomes necessary to go au naturel. I call this the pull-the-fucking-bus-over-now-I-gotta-fucking-shit theory—crude yet highly effective.

While out on a desert highway, I thought my ass was going to fucking explode. Our bus wasn't even moving because we were stuck in some accident traffic or some shit like that. I grabbed a roll of Brawny paper towels, jumped off the bus, ran down into a gully, and squatted to take a shit right there, spraying the nearby rocks with my Black Label shit of doom. I swear when I was finished it looked like someone did a rock painting of three large buffalo.

Although most of the time it is possible to get the bus to pull over for a quick shit break, there are times when you are simply too hungover to make it any farther than the bus's bathroom. (Or maybe you scarfed a couple of McSomethings for lunch and that garbage slid through your system like a pig on a waterslide.) And as your Black Label luck would have it, that's usually when you feel that well-known rumble in your lower bowels alerting you that it's time for your daily disaster. When this occurs, you've got to be prepared. Stock up on biodegradable bags for the bus before the tour. Take one of those bags and wrap it over the goddamn toilet, do your business, wipe your ass, and stick the toilet paper in the bag as well. Then tie that shit bag off and heave it right the fuck out the bus window while driving down the road. I've done this several times and it works perfectly. While this does break the rule of actually shitting on the bus, it's a great way to set it free and get rid of the evidence. So maybe you end up with an infraction of the rules, but nothing a couple of matches couldn't handle to get rid of the fucking stench. Just make sure the bag is biodegradable, because that's the Black Label way—when you're going brown, you've still gotta be thinking green.

World Tour Survival Technique: Rules of the Road

OF COURSE *NO SHITTING ON THE BUS* IS RULE NO. 1, BUT ON THE BLACK Label ride we have a few more that you may want to incorporate into your own rulebook.

Rule No. 2: No tea-bagging anyone while they're sleeping. I say "while they're sleeping" because if someone is awake while the tea-bagging is occurring it either means that they want it to be happening or that JD has some unfortunate dude in his basement and is about to let the Gimp out of the box. Some people find it funny to pinch the nose of their sleeping friend and when the unsuspecting victim opens their mouth, in drops the ball sac for a tonsil dip. Personally I would not find this amusing at all, but when traveling around with the likes of my bandmates, it is sometimes necessary to put down the obvious as a solid rule so no one gets any funny ideas. You would think a rock legend like myself would be safe from a Delta Tau Chi prank like this, but I read in Slash's autobiography that even he wasn't safe from the getting tea-bagged by Tommy Lee back when Guns N' Roses toured with Mötley Crüe.

Note from Zakk: Once again, Father Eric added this little tidbit of knowledge, probably due to something he is trying to forget from his college days. I just figured this is a rule in life. I've never been tea-bagged or tea-bagged anybody. But evidently some clowns find this fucking funny. You want to know fucking funny? Stick your ball sac on my fucking face while I'm sleeping and I'll gnaw your nuts right the fuck off. I can't wait to see the look on your face while I'm biting down on your soon-to-be-severed balls—as you hear them snap, crackle, and pop. Then the next round of comedy will be when you have to explain your stupidity and my oral castration of you to your fucking girlfriend or wife and your doctor. So if you ever want your fucking balls removed, you know where I sleep.

Rule No. 3: No spooning. When you're on the tour bus, spooning your with girl is a hard-ass maneuver, and because of the size of the bunks, there really isn't room for this sort of behavior. But I'm not talking about heterosexual, lovey-dovey cuddling here.

What I'm referring to is oversized and undershowered hairy man-snuggling. Admittedly, this rule was established because of me.

Our drummer Philth and I had been up late one night drinking and he ended up crashing out in the bed that was in the back of the bus, Barb's and my bed. When Barb saw Philth sleeping in our bed, she just went up to the front of the bus to sleep there. Next entered me, thinking Barb was in the back bed waiting for my sweet lovin', so I strolled into the back, climbed in the bed, spooned Philth, and grabbed his ass. That's when I heard his deep, alcohol-dried vocal cords mutter, "Zakk . . . that's my ass. It's Phil, not Barb," as if I wouldn't have figured it out by the deep voice and handful of man-ass I was holding on to. But what really made me realize that it wasn't Barb is that Philth's back is nowhere as furry and gorilla-esque as Barbaranne's.

"Oops, sorry about that, brother. How about that Giants game today?"

"Hell of a game, Zakk, hell of a game," he murmured, still half-asleep.

"We're looking good this season. If we can keep moving the ball down the field and play heavy with our defense, we could make the playoffs."

"That would be great, Zakk. You know what else would be great? Not having your hot breath on the back of my neck or your hand on my ass."

"Well, good talkin' with you, brother. I'll catch ya in the morning."

"Yeah, we'll hit the gym and start drinking early."

"Sounds good, buddy. Sweet dreams, pudding–er . . . I mean . . . Good night, buddy."

"Night, babe."

Fortunately for everyone I'm not Philth's type, because we all know that spooning leads to forking, which actually will feel quite comfortable as you acclimate your gaping asshole to the music business.

Rule No. 4: Never cross international borders with drugs. I don't smoke weed, smoke crack cocaine, or sniff glue. But sometimes I think maybe I should. My affinity for a good time has always been satisfied by a cold beer or twelve—cases, that is. But to each their own. And who am I to lock JD out of the pot-cookie jar? Although, in JD's defense, all of his weed is medically prescribed and cleared. Medically, because he makes all the rest of us sick. That being said, make sure you never cross international borders with any of that shit.

If you're headed up through Canada, you'll want to finish your crack and heroin before you get to the border or get rid of it, because you *will* get searched. Pills, weed, needles, crack, crack lite for your girlish figure, and anything else that makes you tick—make sure it ain't on the bus. Always check the bus before you hit the road, because for all you know, the last band on your bus could have been Bob Marley and the Wailers. They didn't smoke much weed, did they? Go through that motherfucker ahead of time like you're a goddamn German shepherd drug dog, because if you cross a border and that shit is on your ride, my brother, even if it's not yours, you are going down. The border patrol does not fuck around.

Let me tell you about something that happened to a buddy of mine and his band while going into Canada.

Everybody in the band and crew was given the usual "Whatever you got, get rid of it" General Patton speech before they crossed the border. Later that day my buddy was sitting in the dressing room at the gig, noodling on his fiddle, when in walked his tour manager.

"Here's the fucking shopping list I just received from the border patrol," he said. "Let's see, Percocet, Vicodin, Xenadrine, Xanax, muscle relaxers, traces of heroin, and marijuana."

After he rattled this fucking grocery list off, my buddy told me that every guy in the room looked dumbfounded and couldn't say anything but, "Oh man, wow. Where did they find all that? I don't do that anymore. It's not mine."

Now, I don't dabble in any of that bullshit, but if beer and

NOTIFICATION OF SEIZURE

While inspecting your bags for explosives, workers for the Transportation Security Administration (TSA) observed

Drugs & Drug Paraphernalia

and notified the Spokane Airport Police. The aforementioned item is illegal in the State of Washington under R.C.W.:

_6950.401(e)_

And was confiscated by Officer _Creek_

The item was _Confiscated_

No criminal charges have been filed. If you wish to contact us regarding this matter please call (509) 455-6429.

█████████████████

Officer's signature

_3-16-09_   _3/6:09_   ██████████

Time _7:27 PM_ Date   Case number (if any)

SPOKANE AIRPORT POLICE

Crown Royal were on that fucking list, how in the fuck am I gonna go in with a straight face and say, "Wow, how did that booze get in there?" Un-fucking-real.

As the rest of the story goes, they were about to play some shows in Canada and knew they couldn't carry their goodies across the border. So they put their little heads together and packed up all the goodies in band merchandise boxes. They also loaded the boxes with grapefruits and oranges to distract any drug dogs from sniffing out their shit.

It wasn't long before their tour manager received the wonderful news of the band's merchandise confiscation. The DEA informed him that they had all of the guys' party treats. Moral of the story, kids? Don't try this stupid shit at home. But if you're bored and have some time on your hands, go down to the DEA and try to collect the drugs they confiscated. Just say, "I'm just here to pick up my stuff, fellas." See what the fuck happens. You'll have plenty of time behind bars to try to figure out why the fuck you shouldn't cross international borders with drugs, you fucking moron.

My buddy actually saved a copy of the notification of seizure from the police. Good times. That's why I always prefer when me and the guys get together and fist each other while sampling wines from a variety of California vineyards. It really does take away from the stress of the music business, while still achieving the same gaping-ass results.

Note from Zakk: Oh, and as a final caution to junkies, make sure you throw your needles in the garbage and don't get them confused with my steroids. I'm guessing the effect you're looking for will be completely different, as you tear the door off the bus, flip over some cars, and rampage through the nearest city.

Rule No. 5: Smell *everything* before you eat or drink it. Now, this last rule isn't so much a steadfast law of the road as it is a cautionary guideline. There isn't really any consequence of wrath for violating it; it's more like a piece of survival advice—literally.

It all came about during one of the most fun tours I've ever been on. It was the one to support *No More Tears*. The lineup was Ozzy, Alice in Chains, and Sepultura. This one was a blast because of the brotherhood all the bands shared on the road. We'd party with each other, hang on each other's buses, and always stick around to check out everyone else's sets. It was very cool.

After one of the shows, all three bands piled into their buses and began the caravan. I jumped on the Alice bus to hang with all the guys. We got wasted and laughed our asses off all night, listening to Fleetwood Mac, Elton John, Neil Young, and a whole bunch of other ass-kicking classic rock. Eventually, the guys started falling off one by one to go pass out for the night since we had a show the next day.

Mike Starr, who was in Alice at the time, and I were the last two guys standing. The driver for Alice's bus was named Lupe. He was anal about keeping the bus clean and nice for everyone on board, and so he was up early, as usual, cleaning the entire rig. To make his job easier, he had dumped some ammonia into an empty Corona bottle so he wouldn't have to carry around a huge bucket of chemicals while doing the job. When Lupe finished cleaning, he put the Corona bottle in a cup holder near the front of the bus and then went in the back to fold blankets or some shit.

I was the first one up and already had a cold beer in the front lounge when Mikey rolled out of his bunk, still beat the fuck up from the night before. We reminisced a bit about the previous evening's comedy and what a fucking great time we had. As we continued to shoot the shit, Mike saw me firing back an ice-cold Corona and figured he'd join me, as there was a Corona bottle sitting right next to him in the armrest of his chair. Now, he must have had some bad cottonmouth or something, 'cause as soon as he spied the Corona bottle sitting there in the holder, he grabbed it and pounded the fucking thing. I shit you *not*, he drank the whole bottle down in one! Only problem was, it was the Corona bottle filled with Lupe's fucking ammonia!

Next thing you know we're bringing Mike down to the hospital to get his stomach pumped. After that they gave him some charcoal-like medication to soak up anything that was still in his system. It's no mystery that, besides being one of the coolest souls on earth, Mikey had an affinity for pharmaceuticals. He wasn't shy about asking around for them either. Lupe told me that while he was in the hospital, after getting his fuckin' stomach pumped, Mike had the balls to ask the doctor, "Hey, doc? I'm in this rock band and we're always on the road. I have trouble sleeping. Do you happen to have any quaaludes?"

It was hilarious! The doctor just told him to get the fuck outta there and sent him on his way. None of this surprised me though. Mikey had even asked Ozzy if he could sample some of his medication. Ozzy's stuff isn't recreational at all! It totally baffled the Boss; Ozzy would come up to me and say shit like, "Yeah right, Zakk, I'm gonna give him some of my shit. Just my luck the shit that I take would end up fuckin' killing the motherfucker, and there's another lawsuit waiting to happen!"

You know what though, no matter how hard Mike partied, he still made every show and played his ass off. That goes right back to the Black Label spirit: Do what you will, as long as you answer that fuckin' bell every night, and Mikey did just that, without question. Rest in peace, our brother in musical warfare.

The Flagship of the Black Label Armada: The Tour Bus

AS I WAS SAYING EARLIER, GETTING FROM POINT A TO POINT B IS ALWAYS where shit goes down. You wake up in a hotel (point A) and you hit the stage that night (point B), and everything in between is the gray area that no one wants to hear about. That said, getting to the show can be the most intense part of the day depending on where we are. I've been in everything from police escorts through New York City to rolling in a fleet of tour buses to having my wife drop me off at the gig. If you love what you're doing, it doesn't matter how you get to the show, just so long as you get there.

When you first start out you'll probably end up doing exactly what we did: borrow someone's parents' van to get your equipment and the guys to the gig. I revisited the van experience during the *Book of Shadows* tour in 1996. We had no need for more than an Aerostar minivan. The show was just Nick Catanese and I, playin' acoustic stuff. There were four of us in the van, Nick, Dave, Chris, and myself, taking turns driving and sleeping, and no joke, we put sixteen thousand miles on this thing in two months of touring. Some nights I was so deliriously exhausted from driving and playing that during the gig, I'd introduce the backdrop pictures of the angel and the devil as members of the band and forget to introduce Nick—the only other live body on the stage. Needless to say, even as packed as that fucking van was, with the guitars, the backdrops, the amps, whatever the fuck else we needed to keep the acoustical armada of doom rolling, and sixteen thousand miles of us sleeping on the floor or in a chair—we still had a fucking blast.

Out of the Van and into the Bus

Lug Nut Roulette

Gambling and betting is a way of life within the Black Label family. We're always throwing money down on football and baseball games, boxing matches, UFC fights, and pretty much anything else where the outcome is a gamble. To give you an example of this, let me tell you about a game we call Lug Nut Roulette.

The game starts by counting out however many lug nuts are on the front wheel of the bus. Each guy picks one of the lug nuts, for five bucks or whatever, you know, maybe wife swapping, teabagging, or who gets to suck off the radio programmer at the next town we hit so that they can spin our awesome hit singles for the Black Label family to enjoy—all bets are on. Basically, everything and all the money goes into a pot. Then you take a Sharpie and write each guy's name next to their selected lug nut, and make a mark at the top of the wheel well, dead center at twelve o'clock. Everyone gets on the bus and at the next stop, whether it's a truck stop or a whorehouse, you get off the bus and check whose name lines up closest to the mark you made on the wheel well, and that person is the winner of the pot. Each stop you can keep throwing into the pot and getting winners. If you're really lucky you'll end up in the sack with all the guys' wives, girlfriends, even JD's husband. Yeah, I know it sounds pathetic that we're gambling on the wheel of the bus, but when you're out there on the road, in the middle of nowhere, it could be one of the most exciting things in your day. JD loves the game so much in fact that many times he busts into that song, "The wheels on the bus go round and round!" It's like being in a band with a hairy, stinky toddler—who has a husband.

Clicking the Mic

Another way we like to have a good time on the road is by doing something that we learned from our bus driver called "clicking the mic." When we were out near the truck stops, we'd have Dino the truck driver click the mic as we approached one. They call it "fishing." This is where you click the mic on the radio a few times and wait for someone to click back. That is a signal that they're looking for a blow job or something in the truck stop bathrooms. Then we'd jump on the line and have some fun with the guy at the other end, usually concluding with them telling us to fuck off, never a "happy ending." I never asked Dino how he found out about the mic-clicking deal, and I'm not sure I ever want to find out.

Circle of Life

The words *alpha* and *beta* describe the ranking system within the wild animal kingdom and the pecking order of life. When two dominant alphas collide in God's great wilderness, a display of aggression occurs as each animal exaggerates its own features and movements in a threatening manner, often followed by a battle to the death. As this is the case in the great outdoors, it is also so within the confines of a tiny fishbowl.

One time in Wyoming, me, Phil, and Mark rolled into this pet store called All God's Creatures. We went to look at the dogs, since I was looking to buy a couple of Rottweiler puppies. They didn't have any puppies, but we saw a huge display of those Siamese fighting fish, you know, the betta fish. Phil had this idea that each of us would pick out his own fish and bowl, and then take it back onto the bus so the event could begin. The guys would wait in the back lounge with their fish until they were called out. We'd place one large bowl on the front lounge table

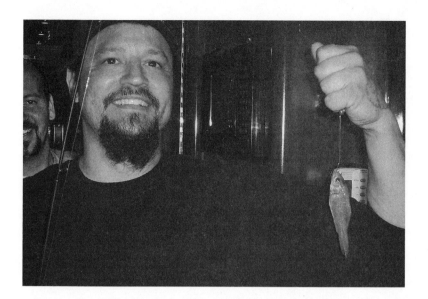

and then the referee would announce the combatants. Each fish would be brought up with the bus lights flickering and its own entrance song blasting ("Hell's Bells" was a crowd favorite!). Once both fish were brought to the table, the referee would lay out all the rules to ensure a fair fight, all bets were confirmed, and then we would start the match with the traditional "Let's get it oooooonnnnnnnn!!!!" The two fish would get dumped into the underwater gladiator bowl and the battle would commence until it was determined which fish was more dominant. That was the plan anyway, but it never happened.

When we went up to the counter to buy a bunch of these fish and one bowl, the lady at the front said that the fish couldn't all live in one little bowl, that they each needed their own. Phil explained to her that it wasn't an issue, and then he filled her in on his idea for the finned gladiators. She became upset and wouldn't let us buy the fish, saying that they would kill each other if you put them all in one bowl. Phil replied to her, "Look, lady, that's the circle of life, the big fish eats the little fish."

The next thing you know, this lady was screaming at us, "The circle of life? The circle of life? You assholes just *circled* yourselves right the fuck out of this store!"

Another time, our fearless leader Mark decided to turn the bus into a sport-fishing boat. He came in one day with a fish tank and a batch of these large feeder goldfish. You know, the ones you buy to feed to your pet eel or lionfish. So we set this tank up in the back of the bus and were casting our lines from the front lounge. We were using your basic tackle, like cheese and salmon eggs, on small treble hooks, and these goldfish were taking the bait. It was hysterical watching the guys reel in their prize fish! Of course, no fish were harmed during these tour bus fishing tournaments—it was all catch and release.

Bus Driver Pete

WHEN WE'RE OUT TOURING, WE CROSS THOUSANDS UPON THOUSANDS OF miles in the tour bus. Usually, after the gig, we'll hang out for a bit, but then it's back on the road and off to the next city. These drives can be anywhere from six hours to twenty hours, depending on where the next gig is. For different tours we get different drivers; usually they work for the leasing company and come with the bus. Now, it's common knowledge that in order to become a tour bus driver you have to be legally insane, not possess a full set of teeth, or have some kind of criminal history that finds its way into the whispered rumors heard throughout the tour. But what is not so common is for one man to possess all of these prerequisites. And when such a man shows up for the job, he becomes immortalized by being included in this holy parchment dedicated to all things Metal. And so begins the legacy of Bus Driver Pete.

Pete was a markedly short and slender old man with unusually large extremities—giant hands, giant feet, and big floppy ears that reached out far beyond the derby he always wore. He told us once, after someone brought up the incredible size of his hands, that he also had a gigantic dick. I never saw it, but Father Ferguson later confirmed that it looked like the trunk of a small elephant. But even with his huge-gantic manhood, Pete was bitter at the world. And as hard as we tried to find out more about him we couldn't decipher most of his mumbled jargon to save our lives. To make matters worse, he always had a smoking pipe in his mouth, so you couldn't even try to lip-read what he was saying—everything came out of his yapper with the same exact shit-eating grin on his face.

As slow as Pete was to physically move from one place to another, he was the opposite with his driving. Mark had made this itinerary tour book that showed how long our bus rides were going to be into each town. We would look at the book and see a seven-hundred-mile drive that should take about fourteen hours to the next city. I shit you not, we would get there in eight hours. I asked Pete if he was running from the law or something. As it turned out, he was, but that had nothing to do with the fact that he drove like the guys in *Cannonball Run*.

One night Pete was driving us over the mountains near Modesto, California, and Mark was up front with him trading stories from the road. I had gone to bed early. Mark remembers seeing the yellow warning signs that Pete did not. Our bus jerked sideways right up on the guardrails, leaning over the mountain-side. I could hear Mark screaming, "Pete, there's another one!" as the bus swerved in the other direction. We were all over the fucking road on this curvy mountain, right next to the cliffs. Then I heard Pete yell, "Wow! That came out of nowhere," and Mark yell back, "Fucking *nowhere*? There were fucking signs, man! Can't you see the fucking signs?"

I woke up to the sights and sounds of shit falling from everywhere in the back lounge, thinking that our submarine was getting hit by enemy torpedoes. I made my way to the front, buck fucking naked, yelling, "What the fuck is going on?!" There was shit all over the place, a total disaster—coffeemaker, cups, dishes, magazines, cans and boxes of food, whatever was on the tables and in the cabinets was now all over the fucking floor. Luckily, we hadn't gone over the fucking rails. Pete started telling me about how the turns came out of nowhere. Meanwhile Mark was telling Phil and me, "Man, we are all dead tonight. I'm calling my wife to say good-bye." We would have been better off taking shifts and driving the bus ourselves because no one slept the rest of the night.

On one Ozzfest tour we headlined the second stage. This meant we were always done at around six o'clock and could head out for the next town. One of those nights we all ended up at a Hooters restaurant to grab dinner and drinks and watch sports. Mark told Pete that we were gonna be there for a while and to go grab a bunk until we were ready to leave. We stayed until the joint closed and then headed to the next town. The next day, Pete wanted to speak with Mark. With his smoking pipe bouncing around in his disgruntled mouth, Pete told him, "I don't play those games."

"What games, Pete?" Mark asked.

"When I leave a city, I go straight to the next city. No bullshit like last night."

So Mark told him, "Well, Zakk's paying you, so you're gonna do whatever the fuck we tell you to do. You made four hundred bucks last night sleeping in a bunk. I would do that every fuckin' day of the week, man."

Pete unzipped his fly, dropped his trousers, and tucked his Snuffleupagus cock and balls between his legs, exposing a seventy-two-year-old silver man-pussy. "Next time I want to be treated like a pussy I'll walk around with one," he said, waving his oversized hands in the air. Mark has never been the same since.

Another time I was woken from a nap to the bellows of Phil cursing at Pete. As it turned out, Pete had removed his false teeth earlier and dropped them into a bowl of water in the fridge so he could grab a quick nap. But it wasn't a bowl of water, it was Phil's soup. When Phil came back on the bus he grabbed the bowl, tossed it in the microwave, and took a few spoonfuls before he discovered Pete's warmed-up choppers in the bowl. Phil went into a volcanic rage of Black Label proportions.

Several years ago we were crossing into North Carolina and we were stopped by the state troopers. It's not an unusual thing to happen and they usually just make sure everything is fine and the driver has a valid license and insurance and stuff like that. After checking Pete's paperwork, one of the troopers escorted him off the bus and into the back of one of the patrol cars. Then more troopers showed up. Mark woke me up and told me there was a problem so I came off the bus to talk to the troopers. Apparently they had been looking for Pete for quite some time for his involvement in an actual train robbery that took place in the South back in the late sixties. Pete had been on the run for almost fifty years, under a new name, picking up jobs around the country where he could keep a low profile. This was the last we saw of Pete and a new driver was sent out to finish the tour.

Recently, I was talking to Father Leslie West and he was telling Mark and me some crazy stories about a bus driver from his tour in Canada. Mark jokingly asked Leslie if the driver's name happened to be Pete. That's when Leslie exclaimed, "Yeah, his name *was* Pete!" Mark showed him a picture of Bus Driver Pete, and sure as shit, it was the same guy!

Black Label Ops: Training Day
BY MARK "FERGIE" FERGUSON

WE WERE IN KANSAS CITY, AND IT WAS RAINING OUTSIDE, SO the guys couldn't shoot their guns outdoors and they decided to do all their shootin' inside the bus. They had these thousand-feet-per-second pellet rifles, and all the guys were crouched down at the front of the bus and shooting toward the back lounge. I said, "*Guys . . . ,*" but Dimebag's girl Rita was out with us that tour and getting her shots in with the rest of us. They had set up all these blankets in the back to catch the beer bottles and cans that they were shooting at. The scary thing was that Nick and some of the guys were actually in their bunks, in their line of fire. I mean, these guys couldn't as much as poke their head out of the bunks or someone'd get shot in the eye.

Next thing you know, the bus broke down, because they blasted the fucking bracket to the fan belt. We found out later these shots had gone straight through the seats in the back of the bus and into the engine. So we had to deal with that debacle, which cost about four thousand dollars after repairing the seats, the engine work, and replacing the carpet that had been ruined from all the exploded bottles and cans of whatever they could find to shoot. That was the last shooting gallery we set up in the bus. After that we reserved target practice for outdoors and in the hotel rooms.

In one of our hotel shooting ranges we were getting complaints from the management about us shooting in our rooms. We had the whole thing set up for target practice in the hotel room, shooting from one end to the other, blowing up shit. After finding out that we were actually shooting in our rooms, the hotel called the cops. I went down to the lobby to try to convince the hotel manager that nothing was going on, but they insisted on getting the cops down there. Phil took all the guns and stuck them in between the mattresses in case the cops decided to enter the room, and we figured it would be best for us to slip out of there until the heat cooled down. We timed it perfectly by cell phone so that as the cops came up to our room, we all went down another elevator and headed out.

Later, we ended up getting busy for the BLS show in New York, and after the performance we left for the next town. It was then that we remembered we had left all the guns back in the hotel room in New Jersey. So I had to call and tell the hotel manager that nothing was going on, in case the housekeeping came in there to change the sheets and found that we left a stash of rifles in our hotel room. I had to explain that we were in Room 405 and not to be alarmed, but we were gonna send someone over to collect all the rifles we left under the mattress. A thousand feet per second; we're lucky no one lost an eye. We had been in there shooting thirty feet away.

How Black Holes Are Created

As I've mentioned before, there is a ton of time to kill while out on the road. When I'm not boozing and goofing off, I while away the hours pondering serious matters of time, space, and the cosmic span of things—for what better place than the laboratory of life itself to lead one to genius? One such discovery deals with, arguably, the most powerful force in the universe—black holes.

There have been many theories put forth on black holes, exactly what they are, and how they have come to exist. But what Stephen Hawking failed to understand is the true secret of how these anomalies are actually created; it is due to the inverse relationship of thrust and launch. I'll explain:

Not too long ago, before making my way to a show, I found myself at the hotel bar enjoying a refreshing adult beverage. I know, it's out of character for me to frequent these types of establishments, but there I was nonetheless. I was waiting for Black Label Special Ops security's "How Ya Doin'" Phil to arrive and toss back a few cocktails and relax before heading out to the Black Label cathedral. As his usual slow self, and given his need to spend endless hours combing his long and flowing locks, Phil was late. This gave me ample opportunity to enjoy my adult beverage and engage in interesting rock conversation with the bartender. Then finally Phil got there and, of course, we enjoyed another refreshing adult beverage. Upon his arrival, I mentioned to Phil that his hair didn't quite look as intimidating as a Black Label Special Operative's should look, as he had it in pigtails, similar to Wendy—you know, the redheaded girl on the Wendy's restaurant logo. He immediately dashed back up to his room for three more showers. With Black Label Special Ops like this, it's a good thing I am well versed in Black Label Five Deadly Venoms kung fu.

When out imbibing heavily, there is always that one Drink of Death that can seriously put you over the edge if it is not consumed properly. Let's just say that I found that drink, and it didn't work out as I had hoped. It's not that it went down the wrong way, it was just wrong. All of a sudden I needed to quickly head to the bathroom. It wasn't clear whether or not I had to shit or puke, I just knew that things were wrong—seriously wrong.

I made the decision to first try to take a shit, thinking that relieving my bowels would in turn take a load off my mind. So I laid down that flimsy ass protector that looks like it's made of a giant butt-shaped rolling paper and sat down to see what would happen. As I attempted to take a shit, I began to feel that all-too-familiar warm rush race through my body. You know, that hot sweaty prickly feeling when you know you are going to fucking puke. Without a thought, I popped off the bowl, spun around, and let the contents of my stomach heave into the toilet. Then, without any warning—it happened. Like Mount Everest itself, my asshole erupted. When it first dilated I knew things were about to go south, but I was so involved with ralphing that I had no time to react. The gasket blew almost immediately, sending a projectile stream of ass soup mercilessly against the door of the lavatory—shit fucking everywhere. And that, my friends, is exactly how black holes are created. Unfortunately for me, JD is still in my life. Some things never disappear.

Of course, being the consummate moral rocker that I am, I cleaned up my shitty mess. I made my way back to the bar, where Phil, unknowledgeable of the deep-space discovery I had just made in the bathroom, had two more drinks on standby for me—pure Black Label Ops! Of course I tossed those down before hitting the road; it would have been rude not to. On the way to the gig I refreshed myself with a cold beer as I and the rest of my Black Label brethren had a great Black Label mass. When you're in Black Label, things like black holes are just part of another day at the office . . . you just have to Black Label/Patton up and GIFD.

At this point you're probably thinking that I have some kind of bowel disorder and should be branding my own line of Black Label diapers. It ain't just me. Ozzy one time, right during Randy Castillo's drum solo, had to make a break for the can. The second he came off the stage he had to shit, and the only bathroom was somewhere way in the back of the fuckin' arena. Oz and his security guys had to make a break for it. All I remember is seeing Ozzy holding his ass and running with these guys, to make sure he got back onstage before the end of the drum solo. Thank God for drummers, and thank God for solos.

One time in Denver, we were backstage getting ready to play a show. I had to take a shit, so I went in the bathroom to do my thing. While I was in the stall, the guys took all the fuckin' fruit—apples and oranges and shit like that—and were pitching those fuckers like Nolan Ryan at the bathroom stall while I was trying to shit. There was fruit flying underneath the stall door and hitting my feet, fucking bananas splattering everywhere around me—I was under fire.

I concentrated as much as humanly possible and pushed out this rock-solid shit. As soon as it splashed into the toilet, I yelled out, "You wanna play shit games, motherfuckers?" and reached into the fuckin' bowl and grabbed this fuckin' thing. It was like a leather football—the only things missing were the laces and NFL commissioner Pete Rozelle's name on the fuckin' thing. I opened up the door, leaned back and planted my feet like Joe Namath. I could already see the horrified looks on their faces as I launched my shit football in their direction. This spiral of shit soared across the room and the guys dove out of the way. John Sinclair, the keyboard player, had been sitting in a chair the entire time and reading a book. My shit soared right above him and stuck to the wall just above his head. John looked up from his book at the shit that was now easing its way down the wall, muttered, "This reminds me of when I was in the Heavy Metal Kids. There was always shit flying everywhere," and then went right back to his reading like nothing ever happened.

But what happens when a band member needs to build a log cabin and there is no drum solo to save their ass? Well, believe it or not, there is a solution for that as well. It is called the Shit Time Out and was invented by the one and only Father Kirk Windstein from Crowbar.

The Penchant for Violence tour was in support of the second Black Label album, *Stronger Than Death*. I'm good friends with the all guys in Crowbar, and we took them along as the supporting act.

It just so happened that around this time, I had discovered a product called Ultimate Orange, which gave off these insane bursts of caffeinated energy. This stuff was a workout booster used by bodybuilders. It was perfect for getting in vigorous workouts, and so I turned everyone on the tour on to it, not even thinking that it could, or would, be abused—yeah right. As a side note, Ultimate Orange has since been banned, totally gotten rid of due to its extreme potency. Swallowing four of these things was the equivalent of pounding twenty-eight cups of coffee! And some of the guys were popping four or five of these fucking pills before going onstage each night. The guys would get so fuckin' wired that they had to continuously drink beer and vodka just to get any kind of sleep. Even with the drinks it was like a bunch of crack-heads ready to run a marathon. Then they'd just burn out and crash. All of the guys were jacked up on this shit.

One of the gigs on this tour was in a small hole-in-the-wall place that had no stage, so we had to literally play on the floor. Crowbar went on and our guys all hung out to watch the show. Everything was cruising along as usual until all of a sudden, right in the middle of a song, the music stopped and I heard Father Windstein yelling out, "Stop! Stop!" I didn't know what was wrong. Then I heard Kirk's explanation: "We need to take an intermission . . . I've gotta take a fuckin' shit!"

He didn't sound like he was kidding around, and right before our eyes Father Kirk had disappeared. The guys were baffled; they were wondering where the hell he'd gone. I relayed to them that I was under the impression that Kirk had encountered a minor emergency and was resolving his bowel issues. I don't blame him. I mean, the guy's bowels must have been torn the fuck up from all the Ultimate Orange and the amount of booze we'd all been throwing back.

After some time Kirk emerged from the bathroom, strolled out across the floor like he was walking on air, grabbed his guitar, and just busted back into the song where he had left off. We all just went along with it, and the audience didn't give them any grief at all. Sometimes shit quite literally *does* happen. Hey, at least he wasn't rude; it's not like he took a massive shit right on the fucking floor. But if he had blown out his pants onstage, which wasn't out of the question with all the chemistry that was going on that night, whoever was behind him at the time would have been taken out by a cyclone of mud.

It is best to try to avoid any of these onstage emergencies, and so my advice is, whenever possible, clear the pipes before going on. But unfortunately there are hazards to this as well.

We were on the tour bus getting ready to play a show at Harpos in Detroit on the same fucking tour. I was sitting on the bus drinking a beer and feeling the urge to shit my brains out. Now, there is nothing more uncomfortable than trying to keep your guitar-picking steady while clenching your ass cheeks tighter than JD in a prison cell. And, in compliance with the bus rules, I needed to find an alternate location to deposit my payload. The closest bathroom was in the venue itself. So I grabbed a roll of paper towels and made a break for the back of the building. Thankfully I found myself concealed in the pitch-black darkness of an alley, with no one in sight, and so I proceeded to unleash hell upon the pavement below. Unbeknownst to me, when I dropped my trousers, my chained wallet fell directly below my hovering ass and smack-dab into the line of fire. I shit all over it and because it was so dark, I had no idea that I had just painted my black leather wallet brown. All I remember is just shitting everywhere, wiping my ass, and feeling like the weight of the world was just lifted off me. Then I picked up my wallet and stuffed it into my back pocket and went straight into the venue to play the show.

It smelled like shit onstage the whole time and none of us knew why. I figured I must have stepped in shit outside or something. After the gig, I rolled back onto the bus, grabbed another brew, and thought to myself, "Man what smells like shit?" I figured it was on my boots but I found nothing. As I thought about it, a horrifying suspicion slowly crept into my mind. And that's when I realized that once again, being in Black Label, nothing can just be simple. Once you put on the colors, the simplest of things becomes a Herculean effort. Even taking a shit can't just be taking a dump and calling it a day. I had shit all over my wallet, credit cards, and everything else.

I ended up spending an hour washing off my credit cards. Afterward I hung my pants up in the back lounge. That's how the Febreze Lounge got its name, for the industrial-sized bottle of Febreze we had to keep back there to mask the smell of my ass that permanently saturated the bus for the rest of the tour—and so, the very evil we were trying to evade had, perhaps through karma, found its way in, poisoning our food, our water, and the air within.

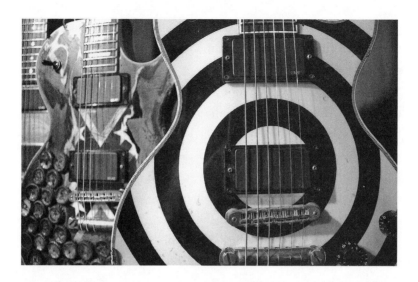

The Guitar Tech, or as I Call Him, My Personal Foot Massager

I MET KEITH "MOBY" LANOUX, BACK IN 1990–1991, THROUGH FATHER Mike Inez while we were recording *No More Tears*. Moby was working with Ugly Kid Joe at the time and came down to hang with Mike and listen to some of the new tracks. It was funny because pretty much every band he was out with either opened for Ozzy or was on Ozzfest, so I saw this guy who was completely obsessed with mail-order brides from Russia all the time.

Besides his own work as a prominent DJ and dance-oriented electronic musician—isn't that the technical term for a guy who works at fucking tit bar?—Moby's been out as a renowned tech with Stone Temple Pilots, Rammstein, Sepultura, Motörhead, and Marilyn Manson, and also took care of our favorite guitar god, Saint Dimebag, along with a bunch of other bands that forge the metals of Valhalla. As the Black Label Armada rolled out on the Mafia tour, we were in need of a general to command the Black Label guitar army. And I was in need of a high-quality foot masseuse. So out came Father Moby and his growing list of numbers for mail-order brides throughout Russia, Poland, the Czech Republic, and the Jersey shore, as he had already run through all of the girls at the Rainbow Bar and Grill in Hollywood—and all the guys on Santa Monica Boulevard.

Moby's been at my side for every kind of performance, whether it's an Ozzy show, BLS show, national anthem performance, prom, bar mitzvah, circumcision, circle jerk, or whatever family fun awaits the almighty Black Label Order! If I'm plugging in, I have Father Moby with me to make sure everything goes smoothly with the guitars. The only drawback to having a "Moby" around is that I had to change the name of my dick . . . it got way too weird when Barbaranne would ask to pleasure "Moby Dick" (it just sounded too close to "Moby's dick"). So that's how the name the Vagina Masher was bestowed upon Barb's relentless wrecking-ball-of-flesh pleasuring device that is conveniently located between my legs. I like to rampage her womb with my jackhammer and pile-drive her body into realms of orgasmic submission, only to leave her conquered and bathed in vaginal defeat by my just and noble cock—not to mention the redecorating of her anal cavity I do with my Nobel Prize–winning man-plow. I'm planning on discussing these techniques in full detail in another literary masterpiece I'm working on, entitled *Just Give Her a Stiff Cock and a Platinum Credit Card and She'll Shut the Fuck Up.*

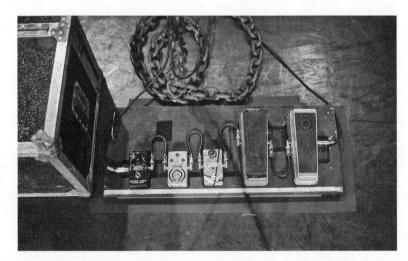

A Typical Day on Tour

WHEN WE'RE OUT ON TOUR, THE SHOW ISN'T THE ONLY THING ON MY mind. In every town we hit there are interviews, press conferences, contests, appearances, TV shows, radio shows, Black Label family meet-and-greets, record-release in-stores, and other happenings and events to be done. It's not like we kick back all day long drinking beers and playing video games until it's time to hit the stage and then party all night until the sun comes up. Wait a second . . . It used to be exactly like that. What the fuck happened???

I thought it would be interesting to share what a typical day on tour looks like for a Rock Hero like myself, as compared to my personal wizard Moby's day. To give you a good perspective on our routines, we both kept a daily journal and wrote down some of the key events that happened to each of us during the day.

7:00 A.M.

Moby: I woke up with a stiff neck and sore back, unable to feel my left arm. Struggled to make it out of bed and find a cup of coffee to wash down the anti-inflammatory on an otherwise empty stomach—empty because I missed dinner last night. After I finished packing up the stage and loading the trucks, there was no fucking food left. I checked my e-mail and phone messages to see the never-ending burdens that will consume my day. Had to wash up quickly and get out the door. I wonder how it will be possible to make it to the end of the day when this one already sucks so badly.

Zakk: These goose-down comforters and oversized satin pillows are fucking unbelievable. Zzzzzzzzzz . . .

8:00 A.M.

Moby: I got to the venue only to show a crew of ex-convicts how to unload the gear. It's the same equipment every day, but we always have new workers who don't know what the fuck to do. One of them dropped two six-hundred-pound road cases off the edge of the truck and smashed my foot. The ice for the drinks hadn't arrived yet, so I had no way to ice my foot.

Zakk: While groping Barbaranne's lifeless and sleeping body, and whilst inside her morning-mist vagina, I jackhammered my cock into submission. It's so awesome treating my body, and Barb's lifeless one, like an amusement park. I blew my load and passed the fuck out. Zzzzzzzz . . .

10:00 A.M.

Moby: Trucks were finally unloaded, with no thanks to the day laborers, as they mostly watched me limp around with road cases. It was one hundred degrees and 90 percent humidity. All the guitars were going out of tune because of the heat and all of the strings were rusting because of the humidity. Then I had to get the backline set up while I fixed the guitars.

Zakk: Woke up to Barbaranne completely unaware what happened to her, until she felt me running down the inside of her leg. She then rewarded my greatness with a *Kama Sutra* position where I do very little of the work. After that I dozed back into dreamland for a bit while she rubbed my feet and ordered coffee and a healthy egg breakfast from the hotel's room service. This is one of the nicest five-star hotels I've stayed in. It could actually be a six-star if there were such a thing. By the way, my cock told me that the goose-down-feathered comforters were amazing as well.

11:00 A.M.

Moby: Slammed my hand closing the roll-down door on the truck. Changing strings and tuning guitars was painful all morning. I forgot one of my tools back at the motel and when I got to my room, everything was completely soaked: the carpets, bed, tables, and all my stuff. I guess some assholes set off the fire sprinkler system on my floor while I was gone.

Zakk: Met up with Father Eric for a cup of Black Label Valhalla java. We had some good laughs and talked about the book you are reading. We set off the fire alarm over at Moby's motel and then ran back over to our place. After some more laughs, we grabbed a pre-lunch snack and then I received a call from my manager that the new Black Label record landed No. 1 on the *Billboard* charts. I went down to the hotel spa to celebrate by getting one of the best massages of my life. That's when my cock told me, "That omelet was simply amazing. The hollandaise sauce was undeniably perfect!"

12:00 P.M.

Moby: While changing strings, intonating the guitars, and setting the backline, got power to everything and did a line check of Zakk's guitars. I'm not sure if the pounding headache is from lack of sleep, lack of food, or an extension of the back and neck pain I've had all day.

Zakk: Grabbed another freshly brewed cup of Black Label Valhalla java and headed back up to my room. Saw JD on my way up to the room. I ducked behind a column in the hotel lobby to avoid his seeing me. After the coast was clear, I continued my stroll back to my room. I was still in my bathrobe and slippers from this morning. My cock was also in a bathrobe and slippers. Yes, six-star hotel.

2:00 P.M.

Moby: Sound check went way over time and I missed any chance at getting a meal. Headed out in a rental car, in tons of traffic, in search of a music store for some parts I needed. Had to hurry and get back to setting up Zakk and Nick's guitars for the night.

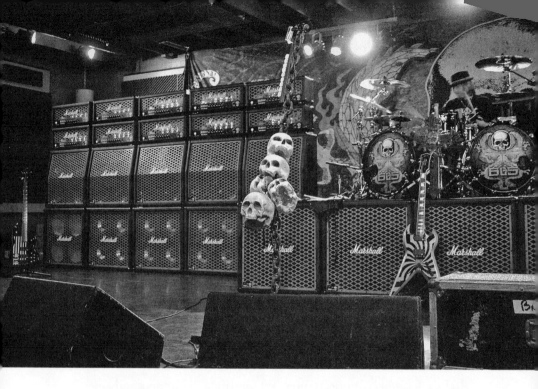

Zakk: Knocked out a couple of quick phone interviews while getting a deep-tissue massage and then took a short nap in front of *SportsCenter.*

5:00 P.M.

Moby: Had to run for a quick tetanus shot. I stuck my hand with a rusted tool while adjusting the intonation on Zakk and Nick's guitars. We've had the same rusty tools for years and no budget for new ones. Zakk says there isn't a dime left in the budget for tools.

Zakk: Just blew a ton of money on a delicious filet mignon dinner, ordered a couple to go in case I get hungry later as well. Then I went to the hotel's gym to get a solid workout. It's not as nice as my gym at home, but it did the trick, plus I was able to watch the game at the same time. Afterward, I headed back to the room to warm up with my guitars while the wife caressed my balls and told me how bountiful they are.

8:00 P.M.

Moby: Headed back from urgent care to the gig. Found a small, day-old side salad in the backseat of the rental car—first meal in twenty-four hours. The lettuce was rubbery from being in the car and heat all day. There was a half-empty water bottle as well, also warm.

Zakk: Phil picked me up at my penthouse suite and brought me a fresh triple-shot mocha. We headed downstairs. I signed a handful of autographs for members of our Black Label family who had been waiting for me in the lobby. We had some laughs, took some pictures, and then we jumped into the tour bus and headed off for Black Label church services.

9:00 P.M.

Moby: Zakk played all sixteen guitars tonight for twelve songs. He actually had me hand him a fresh guitar in the middle of several songs, so the crowd would see every single one we brought out on the road. After the set he handed me his guitar and told me to clean and restring every single one of them by five A.M. for his satellite radio appearance, where he will be performing two songs on the piano only.

Zakk: Had a kick-ass Black Label church service with thousands of Berzerkers. Everything went perfectly except I noticed that the B string on one of the sixteen guitars I played tonight was slightly sharp. I have a sneaking suspicion that Moby is slipping. Gonna have to hire someone to keep an eye on him, which will be deducted from Moby's pay.

11:00 P.M.

Moby: Spent three hours taking down the stage, backline, and guitars and packed everything up on the truck. A homeless guy wandered into the venue collecting cans and threatened me with a rusty knife. I told him if he could stab me deep enough that I could take a few days off work, I would give him one of Zakk's guitars. He gave me a deranged "crazy eyes" look, said something to me that sounded half-Chinese and half-Mongrel, and then staggered off into the night.

Zakk: Stepped off the stage and the Black Label Special Ops escorted me to a limousine waiting to take me back to my hotel suite. Checked my phone to find provocative photos sent from my wife, waiting in bed for me to come bathe her in my conquest.

2:00 A.M.

Moby: Stranded in the venue parking lot. I told those fucking guys I would be right back and they left me here. Have to find a way to the motel we are staying at. It's forty miles from here, so a cab ride is going to cost me at least a hundred bucks. Between the hospital trip and getting left behind, I actually lost money by working today. Gonna look for that homeless guy again and see if two guitars will convince him to stab me with a rusted blade.

Zakk: After conquering the Immortal Beloved, I snacked down one of those savory and delicious steaks I bought earlier (smart planning, that's why I'm the boss). Did a quick interview with China. I'm looking forward to rolling with the China Order of the Black. Got ready for bed; this Viking needs his beauty sleep. Barb frolicked among my balls, sucked me off, and then thanked me for allowing her to be my wife. I gazed right into her gorgeous, almond-shaped green eyes and said, "You're welcome. And since my personal foot masseuse is nowhere to be found, rub my feet."

There you have it, pretty much exactly how it goes down each day.

Bo Gacko

WHEN WE'RE OUT ROLLING WITH THE BLACK LABEL ARMADA, I LIKE TO meet our extended Black Label family in every town we pass through. And then there are radio performances, in-person interviews, and telephone interviews. When I call into a station, I generally get instructions like "don't curse" if it's a broadcast radio station. But sometimes it's satellite radio and they tell me I can say whatever the fuck I want. On one particular occasion, they forgot to let me know it was broadcast radio.

I got on the phone thinking it was a satellite radio station, and I could hear this old timer saying, "Zakk Wylde here today from the Black Label Society. How ya doin' today, Zakk?" So of course I answered, "It's a sad day in rock 'n' roll, guys. I just got done sucking off a couple of guys for beer money . . ."

CLICK!

They took me right off the air. But from my end of the phone, I could still hear them talking.

"See, with idiots like this, no wonder broadcasting is in the state it is."

A few seconds later Mark's phone was blowing up, and you know those calls weren't friendly.

Back in the Pride & Glory days, we were in Idaho doing radio promotion gigs. We walked into this station, still loaded from the night before. I was irritated, trying to figure out how this AM radio station gig was gonna help us in any shape or form. I knew there weren't any of the P & G family listening to this bullshit radio station. To make things even better, the DJ didn't know who the fuck we were; this guy wouldn't have recognized Ozzy if he was stuck in a fuckin' elevator with him. So I decided to have a little fun with this one. I had Brian and JD play some fucked-up song they came up with called "Bo Gacko," about a really nice guy who would do anything for you. At the end of each lyric line, Brian would play this riff on his guitar that sounded like the phrase *Bo Gacko*—which JD came up with when he was stoned out of his gourd one day. So these guys go into this ridiculously goofy-ass shit:

> *When you need him to walk your dog for you*
> *he will . . . Bo Gacko*
> *He'll wash your car for you when you're not*
> *home . . . Bo Gacko*

"*And then . . . ,*" JD sang as he and Brian broke into the next part of this musical masterpiece . . .

Meanwhile, I was fucking dying laughing and the DJ, with a deadpan stare, wasn't saying a fucking thing. He thought this shit was for real.

They finished the song, live on the air, and the DJ came back in saying, "Okay, well that was Pride & Glory with Bo Gaaaacko."

Un-fucking-real.

And these pointless little radio and TV things still continue to this day.

You're a Viking from New Jersey? You Must Have Grown Up and Lived Right Next Door to Bruce Springsteen!

HERE'S A GREAT BLACK LABEL SUPER BOWL HIGHLIGHT REEL OF HOW amazingly the publicist and record company can perform when left to make decisions at will. Just recently, on tour for the *Order of the Black* record, we had just finished three Black Label church services and were about to play the fourth consecutive show in New York City. Now, when you're playing the guitar and staying up all fucking night getting fucking hammered, it ain't a big deal when you've got a gig the next day. That is, unless you're the douchebag lead singer of Black Label, which is the other half of what I do, making me half *more* douche, thus completing my full-bore doucheness. Anyway, ask any lead singer and he or she will tell you that the only way to get ready for the next gig is to sleep and shut the fuck up. For guitar and bass, you change the strings. For drums you change the drum heads. But for vocals, you gotta rest the pipes until it's showtime. So now that everybody knows that, what does my Black Label Special Ops publicity team arrange? This is how they show me why I pay them the big fucking bucks—my publicity think tank of doom threw this atom-splitting idea at me.

Before I get into this brilliant idea, realize I don't go to sleep after a Black Label mass until three A.M., or even five A.M. I'm up from all of the adrenaline of the Black Label church service. So the game plan is to get me and Mark to some fucking radio station in the city at about six in the fucking morning to tell them what my favorite fucking Bruce Springsteen songs are and what memories I have connected to these fucking songs! Are you for fucking real??!!

Then I was told it's the E Street satellite radio channel, where all they play is Father Springsteen 24 fucking 7!!! Now, I dig the Boss, but I asked my team of specialists, "What in the fuck does this have to do with me promoting Black motherfucking Label?"

The answer was, being that I'm the fucking Viking douche that rose from the frozen tundra of the Nordic New Jersey parkways, where Odin resides—and if you notice, the only fucking birds that fly around New Jersey are ravens—they thought it would be cool publicity because I was playing NYC that night.

I then asked, being the dumb motherfucker that I am, "Are they going to announce that we are playing in town? Are they going to play Black Label? Are they going to even mention Black motherfuckin' Label?"

Well the answer, gang, is one that you'll soon become all too familiar with in the glory-hole-filled music business. And that answer is a resounding, "No. No. No."

After I got done fucking laughing I just said, "Lemme get this straight. You want me on no motherfuckin' sleep, getting ready to play NYC, which is going to be a fucking madhouse tomorrow between friends, family, record company people, radio people, the whole nine yards, and it also being the fourth Black Label mass in a row, which means at some motherfucking point I gotta fucking sleep. But all I'm gonna do is talk about Father Springsteen's songs and whether Barb was sucking me off or I was mounting her from behind while 'Born to' fucking 'Run' was blasting on the radio in my old 1978 Delta 88 Royale. Get the fuck outta here. Tell the gang down at E Street Radio that Bruce and company rule, but I have a Black Label church service I have to attend. And I apologize for not being able to come down to the station. Now that *that's* done, see if you can put your heads together and come up with some more brilliant shit for me to do."

And so the joyous musical journey continues, which will be well documented in yet another one of my future masterpieces, titled *How to Get Your Wife to Tickle Your Prostate, Suck You Off, Change Your Newborn, and Make You a Sandwich at the Same Time.*

World Tour Survival Technique: STDs, and I'm Not Talking About Stronger Than Death

The Adventures of Itchy the Crab Catcher

After you've thrown down a crushing show of Metal alchemy it's time to pat yourself on the back for a job well done, crank up the stereo, and enjoy the spoils of your conquest. At every gig we play, there's a lineup of girls who'd love to be on the receiving end of an extreme rear-end makeover masterminded by yours truly. This is great for the single guys in the band, but it doesn't come without its itchy, crawling consequences.

Over in Tokyo, one of the guys, whom we'll call "Itch" for the

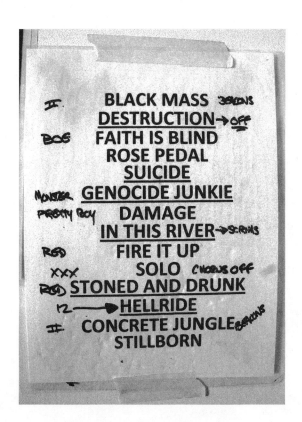

sake of this story, came down with a nasty batch of crabs. This wasn't his first experience with crabs. Itch has had a plethora of burning and bumpy gatherings on his junk over his many years in rock. It's pretty safe to say that he's had every STD in the book a dozen times over, and quite possibly a few that haven't been discovered yet. Let's just say he's a huge fan of *skinning it*.

The day after he banged these Japanese girls, he found a colony of crabs in his crotch. He could literally pick them out, set them on the counter, and watch them race straight back to his nut sac. I mean, if these things were any bigger, he could have named them and walked them around on a leash.

All day long, Itch was scratching like a hound dog. He went to every pharmacy near the hotel, but the language barrier, and the fact that he was yelling and pointing at his own crotch, kept getting him thrown out the door.

Finally, he found help. In one pharmacy, the clerk watched his reenactment of what looked like some fucked-up sign language for jerking off, and right before getting ejected from the store, Itch put his hand on the nearby counter and ran it across, mimicking what a running spider would look like, or in this case, a giant STD crab. The pharmacist's eyes widened and he began nodding and yelling in Japanese; Itch was nodding, yelling back in English, pointing at his crotch, until the clerk disappeared into the back. Moments later he returned with a shampoo that would, to this day, be the best cure for crabs that Itch has ever used. (Yeah, he's had several visits from these sexual crustaceans over the years. While this is quite vile, it's also very, very Metal.)

Groupies and Swedish Fish: Not Just an Appetizing Snack Anymore

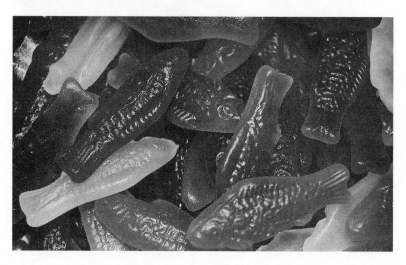

METAL GROUPIES WILL DO SOME SERIOUSLY FREAKY SHIT WHEN LOOKing to win the attention of rock stars. I've seen chicks making out, fighting, getting gangbanged, begging for the clothes I'm wearing, even shooting Swedish Fish candies out of their pussies (yeah, you might want to read that again before moving on).

We were over in the UK, where the groupies are proven to be far kinkier than in France. We had just played a killer show in London, and I planned to hang out for a while with the London chapter, wash up, get a steak dinner, and then do what any real rock star should do in London—go drinking. London has some of the best pubs in the world and the coolest people. It's always a good time in the pubs, and I love it when everyone in the joint starts singing. It's usually theme songs for their soccer team, or drinking songs, but you don't really see that in the U.S. except for a few places, like in Boston.

After hanging with our Black Label family and deciding that taking a shower wasn't on my to-do list after all, I went to go rally the guys for some pub-crawling. The second I walked into their room, I knew something fishy was transpiring because everyone in there was dead silent standing in a half circle. As I walked up from behind them and looked over their shoulders, I saw this girl completely naked, legs spread wide open and in the air. Just as I started to ask the guys who was going to be plowing this girl into primal submission I was interrupted with, "Here it comes!"

I thought I had seen pretty much everything there is to see in the world of Metal, but this day in London, England, proved me wrong. Within a couple of seconds, this girl shot a Swedish Fish candy out of her pussy and six feet across to the guys, one of whom caught it in his mouth. She literally had fired the fish like a cannonball right down the gullet of a Doom Crew member. The result was cheers and celebrations. I could tell by the batch of candy on the floor that they obviously had been trying to make a shot like that for a while. I was just as impressed as the rest of them, astonished really. Some of us eventually made it out to the pubs that night, but not before this chick's phenomenal display of skill racked up a few more points.

Porn Shops: An Oasis in a Sea of Time

PEOPLE ALWAYS ASK ME WHAT IT'S LIKE WHEN OUR WOMEN COME OUT on the road with us. Well, what usually happens is that all of us slobs travel around for a while on our own, and the ladies, not wanting to spend too much time with a bunch of smelly, farting, drunk, and overgrown children, fly in and out at various spots and hook up with us en route. When they do come in, we know we are going to have to be at the top of our game in the sack, and so, since we know exactly when they are coming, we have time to prepare. What that means is that we have time to hit up a porn shop and pick up all sorts of fun things to enhance the experience and make sure our ladies don't forget who is King of the Love-making Castle.

On one occasion, my Immortal Beloved and Philth's girl decided to come and meet up with us. In eager anticipation, our drummer Philth and I headed on down to the local adult toy store of the town we were in. We had just rolled off the bus, and so we were all decked out in full Black Label fashion: leather vests, chains, boots—the works. So we started shopping around for various dirty items and eventually brought our take to the counter, where a nice older woman was working. She looked down at the pile of dildos, Anal Eaze, and butt plugs and said quite matter-of-factly, "So, you boys planning on having a good time tonight?"

Not thinking anything of it, we told her that indeed we were. She bagged up the items and the two of us exited the store. As we were leaving with our sack of goodies, it simultaneously dawned on us how this must have looked from the outside. Two guys decked out in denim and leather, strolling into a porn shop together, and buying a veritable stockpile of dildos, Anal Eaze, and butt plugs! The only thing missing was the Village People's song "Macho Man" soundtracking the whole episode. We just looked at each other and then burst out laughing. Next thing I knew, we were sixty-nining each other, lubing each other up with the Anal

Eaze, and blasting each other's assholes with the butt plugs. At that moment, neither of us was laughing anymore. Neither were any of the record company executives who were all sitting around the boardroom we were in, trying to plot how to promote the next Black Label single. At the end of the day, it's all about the art of things—no matter how stretchingly painful.

What we go through to please our women and the record label! Not only do we put the security of our sexuality to the test, but many of us take it one step further and push our physical boundaries to the limit—those butt plugs were fucking huge. I couldn't feel the shit coming out of my ass for two months. And Philth said it was three months for him.

Cock Pumps
BY NICK CATANESE

IN 2005 WE WERE ON TOUR IN SEATTLE. WE HAD A FEW DAYS off leading up to the show because Zakk had destroyed a bar with a baseball bat and that night's show was canceled. Our tour manager Tim and I were hotel roommates for that tour. So one of those days we were bored out of our minds, wandering around downtown Seattle, and we stumbled into this sex shop. We were browsing around the store and Tim showed me this cock pump that said it would make your cock huge. Next thing you know we were back in our hotel room, each in his own bed, pants down to our ankles, staring at the ceiling and pumping our cocks. As it turns out, these things work. But I don't think you can do anything with your swanz when they're all monstrous like that. The pump pretty much pulls the blood from the rest of your body and fills up your dick with it.

I couldn't wait to go tell Zakk about it and the next thing you know, we're back at the sex shop, but with the whole band and crew this time. Zakk spent like twelve hundred dollars in the joint on these Black Label pocket pussies for the entire crew, a big rubber fist, and a bunch more of the cock pumps. Then, for his wife, he got this sex chair contraption with a vibrating dildo that went up and down. She'd obviously never use something like that, but I guess he thought he'd surprise her with it anyway.

On the night of the show, Zakk decided that all of the sex stuff was gonna be stage props. So we were up there trying to play the set and the stage was covered with cock pumps, pocket pussies, and Barbaranne's undulating dildo chair. The whole while, Sean Kinney (of Alice in Chains) was waving the big rubber sex fist in the air.

Every night for the rest of that tour, you could hear the *squish-squish* sounds of the dick pumps coming from the bunks on the bus.

There are three medical breakthroughs that, when perfected, will change mankind's quality of life forever: a cure for cancer, a cure for baldness, and the ability to substantially increase the size of a man's cock. Now, I don't care if a guy's got a fourteen-inch dick; if you tell him he can get three more inches by simply taking a pill or something easy, he'll be all for it. There are all types of herbal concoctions and strange devices that are sold on late-night television and in porn stores that attempt to accomplish this. One such contraption is—you guessed it—the cock pump.

As Nick mentioned, he had already done some recon on the place; he led us straight to the cock pumps. I had my doubts that they actually worked, but Nick said he had already tried one out. I figured it was my duty, as a friend and leader, to purchase a batch of these for the fellas in the band and the Doom Crew, and so I grabbed about fourteen of these cock jackers and brought the haul back to the bus for distribution. Even Thick-Stick Nick received a brand-new one, despite the fact that he's already got it going on in that department—we call him Thick Stick 'cause he's got one of those thick fuckin' beer-can dicks.

Although being on tour itself is a blast, there are long stretches of time that need to be filled. That's why we all drink so much on the road. The other pastime is, apparently, pounding one's radish, as I found out in a horrifying situation, which ensued soon after I handed out the batch of cock pumps. It happened in the early hours of the morning, probably around three A.M. or so. I woke up and was a little thirsty, so I decided to head to the lounge to grab a beer before going back to sleep. Being considerate, I walked very quietly so I wouldn't disturb the other guys, who were fast asleep, or so I thought. As I made my way to the lounge I heard something strange.

Squish, squish, squish, squish, squish, squish, squish . . .

I stopped dead in my tracks. It actually sounded like a fucked-up version of the Jason Voorhees theme music from *Friday the 13th*. After a brief pause I resumed my trek, and once again . . . *Squish, squish, squish . . .* It was coming from everywhere. Then, in grotesque astonishment, I realized what it was. From every bunk on the bus I heard the sound of cock pumps working! It was like I had been instantaneously transported into a mystical forest of cock pumps. Even with the trauma of my realization, I was able to obtain my beer, and I stealthily made my way back to my bunk.

The next day I brought it up with Nick. He broke out his pump right there on the spot and showed me this thing that sported a shiny new sticker that read MULLETS RULE.

"I blew out my cock pump, dude!" he said to me.

And he had. Thick-Stick Nick had blown out the damn rubber gasket in that thing already! Then he whipped out his schlong to show me the self-inflicted damage he had done. Nick's poor fuckin' dick was beat to hell! It was purple and black and had welts all over it.

"Nick! You gotta stop, man. Look at the state of your dick!"

But Nick wasn't the only one physically abusing his johnson.

After parting ways with Nick I went to the back of the bus to hang out with some of the guys. I got there and was met by the sight of two of the Doom Crew kicking it on the couch together, equipped with cold beers and strapped into those damn cock pumps, watching porn. These guys didn't get it that all the cock pumps did was engorge their dicks and swell them up; it wasn't going to make them cum! It's not like the cock pumps were sucking them off or anything like that. But the band and the whole damn crew seemed addicted to these things.

The pump was actually called the Typhoon, and so from that point on, that tour was referred to as the Typhoon Tour, for obvious reasons.

Cock pumps—unbelievable!

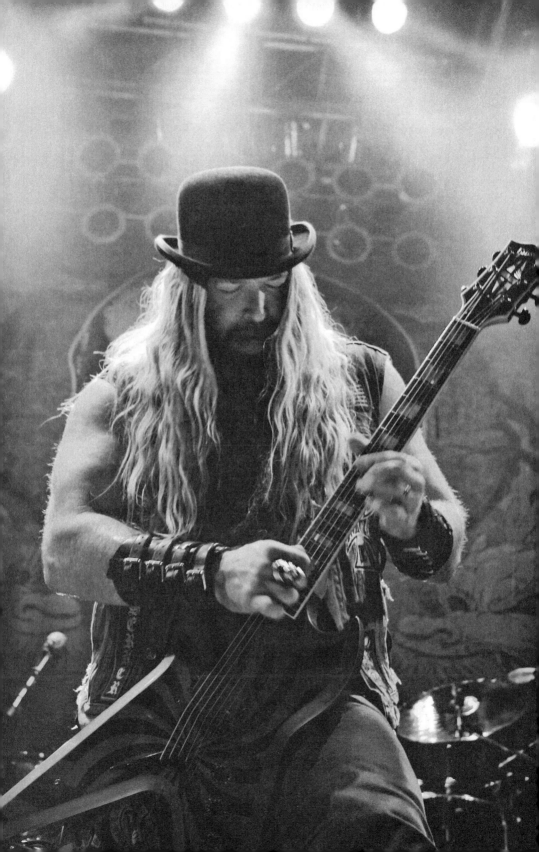

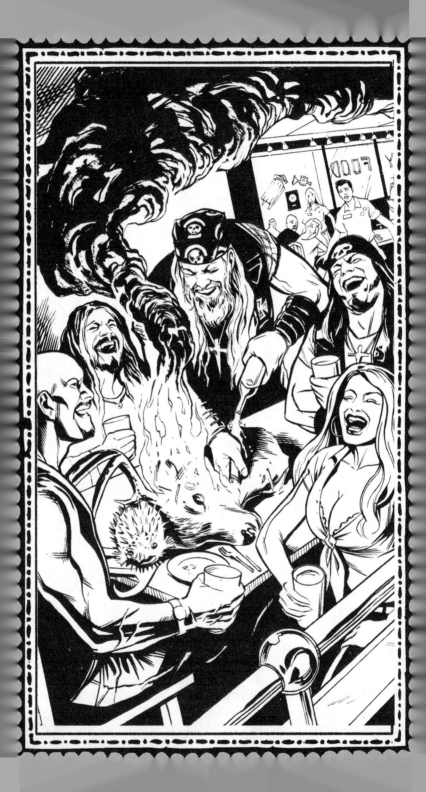

CHAPTER FIVE

Perils of Valhalla

O, woe is the day. Our quest hath been wrought with peril and dismay. Ravens, as black as night, clouded in turbulence the skies above. Our men grew ill at ease as they felt the curse of the Underworld set in around them. The high demon Pazuzu himself has led our legions to imminent doom! The seas ran wild with anger, and capsized their vessels, and took lives to its fathomless depths. And the tide of battle was set against the Order. Every tactic outmatched. Every victorious stride thwarted. But in the true tradition of our combatant ancestors, the Berzerkers pressed on, raising their axes high and unleashing a command of "No surrender!"

Follow my lead into battle, my legions, as our own faces twist into the scowls of war. For with blood and sword and fire we shall win our right, as did the former lions of our blood! With reckless abandon we wage war in thy name, Odin! We shall take upon ourselves revenge, we shall retaliate tenfold, and his magickal wolves shall flank our valiance, as thy redemption nears.

And as the anus of the Underworld yawned in disapproval, our band of warriors fought heroically. With spear and axe, and sword and dagger, they surged forward and squeezed themselves forth from Fate's tightening Rectum of Despair! As we raked across the blistering earth with the hand of the Gods, no man left unscathed. All were inaugurated into the Berzerkers. And as the contour of the land shook and trembled, our emergence from the steamy Bowels of Destiny was one of Victory! The image of the Skull was raised the world over.

Note from Zakk: It's amazing how all this shit usually goes down between waking up, taking a piss, and having my first cup of Valhalla java. It's fucking rough being a Viking from Springsteen and Bon Jovi country. And you know what else is rough? Father Eric's ridiculous fucking imagination. "Scowls of war"? "As thy redemption nears"? What I want to know is this—is my death getting any nearer by reading this nonsensical fucking slobber? It's not so much *am I gonna die,* it's more like *when am I gonna die?* Probably soon if I have to read any more of this stupid shit, although it is rather amusing.

The life of the rock star is fucking awesome; I am not going to lie. I've truly been blessed and I love what I do. But it's not all beer and cock pumps, my friends; as you've already seen, there is a good deal of work that goes into this lifestyle. If you are striving for success in music, remember, nothing is given to you; you have to literally forge it out of your blood, sweat, time, and energy. This is not a quest for the weak or for those who are discouraged easily. When you finally do reach your goal and get on that tour bus, things can get crazy, and when you hit the stage things can, will, and always do go wrong. If you can't maneuver the mental and real perils that litter Valhalla's landscape, then just buy yourself a pair of pink panties and skirt, and kick yourself in the balls the rest of your life for being a weak-willed pussy—kind of like JD. Actually, that's not a fair statement, so allow me to rephrase: *exactly* like JD!

I have encountered so much downright lunacy in my personal quest. But that's also part of the fun. Things that I would have never experienced in life are right in front of me on every tour and at every show. I've been able to see the world, but not without running into my share of danger.

Pazuzu Gone Wylde

WHETHER IT'S GETTING TO THE GIG, SOMETHING YOU ATE, AN OVERCRAZED crowd, or maybe you just got completely plastered at the airport, you're gonna run into catastrophes. And when they strike, you've got to Black Label/Patton up, make the best of the situation, and keep the machine rolling. I would suggest writing all of those instances down, so that one day when you write a book you can include all of those fantastic stories. Maybe you'll actually benefit a little from all the chaos you've been through over the years. And if you didn't learn from your mistakes, at least someone else might be able to. Here are a few tales from the road when things didn't go exactly according to plan. Whether it's through an act of man or of God, even just getting to the gig itself can be perilous.

So there we were in London—tiny little streets, double-decker buses, the whole nine yards. The Ozzy crew was relaxing in their bunks as our tour bus made its way through town and toward the spot where the show was going to be. Then, all of a sudden, *bang*—a forty-car fucking pileup! I still have no idea what actually happened to cause the accident, but I do remember that the crew got it bad, flying out of their bunks and getting pretty well banged up. Thank God no one was killed. But you know what? As badly as those guys were bruised and hurtin', they still got their asses to the show and actually made it on time! It was just another example of a GIFD moment.

We spend enough time on the buses that it's nice when we are afforded the luxury of flying to a gig, but sometimes getting off the ground isn't always a foregone conclusion. On one occasion, I found myself stuck in this little airport-hotel bar somewhere in

Europe. It was just me, Ozzy, Randy Castillo, and Geezer Butler hanging out and just fuckin' drinking. It was raining like a damn monsoon outside and we were stuck there for quite a while. Needless to say it didn't take long before we were all pretty wasted.

While we were knockin' them back in the bar, our leader Nick Cua (Ozzy's tour manager) was busily trying to figure out how we were going to get to this next gig. Of course things were totally fucked. We were a good four hundred miles away from our destination. All the flights were grounded and it was looking like we weren't going anywhere. Nick was losing his damn mind, on the phone trying to pull something out of thin air. Nick basically just said, "Fuck it!" and rounded up a couple of rental cars. Of course by the time all the cars were ready to head out, all of us were pretty well hammered; even the Boss had taken that step beyond drunk into fucked-up land. Nick on the other hand had spent the last several hours trying desperately to figure out how to overcome all of the obstacles and get our asses to the show, so he had pretty much had it by the time he told us, "Get in the fuckin' cars!"

We all stumbled out of the bar like a small hunting party of drunken Neanderthals and made our way out to where the cars were parked and ready. All I remember is Ozzy coming onto the scene, looking around, and saying, as only he can, "What's going on? Isn't there any organization around here?"

Nick, in complete frustration, just looked at the Boss and told him, "Get your ass in the *fuckin' car!*"

My God, it was comedy hearin' those two! But we still made it to the show. We Got It Fuckin' Done.

Ozzy's a What?

I REMEMBER THIS ONE NIGHT OVER IN EUROPE, WE WERE PLAYING SOME small club, and Ozzy and Geezer were feeling a little under the weather, so the gig was getting canceled. I think at this point they

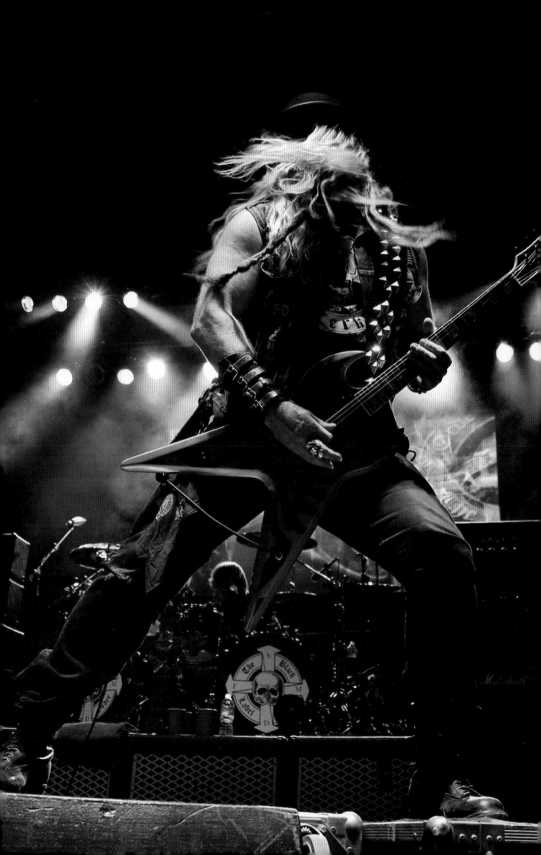

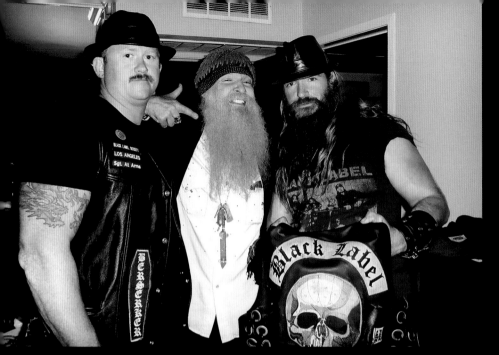

With Jeff "The Grimm Cracker" Graham, Black Label Special Ops, and the legendary Billy "F" Gibbons, from whom I stole all my pinch harmonics *and* the beard. Thanks, Father Gibbons. You rule!

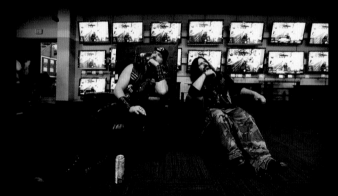

Me and JD–TV shopping with Meatball Lasagna. If I could somehow get all those TVs to continuously show footage of me, I'd never have to worry about seeing JD again.

JD, me, and Adam Klumpp, the Black Label engineer extraordinaire as well as our favorite Irish Catholic rabbi.

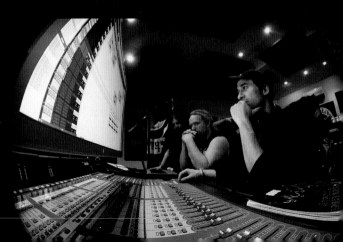

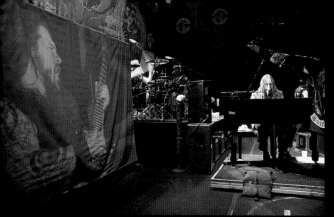

Dime, the boys, and me. Playing "In This River"—Dime's song.

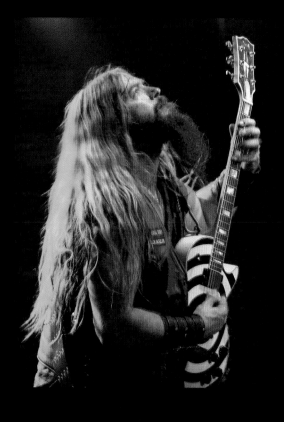

Me, looking up to my savior, Jesus Christ, knowing that his eternal shield of strength protects me from all that is evil, since JD is standing just to my right.

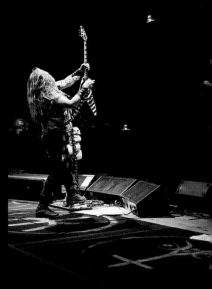

My guitar solo—one of the highlights of the show, not so much my playing but the opportunity it presents for everybody to gather at JD's Bar and Grill. People hang out over at his side of the stage, drinking and having a good time while JD picks up some guy to have sex with after Black Label Mass.

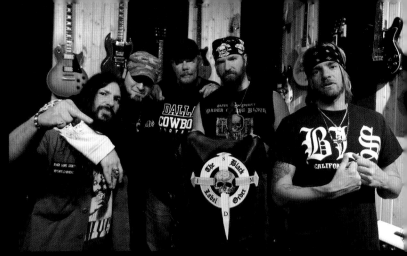

Rockline Radio with JD, Nick, Father Bob Coburn, me, and Will Hunt.

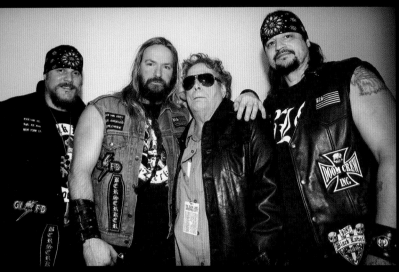

Phil Ciulo of Black Label Special Ops, me, Father Leslie West, and Mark "Field General" Ferguson. As Leslie says, he's my father, but neither of us has any idea who my mother is.

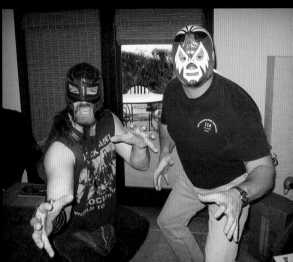

Z-Man and the Cracker, Black Libre Society—a tag team of Doom.

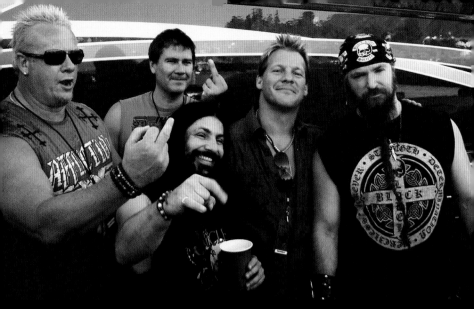

Hanging with Father Jericho and my Black Label brethren at Ozzfest. Everyone is having a great time and drinking adult beverages except for me, the pussy with a Shirley Temple.

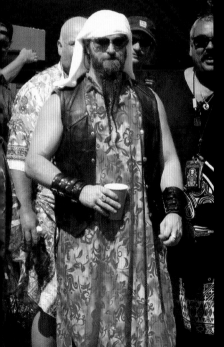

Ozzy's birthday. After a couple of cocktails, wearing a dress sounded like a great idea.

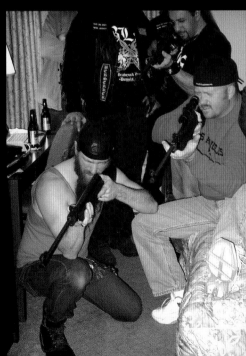

JD's surprise birthday party. And, man, was he surprised when Father Fergie yelled, "Open fire!"

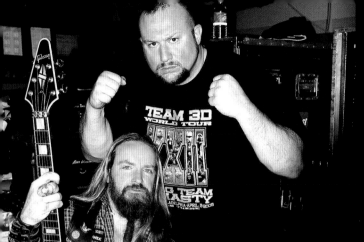

Father Bubba and me backstage. I'm about to play the national anthem fo a TNA Wrestling event.

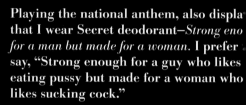

Playing the national anthem, also displa that I wear Secret deodorant—*Strong eno for a man but made for a woman.* I prefer say, "Strong enough for a guy who likes eating pussy but made for a woman who likes sucking cock."

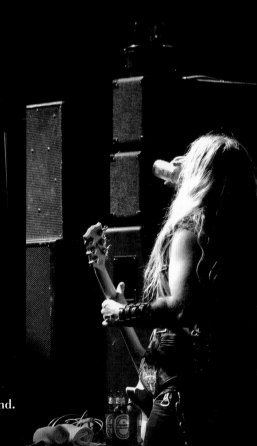

We had a good run, old friend.

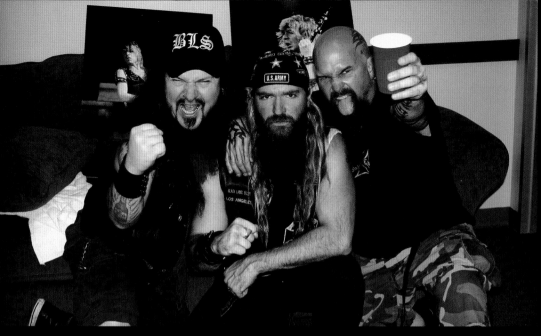

Father Dime, me, and Father King on August 8, 2004, at the Cynthia Woods Mitchell Pavilion in Houston, Texas. Father Dime gave me the posters of our hero, Saint Rhoads, in the background, and they still reside in my music room at the compound.

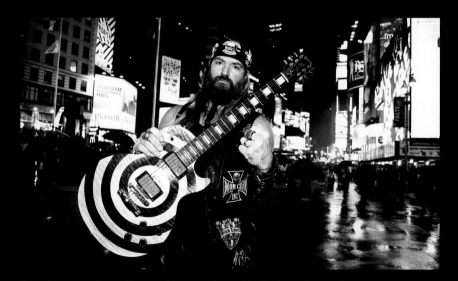

October 31, 2009—Times Square, New York City. Several minutes after this photo was taken, Eric and I were beaten up by a bunch of senior citizens who took Eric's wallet and my guitar, and they hurt our Black Label feelings. I fully believe in taking care of our elders, but after being on the receiving end of this ass-whooping, I found myself questioning this belief. What are they getting in Medicare packages these days—STEROIDS??? I mean they beat the living fuck out of us!

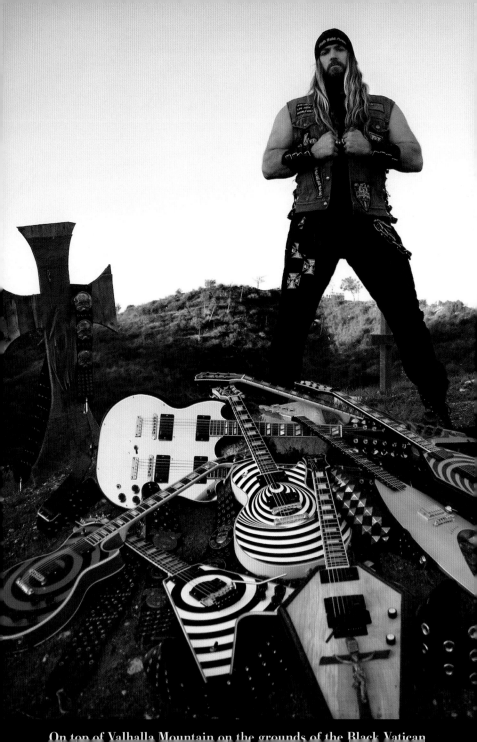

On top of Valhalla Mountain on the grounds of the Black Vatican

were both back at the hotel, which was actually across the street from the venue. So our fearless tour manager and guardian angel Bobby Thompson, bless his soul, came up to me as I was warming up on my guitar in the venue and said, "Zakky, would you mind going up onstage and telling the audience that Ozzy and Geezer are feeling under the weather and that the show is canceled? But we'll be back soon and all their tickets will be refunded?"

I looked at B.T. and said, "Fuck that, Bobby. I ain't going up there and saying that shit."

Bobby just said, "All right, just get your stuff together so we can get your asses over to the hotel."

Me and Father Castillo started walking out the back door and across the street to the hotel. We went up to the top floor to the Skybar to have some cocktails. As we were having our drinks, we could literally see the people down below, waiting to get inside the venue for the big hot-rockin' show. Me and Randy went downstairs to ask if there were any cool rock bars in town. Just then a kid came up to us and asked, "Oh man, were you guys going to the show tonight?"

"Yeah, it really sucks, man. We really wanted to see Ozzy," Randy and I responded.

Then the kid told us, "Yeah, I had tickets and a recorder. I was going to tape the show tonight. Here, check it out."

He hit play on his recorder and I could hear people talking and chattering, and next I hear Father Thompson's voice over the PA system announcing that Ozzy wouldn't be performing that night.

First, B.T. thanked the crowd for their understanding before the comedy ensued. There was mumbling and then utter disgust. And then chanting: "Ozzy's a wanker . . . Ozzy's a wanker . . . Ozzy's a wanker." All one thousand of them in unison and sheer drunken delight blasting out our fearless leader's name.

Me and Randy just started fucking cracking up. Then the crowd turned into an angry mob and destroyed the whole fucking place. John Sinclair's keyboards, which were behind the PA, got completely demolished as they tipped the whole fucking PA over. Thank God John wasn't behind there. Needless to say, I don't think the cancellation was well received.

Just because you actually make it to a show alive doesn't mean you're out of the woods by any stretch of the imagination. Once the show begins, expect that anything that can go wrong—will go wrong—and sometimes it gets downright hairy out there.

Of Fire, Indecent Exposure, Vomit, and Cleveland

Now, ANYONE WHO HAS EVER SEEN AN OZZY SHOW KNOWS THAT THE Prince of Darkness loves to play with water. Whether it's with those big fire hoses he drags around, the water guns, or the big-ass two-gallon buckets, dowsing his fans and bandmates is a particularly inspired pastime for the Boss. The buckets were first; they came about well before any of the other contraptions were developed, and he was never hesitant about using them. All of these satanic water sports came to an electrifying climax at Mc-Nichols Arena in Denver, Colorado.

We were probably about four songs into the set, heading into the outro for "Shot in the Dark." I was jamming away, Randy was pounding the skins, and Geezer was going from one side of the stage to the other while Ozzy ran around with those buckets soaking the first ten rows of the audience. Then Ozzy spied Tony Dennis, his personal assistant, who had made the unfortunate choice of standing at the side of the stage, right in Ozzy's crosshairs. It was Tony's time to soak.

Now, Tony was standing just in front of where the stage monitor engineer was positioned, working the monitor-mixing console. With that evil Ozzy gleam in his eyes, the Boss launched the water at Tony, but, as if by merciless fate, the flashlight that Tony was holding fell and Tony bent down to pick it up, right at the exact moment that the airborne wave was hurtling toward him. Two full gallons of water went right over Tony and broke over the monitor console. I kid you not, six-foot fuckin' flames began shooting off that thing. It was like a perfect storm of disaster.

There was this huge crackling noise, and then the monitors went dead. And there was no sound at all onstage. All I could hear was the sound from the front of house echoing throughout the arena. At first I thought it was my fuckin' rig and I bolted over to check it out, but I soon realized it was much more serious than that. And then I saw those fuckin' flames spewing from the console. That shit could have easily killed someone.

Since the onstage sound was out, none of us could hear shit, especially Ozzy. We ended up finishing out the set all huddled up in a bunch so we could cue Oz when to come in. It was so bad that Randy's drums sounded like cardboard boxes because he was set so far back, and good luck hearing the cymbals. Mind you, this was a massive fuckin' stage. I was singing the first line of each verse so Oz would know when to come in. We had to do pretty much the whole set like that, with Ozzy's head right next to mine so he could get the cues.

We got through the show of course, but I remember thinking, "Thank God it wasn't me!" I mean, it's Ozzy's show, and he's earned the right to do pretty much whatever the hell he wants. Bottom line though—shit happens. And when it does, you've got to power through it regardless of the circumstances. After all, this is Metal, and as the saying goes, "Rock out with your cock out!"

It was at a show in Albuquerque, New Mexico, where I found out, in a somewhat obscene twist of fate, the true meaning of this classic adage.

The whole grotesque incident wouldn't really have been that bad, except for the fact that Randy Castillo had some family out for the show that night; his nephews and his nine-year-old niece were standing right there by the side of the stage. I was out there, onstage, doing my moves, busting into my wide stances and so forth when, right as I was lifting my guitar, I hear this loud RIIIPPPP!!!!

My fuckin' pants had split, right up the crotch to the waistband! In fact the waistband was the only damn thing holding the rest of my pants on. It looked like I was wearing a pair of assless chaps. Of course this happened right at the point where I was raising my axe high in the air, and so there I was, standing with my legs spread apart and my dick and balls hanging out in all their glory for the world, and Randy's bewildered nine-year-old niece, to see.

Of course I couldn't stop playing, so I just kept on at it, doing all my usual bullshit, with my junk flappin' around, until Randy finally took his drum solo. You'll find that the Almighty Drum Solo is one of the most opportune moments in a show to fix your shit when it goes wrong. I threw on some new pants and finished the show. Even though I'll never forget that gig, I hope that Randy's nephews and niece will and that I didn't traumatize anyone too badly.

Besides keeping an extra pair of pants with you at the gig, another valuable piece of advice I will offer the would-be rock star is to never eat before a show, especially if the food in question is itself questionable. When we were playing with Mike Bordin behind the drums, he had a stomach of steel and could power down whatever the fuck he wanted before a show. He could kill and eat a three-pound porterhouse, pound a beer, roll onto the kit, and blast it out no problem. Some can. Not me. These days I won't even eat a meal five hours before a show, and with good reason.

It all went down while on the Mafia tour and while we were playing the Fillmore in San Francisco, California. A classic venue: the Doors, the Stones, Led Zeppelin, Jimi Hendrix, you name 'em, they've played there. We made it into town a bit early, and JD, Barb, and I were a bit hungry so we decided we'd go scout out something to eat. Of course, being in San Francisco, we figured that we needed to partake of the town's legendary Chinese cui-

BRINGING Metal TO THE CHILDREN

206

sine. Unbeknownst to many, I have really terrible acid reflux, and at the time I wasn't taking anything to treat it.

I couldn't tell what exactly was on my plate, but it was definitely spicy. We got enough in us to feel full and then headed over to the show. Things were fine at first as we laid into the set, but as time went on, I began to feel a little off. As we began to play "What's in You," things took a turn for the worse and the song became eerily prophetic. I got through the first verse all right, but by the time we were beginning the riff for the second, I could feel my stomach churning. My mouth wasn't going to open without a disaster, so I just kept playing the riff, confusing the hell out of JD, who was wondering what the fuck was going on. My mouth began to drip with saliva like a rabid dog's, and I was spitting on the stage to get the shit out of my mouth. Finally, I decided it was time to power through the queasy feelings and GIFD, so I opened my mouth with the intention of getting through the song, come hell or high water.

"Helter Skelter's comin' 'round the bend, Satan's on his way . . . What's in you now . . ."

Motherfucker! Once again, that warm rush I knew all too well washed through my body. Vomit launched out of me like I was some kind of Chinese puke dragon, spraying all over the mic, the pedal boards, and everything and everyone else that was of the bad fortune to be too close to the disaster.

All I heard while I was unloading my bile-ridden payload was JD saying, "Yeah . . . What's in you!"

Apparently it was Chinese.

JD felt the need to continue with, "Hey, Zakk, I see you had the beef and broccoli . . . Oh, and that you were enjoying a little bit of the garlic chicken as well!"

So there it is. Now I never eat a thing before a show, and if anyone has a touchy stomach, I would seriously advise against a preshow meal for them as well. Otherwise everyone at the show may just find out exactly what's in you.

While I'm on the task of dropping all of this wisdom on your spongelike gray matter, I might as well remind you of the obvious. Try to find out what city you are in before you get inspired to give a shout-out. It's tough when you are hitting as many cities as I do per year, and there aren't too many topics for discussion that I will bring up onstage, but anyone who knows me knows that I'm a huge football fan, and given the opportunity I can't help being a fanatic. That said, being from the East Coast, the New York Giants are my all-time favorite team. Unfortunately, the Giants can't win every Super Bowl, and so I still, occasionally, have to recognize other great teams for their prominence and talent. I'm good that way, as long as it isn't the Steelers. It's not because they don't have an awesome franchise, it's because Father Eric and Father Fergie love the Steelers as much as I love being the bad guy. In fact, any team that JD, Eric, Nicky, and Mark are going for is always on my hope-they-lose list.

We were traveling through California and ended up in Oakland for a show. Now, Northern California might as well have been Guam to me at the time, and I didn't know the lay of the land whatsoever. The show was being played just after the Super Bowl, where the San Francisco 49ers had recently won another title. I got it in my head that I'd be Mr. Sports Ambassador and relate to all the sports fans in the audience, and so I jumped on the mic to extend my congratulations.

"Being a Giants fan I just gotta give you guys fuckin' credit," I screamed out. "Your Niners have one badass motherfuckin' football team! Congrats on the Super Bowl!" I waited for the cheers of approval and gratitude. The crowd erupted loudly, but not as planned. Instead of roars of acceptance and brotherhood, my heartfelt props were met with a resounding "BOOOOOOOOOOOOO!!!!"

Randy leaned out over his kit and yelled to me, "We're not in San Francisco, asshole! We're in fucking Oakland!"

It was truly a Spinal Tap, "Hello, Cleveland!" moment.

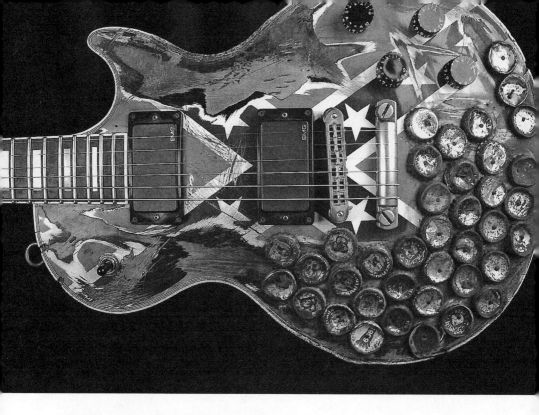

Take That Boy to Hollywood!

WE WERE DOWN IN CHICAGO, IN NITRO MODE—DRINKING EVERYTHING. I was down there with Phil and Mark, drinking Crown Royal by the gallon, literally. We went to Buddy Guy's blues bar and it was killer because Buddy Guy's band was playing. The guitar player came over and gave us a bottle of Buddy's beverage of choice, Louis XIII cognac. He asked if I would come up and do a couple of songs with them. I was stoked to jam with these guys; it was a killer session ripping it up with the saxophone player, just smokin' solos back and forth. While I was up there playing, Mark and Phil dusted the cognac. Mark went into the bathroom to take a piss, and there was this old guy in there who looked just like John Lee Hooker. He said, "You with dat white boy out there?" And Mark said, "Yeah." The guy answered back, "That boy's gooood! You oughtta take that boy to Hollywood!"

And we did. And that's when everything changed for me—

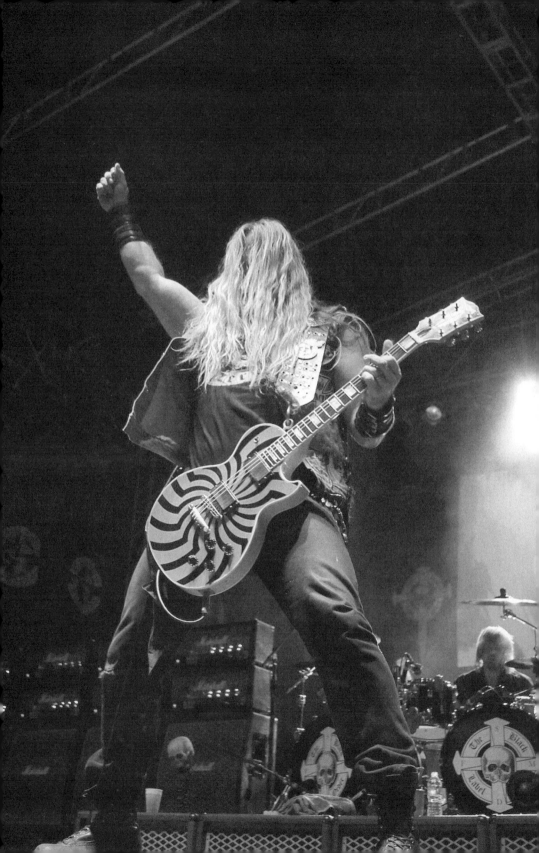

music, gay porn, sex change, then another sex change, and now a happy father of three married to a cock-gobbling whore whom I worship and adore.

Twenty-four Hours Drinking with Zakk Wylde
BY JIMMY HUBBARD

IT WAS MY SECOND YEAR WORKING AT *GUITAR WORLD*, MY FIRST magazine cover shoot, the first time I met Zakk, and my first time photographing him. He came to our building in New York City, down on Twenty-first and Fifth Avenue, to give a guitar lesson and have photos taken for our July 2004 issue. I was immediately surprised at the juxtaposition of his larger-than-life appearance and his down-to-earth personality. He's really just a guy you can talk to and bullshit about music with, all day.

We started drinking early that afternoon. I definitely wasn't drinking as much as Zakk; I wouldn't have been able to keep up. We did our photo shoot right after he finished with a guitar lesson, at about five o'clock in the afternoon. An hour later, Zakk wanted to go get some steaks, so me, Zakk, Nick Bowcott (Nick had worked with Zakk a lot over the years), and our publisher Greg Di Benedetto all went to some fancy steakhouse in the lower West Side. We got tons of ridiculous food and a whole lot of alcohol again.

I can't remember exactly what the conversation was, but Zakk ended up faux-strangling Greg, our publisher. He was describing what he was gonna do to someone that he was really pissed at and then went through the motions on Greg. It was kind of this awkward thing where Zakk didn't mean it to be a real strangulation, but Greg was pinned up against a wall nonetheless, laughing nervously while the blood evacuated his head. Bowcott was sitting at the table in absolute fits of hysterics, and I was watching in utter disbelief that Zakk was choking out our publisher.

After dinner Zakk wanted to go to an Irish pub and keep drinking. Greg was out of there quick, and Bowcott left too, but not before giving me instructions: "Jimmy, make sure Zakk gets back to his hotel." He gave me the address of the hotel, which was on Forty-ninth in the middle of Times Square, and bolted out of there.

I decided to find an Irish bar along the way back to Zakk's hotel, so we could get a beer and then get him back. We hopped into a cab and I told the driver to take us to a bar on Eighth Avenue somewhere near Times Square. The driver said, "Yeah, I know a place I can take you to."

Zakk started in right away with this *thing* that he was doing all night with everyone he came across—"Hey, bro, who would win in a fight, Mike Tyson or Evander Holyfield, both in their prime?" The cab driver picked Tyson. This was one of those things where there really is no correct answer, because Zakk just wants to engage people and have a conversation. If someone answered Tyson, Zakk would respond with, "No way, man, Holyfield." If they went with Holyfield, Zakk would take Tyson's side.

Once inside, he handed me some cash and told me to get us a couple of beers while he went to take a shit. And then it struck me.

"Hey, Zakk, dude, do you see any chicks in here?"

"Aww, dude, that cab driver dropped us off at a *homo hang*." (You can't even make this shit up.)

After leaving the gay bar, we grabbed a case of beer and sat in the middle of Times Square until the sun came up. I remember at one point jumping over a fence and peeing on a statue, just total inebriated retardation. Next thing I knew someone was tapping on me. It was Barbaranne with a handful of aspirin. I had passed out on the couch in their hotel room and she was telling me that I should probably get out of there before Zakk woke up and wanted to start drinking again.

I called my boss, told him that I was running a little late and had just woke up on Zakk's couch, and then I just passed out again. Then another tap, but this time it wasn't Barb, it was Zakk, and I could hear him opening beers.

"Bro, here, have another cold one, buddy." And we started drinking again.

I think by that time it was almost noon. I called my editor and told him I'd be at work in about an hour. He suggested, since I was still with Zakk, that both of us simply drop by the magazine's headquarters so Zakk could pick up his guitars. It sounded easier said than done.

We drank more and I told Zakk he needed to come back with me to meet Bowcott and get his guitars. So we finished off the beers in the room and headed downstairs to the hotel bar and continued drinking there. I kept looking at my watch to make sure we would make it to my work in time. At one point my mom called and I put her on the phone with Zakk. He told her the whole story from the night before, the peeing, the gay bar, everything. Finally, around five o'clock (I was completely fucking hammered again) I told Zakk that we really had to grab a cab and start making our way downtown.

We headed out to grab a ride, but before I could hail a cab, Zakk decided to duck into a corner store to pick up some "road beers" for the trek downtown. As he emerged from the shop with a cold six-pack, he spied a pedicab and stopped the driver (a pedicab is one of those carts pulled by a bicycle). Zakk asked this guy how much it would be to take us down to my work, but the biker said he didn't go that far, until Zakk pulled out a wad of cash and told him, "Yes you do." And so there we were, in the middle of rush-hour traffic

PERILS OF VALHALLA

213

and on one of the busiest streets in Manhattan, riding in a pedicab and drinking beers.

I called my boss and told him, "You gotta grab a camera, I'm on a bike with Zakk and we're headed down there." We finally arrived at my work at about six o'clock in the afternoon. I couldn't believe I had managed to survive a full twenty-four hours of drinking with Zakk Wylde. Then I stepped out of the pedicab cart and puked.

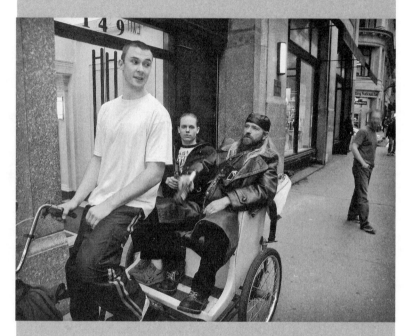

Note from Zakk: Father Jimmy, too bad I don't drink anymore. But if my blood clots ever give me a free hall pass for a day, I suggest we go back out for another pedicab ride! Good times indeed, my Black Label brother!

Have a Nice Trip! See Ya Next Fall!

So NOW THE SHOW IS OVER, AND YOU THINK YOU'VE FINALLY MADE IT through the Metal gauntlet—WRONG! You're only partway through, my little Metal brother. The simple act of getting off the stage can be an ordeal in and of itself, and sometimes even an opportunity to test the true valor and toughness of you and your crew. One such trial by fire befell a friend of mine while Black Label was rolling with our New Orleans chapter.

Let me start by saying that, in my book (and whaddaya know, this is my book!), Louisiana isn't a state at all. In fact it really is its own planet, floating around in its own beautiful, swampy galaxy. One of that planet's more hilarious creatures is a friend of mine named Frey, who is part of the New Orleans chapter of BLS. Frey has a band called Valume Nob, and no, that's not a typo, it's "Valume," kind of like the little pill that was used to calm down housewives in the seventies—Frey's quite the wordsmith. Hanging with Frey and his crew is always interesting. At that time, there was all sorts of shit flying around: smoke, drink, all sorts of pills, what you'd expect on a good, old-fashioned rock 'n' roll tour.

Traveling around with the New Orleans Berzerkers really is comedy beyond comedy, and so we took a bunch of the New Orleans guys out on the road with us for a few cities. BLS was on one bus, and those crazy bastards all piled in another. I figured we'd put the New Orleans chapter to work, so they were always helping us load in and load out, and the band always stuck around to hang as well. We'd get the trailers loaded and situated, then begin the party as one big family.

At one show, Frey was doing load-out, and so of course I was kicking it with some of the guys in the band, having a few post-show refreshments. Frey had to go up and down this rickety flight of stairs to get the shit loaded out of the club, a recipe for disaster. Sure enough, our twinkle-toed friend, with all of his grace and nimbleness, ended up taking a serious tumble while attempting to maneuver a bass drum down the narrow stairwell. I was outside chilling, when all of a sudden an ambulance came, hauling ass around the corner, lights blazing and sirens blasting. We all ran for the front of the club to find out what the hell was happening and found Frey being strapped to a gurney. He appeared all right, but he was shrieking like Harvey Fierstein and grabbing at his leg.

"It snapped! I heard it snap! It SNAAAAAAPPED!!!"

This guy needed calming down, and quickly. So I sprang into action and ran to the bus to procure the necessary supplies. He was thankful for the Crown Royal and beers I fed him while he waited to be loaded into the ambulance. Since I was the one with the credit cards, I ended up having to jump in the meat wagon with him, and so I hauled along a pillowcase full of beer and a grabbed a bottle of Crown for the ride. The rest of the guys followed us to the hospital. Of course we were drinking the whole ride there.

Once we got to the emergency room, they loaded him out and set him up in a room. The rest of the guys hadn't arrived at the hospital yet. Since Frey and I rode in the ambulance, we got there right away, going through stoplights and all that. He was lying there all jacked up, but there wasn't a doctor or nurse there yet, so it was just me, Frey, and a shitload of booze. I figured someone had to be coming in sooner than later, and so I got to work quickly.

First I strapped him into a neck brace, threw on a couple of splints, and hung a stethoscope around his neck. But that wasn't enough, not by a long shot. I bandaged him up like he was a fucking mummy! By the time I was finished taping him up and wrapping gauze around his head he looked like a wounded Civil War soldier. To finish off the masterpiece we put rubber surgical gloves on his hands and on his fuckin' feet! Just as I applied the final touches on Frey, the nurse walked in. She was pissed.

"You guys get the fuck out of here!" she yelled. And we actually ended up getting kicked out of the hospital altogether. Go figure.

After all the wailing Frey did at the scene and all of the ensuing hospital bills, it turned out that all he really did was bruise his fucking shin! He definitely didn't earn any kind of Black

Label Purple Heart for that one, but he did win the award for Biggest Pussy of the Year, putting an end to JD's six-year winning streak.

This stuff is all pretty fucking funny, but I don't want anyone to think that the dangers of the road are all cock 'n' balls, puke, and Baby Hueys with bruised shins. It's the times that you have to get offstage a lot sooner than expected that can be the most perilous of all, and some of these incidents, for better or worse, end up being written into rock 'n' roll lore.

Madness at the Meadows

ONE OF THE MORE LEGENDARY CONCERTS IN THE HISTORY OF METAL occurred at Irvine Meadows in California. It was a special benefit concert that Ozzy was holding to honor Randy Rhoads and to raise money to build him a mausoleum, because all of these sick assholes kept stealing his gravestone. It was a very emotional evening for everyone, and I actually had the honor of playing "Dee" for Randy's mother during the gig.

Things were going great until we got near the end of the show. When we came out for the encore, ready to play "Crazy Train," Ozzy grabbed his mic and yelled out to everybody, "All right, who wants to get crazy with Ozzy? Who wants to dance with the Oz? I need every single one of you to go extra, extra crazy!" And oh boy did they go crazy.

The next thing you know, a wave of humanity rolled through the amphitheater and smashed onto the stage. The security at the show was completely overwhelmed by the number of fans. People were jumping barriers and clawing their way onstage. In only seconds the whole situation got completely out of hand.

Some guy jumped up next to Ozzy and started trying to grab the mic out of his hand. The whole stage was packed with people. The mob started tearing everything apart. I saw one group of guys dismantling Randy Castillo's drum kit, and others were tearing up the monitors. It seemed like there were more people onstage than in the audience. I looked up and saw a bunch of kids sitting on these metal trusses that were suspended above the arena by chains; I watched as the chains snapped and the kids fell to the deck below. I heard later that they had survived, but not without a few broken bones.

I caught two motherfuckers trying to steal my fiddles. I went ballistic on those motherfuckers, pummeling them, head-butting them, just beating the living shit out of these guys. One of them was actually on my back while we were fighting. Finally I was able to secure my gear and get the hell out of there. Randy wasn't so lucky; his drum kit was completely gone. Some kids even got ahold of Ozzy's water buckets and of course they started heaving them right into the monitors. Flames were shooting out of the monitor console. The stage was fucking annihilated.

I found out afterward that they even took Ozzy's forty-inch monitor that he uses to scroll the lyrics! Seriously? I mean, somebody actually walked out of the venue with a forty-inch television! How the fuck they walked out of there with that, I don't know. But they took everything: mics, cymbals, drums—everything.

The total bill for the damage was over a hundred thousand dollars, and then of course Ozzy started getting hit with all the lawsuits. We still ended up getting the mausoleum for Saint Rhoads, so that all the fans can go down there and pay their respects to Randy.

One thing about being on the road is that it isn't just perilous for the Vikings themselves. When we storm into a town to pillage and conquer, there is always a great deal of collateral damage, but thankfully, in the past I was usually too fuckin' hammered to remember all of the craziness.

Crabs and Deer Heads

by Nick "E.T." Catanese, Pittsburgh Chapter

We were in San Antonio, Texas, with Rob Zombie, playing one of the last shows of Ozzfest. Rob and all of us decided to hit up Joe's Crab Shack. John Tempesta (of the Rob Zombie Band), Stone Cold Steve Austin, and his wife Debra were with us as well. Picture, if you will, a table with Zakk Wylde, Rob Zombie, Stone Cold and Debra, John, and myself, surrounded by tables with families trying to have a nice, normal dinner.

Zakk was sitting there wearing a bib, drinking beer from these huge hurricane fishbowls. After every chug, he slammed the fishbowl down and beer splashed all over. He had all these crab chunks and bits of food all over him and in his beard. Then, out of nowhere, Zakk stood up and punched this buoy that was hanging from a wall. It went flying across the room and hit some lady in the head; of course Zakk ended up going over there, apologizing, and buying their dinner.

Inspired, John got up and tore an oar off the wall and smacked a hanging blowfish, sending the fat little bastard sailing. We were already roaring with laughter when Zakk ripped this deer head off the wall. He got the head down, put it in the center of our table, then poured 151-proof rum on it and set it on fire. Then he stood over this fucking burning deer head and yelled, "How do you like your venison?"

There were these mortified people around us who were trying to have a nice dinner, and then these Viking deer-head-burning banshees at the table across from them. Zombie and everybody were absolutely hysterical with laughter. And the next thing you know the cops showed up. They came up to the table and recognized Zakk, Stone Cold, and Zombie. Instead of making any arrests, the cops wound up asking for pictures and autographs. In the end, we paid for the damages, but Zakk said if he was going to pay for the deer head, then it was going with him. The result was that we ended up with this burned deer head on the bus, as well as the blowfish and all that shit.

The next day we had a show with Zombie. At the show, Zakk took the deer head out during Rob Zombie's set and was dancing around with it, trying to mess with him and make him laugh during his performance. Later that night, Zakk was onstage playing with Ozzy. Rob and I were in the back watching the show on the Jumbotron and he tells me, "Dude, I gotta get him back. Go find me a black sheet."

So I went out and found a black sheet and brought it back to Rob. He already had the deer head tied on, and it looked like it was coming out of his stomach. He pulled the black sheet over his head, making it look like the deer head was just levitating in the dark. He decorated the head with beer cans on the antlers and a cigarette in its mouth and stuff like that.

Next thing I knew, I was steering Rob Zombie through to the stage. Zakk was out there in the middle of his solo when all of a sudden you saw this deer head peek over his shoulder and start jumping around. I could see tears rolling out of Zakk's eyes because he was laughing so hard. You can't make this shit up.

Note from Zakk: What Father Nickolas forgot to add was the fifteen-hundred-dollar tab for all the king crab legs, lobster, and titanic quantities of booze all the Berzerkers helped themselves to. Ever since I added "legendary vocalist" to my iconic death-defying guitar skills, along with Father of the Year and whatever else is on the growing list of douchebag awards that have come my way, another awesome award that I seem to receive without ever entering a contest is the Recipient of the Check at the End of a Behemoth Meal Award. So at this particular Berzerker buffet of doom, I reached into my wallet and handed our tour manager at the time, Father Bolin, my Black Label American Express card to handle the damages.

Timmy said, "Fuck this. Hey, motherfuckers, everybody throw forty dollars on the table for all the fucking booze and goddamn food you all helped yourselves to."

At this point I looked at Father Tim and started laughing, saying, "You're fucking dreaming, Tim."

Grand fucking total from eighteen working guys for a fifteen-hundred-dollar tab: sixty fucking dollars and thirty-six cents. Mind you, there was some pocket lint thrown in for good measure.

So there is my answer to myself when I ask the question, "I wonder when I can retire?": "Well, asshole, with brothers and friends like this, let's see . . . like a long, long, long fucking time from now!" It's just like when we pulled up to our new house and I asked my Immortal Beloved, Barbaranne, "Can we afford this?"

"Just keep working, asshole, we'll be fine."

Disciples of the Mosh Pit

DANGER LURKS IN EVERY SMOLDERING, STICKY CREVICE OF THE METAL labyrinth. From being on the road to getting on- and offstage, all of those who are merely in the presence of Metal's aura are at risk. Never is this risk greater, however, than for the diehard fans, for whom we as a band bleed. It is because of my deep caring for all of those Metalheads out there that I feel it is necessary to explain some crucial facts regarding your very survival when gathering for the Metal feast.

We all love going to a killer Metal show, watching our favorite bands tear it up onstage while banging our heads, thrashing around, and tossing up the Dio horns. If you're a purist Metalhead you might even take it a step further and dive into the mosh pit— you know, that swarm of Berzerkers below the stage at every Black Label show that sweats and bleeds as much as we do up onstage. I was going to give you a Black Label mosh pit tutorial packed with how to survive those crazy fuckin' things, but I realized I haven't been in such a place since my early teens, so I decided to bring in the most credible person I know. This wasn't such a simple task. In order to make sure you received the best possible edification on moshing, I needed to make sure I chose someone with verifiable experience not only as a one-man wrecking machine but also as a true disciple of the mosh pit. This crazy mongrel needed to be a true fan of Metal as well. You know: the kind of guy who eats Metal for breakfast and craves it throughout his day. If there were ever a vitamin for Metal that you could take to become more Metal than you already are, they would find the ingredients in this man's DNA. Fortunately, I've got our man.

Let me tell you a little about this crazy fuckin' Berzerker from Queens, New York. This is a guy who has no boundaries when it comes to destroying his own body in the name of all that is kick-ass. His professional wrestling career spans twenty years of leaping off ringside ropes onto barbed-wire tables, falling off fifteen-foot ladders onto his skull, and pounding his opponents into the ground with his backbreaking power bombs (all of the same things I like to do in the sack with my wife; she's very athletic). This man has had as many concussions as he's held championship titles, and if he weren't out dominating the wrestling circuit with his tag-team partner Brother Devon, he'd probably be out touring with his own Metal band playing and shows with Black Label. I reached deep into the Black Label directory and called on the ultimate mosher and one of my best friends, Black Label Brother Bubba (a.k.a. Bubba Dudley and Brother Ray).

Let's talk a bit more about this three-hundred-and-thirty-pound behemoth of verifiable Metalness. Over the years my brother Bubba has come out to many Ozzfests and Black Label shows to hang out and enjoy the music. At one of those Ozzfest shows we got into a little trouble with Mom (Sharon Osbourne). Before the show there usually isn't much for the bands and their friends to do other than hang out and get ready for the gig. And if you leave a few Black Label brothers with too much free time on their hands, and then mix in the booze, they're bound to get into some kind of trouble.

One of these debacles came about in 2003 at the San Antonio Ozzfest, when I invited Bubba to come out and play baseball with the guys in the tour bus parking lot. We set up all the bases, grabbed some gloves and bats, invited a bunch of rockers to join, and threw a game down. Sharon kept getting pissed, because when we'd play baseball the buses would get dents in the sides and more than once a ball went through one of the windows. And this particular day was no different; if anything we were more destructive with Bubba there (strength in numbers). Pitches were flying and balls were being smashed deep into the sides of fences, buses, buildings, and anything in our way. Finally, out came Sharon from one of the buses screaming at us like we were thirteen-year-olds, probably because we were acting like it. We tried hiding around the back of our bus until we thought she was gone, but she busted us and said we couldn't play anymore.

In 2009 Bubba came out to a Black Label show at the House of Blues in Atlantic City. As usual, we had our share of beers and storytelling. That night I watched him exude maximum Metalness as he cometed into the mosh pit, sweating and bleeding while we played. He broke his finger and at one point grabbed this chick's long hair, making her head bang to "Stoned and Drunk." Moments later, Bubba was standing there with a crazed look in his eyes, the girl's hair in his hand, but no girl! She had extensions and Bubba had literally yanked them completely off her head. With all the sweat and blood, and his broken finger, and his standing there looking like he had just scalped someone, I could tell it was a good night for my brother Bubba. More importantly, I knew this was the master who could teach you, young Metal Loki, how to survive a mosh pit.

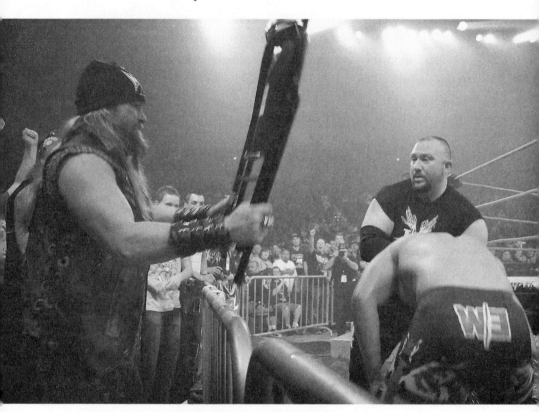

Bubba's Mosh Pit Survival Camp

WHAT IS GOING ON, YOU INSANE BERZERKERS? THIS IS BUBBA DUDLEY, one-half of the greatest professional wrestling tag-team champions in the world, here. Three hundred and thirty pounds—WTF? Try three hundred and thirty pounds of twisted steel and sex appeal! I eat T-bone steaks and lift barbell plates. And to build this finely tuned sex machine, you've got to get the food down and the weights up. Ever find yourself in the middle of a mosh pit at a Thrash Metal concert with your face pressed firmly into the ground beneath the boots of another mosher, your teeth bleeding, and the rest of your body being trampled relentlessly by Berzerkers who are completely oblivious to the fact that you have become one with the dirt below their feet? If your answer is no, then you need to read this section worse than we thought. Chances are that you've handed in your man badge for a vagina pin, you're carrying around some kind of man bag, and your nut sac has become a detachable accessory that you more often than not leave at home in your nightstand drawer. We've got to get you back on track, my brotha.

Ever since I was a little kid I wanted to be three things: a professional wrestler, a rock star, and in porn. I've done two out of the three, and since Meat Loaf already cornered the market on the three-hundred-pound rock star, I enjoy my Metal from the audience and from my favorite place during a Black Label Society show—the mosh pit. This is where you can truly test your body and mind to see what it's capable of as you collide into dozens of other Berzerkers sweating, bleeding, and breaking themselves in the name of rock 'n' roll.

In order to survive a mosh pit, you're gonna need to learn how to prepare your body for the impact it's gonna take. What I mean is that you've got to stay in shape. Different guys have different workouts. Some guys roll into the gym trying to bench-press five hundred pounds. I'm not one of those guys. As a pro wrestler, I'm constantly working day in and day out. I'm like an offensive lineman, but there is no off season in pro wrestling. I'm built for power, so that I can wrestle for thirty minutes a night in the ring, 365 days a year, and still be ready to go. The workouts that I do are for cardio and strength. Now, you bring that into the circle and you've got exactly what it physically takes to be true disciple of the pit.

Just like there are different types of dancing, like the tango, the mambo, break dancing, and the Robot (which Zakk tells me JD used to do down at Wildwood for some coin), there are also different types of moshing.

1. **The Slam Pit:** This is probably the most basic type of pit, where the fans slam, bounce, and push off one another as they raise Cain to their favorite Metal band. You'll see rockers popping up and down, devil horns and fists pumping, and both guys and girls displaying their aggressive approval of the music.

2. **The Circle Pit, or as I like to call it, the Swarm:** This is when the entire crowd below the stage, much like bees, instinctively moves in unison to create something that looks like a tornado. Moshers stomp, trample, and jump as they circle around the pit. Sometimes you'll get a really crazy bee circling in the opposite direction. This is a great way to reduce the amount of teeth you have.

3. **The Thrash Metal Pit:** Similar to the Slam Pit but the music is faster-paced Thrash, like Slayer or Anthrax, and the fans move accordingly. Everything is exaggerated in Thrash Metal, like the foot stomps, the fists in the air, and the amount of headbanging. Much like a cage match, you'll find plenty of elbows, punches, and kicks being thrown here. If you wake up the next day without whiplash, bruises, scratches, and a black eye . . . then you did it wrong. Obviously this is my favorite type of pit.

4. **The Black Metal Pit:** From our Nordic ancestors descended the Black Metal legions. These pits are similar to Thrash Pits, except that everyone in the audience is wearing black clothes covered with spikes and studs, and their faces are painted to look like versions of King Diamond and Cradle of Filth. I think the key here is to find a Halloween shop before the show and make sure you have enough fake-blood capsules to last through the night.

5. **The Alternative Pit:** This is the safest pit, where you might actually make friends or meet your future husband, wife, or domestic partner or whatever. There is lots of hopping around but with very little crashing into one

another. This pit is probably better characterized as the tossing of a fruit salad than a real-deal mosh pit.

Now that you're educated on how to train for a pit and what types of pits you'll find at various shows, you're just about ready. However, every great plan has an exit strategy, and this plan is no different. So in case you find yourself in a Thrash Metal Pit and you've decided you're more of an Alternative Pit type of person, here are a few ways to escape such a predicament. Remember, you'll need to react with catlike reflexes to escape, mostly because you are a complete pussy, but you'll live to mosh another day.

1. **"Crazy eyes" will always buy you a little time.** Throw your head back like Linda Blair from *The Exorcist* and shove out your tongue while shaking your head frantically and rolling your eyes in every direction, giving the illusion that you actually, in fact, have crazy eyes. Moshers around you will be momentarily stunned by your apparent demonic possession, buying you enough time to dart into the crowd. If you continue this evasive maneuver on your way through the crowd, people will clear a path for your escape.

2. **Shit yourself.** This doesn't need an explanation. It's not a clever title for something other than shitting yourself. Just shit your pants and watch people back away once they know and smell it's you.

3. **Fake an impalement.** Pick up an object and make it look like you've been impaled. Preferably someone's prosthetic leg. If you happen to be in a Black Metal Pit, you should also bite into a few of those blood capsules you're carrying around and spit it on the prosthesis to make it appear like a legitimate injury. If you can't find anything to use as the apparent impaling device, then go with the old wrestling cut-your-own-forehead move. Slit your fore-

head a little until you bleed a fucking red waterfall. Your face raining blood will buy you a few moments in most mosh pits. Once you get into the Slayer category, this will not work, as the band is likely to also be covered in blood that will be spewing from the stage and painting the first twenty rows of the audience.

4. **End it quickly.** Just stick out your tongue and make angry faces at the toughest sons of bitches in the pit. Make sure to maintain eye contact with them as long as you can. It will be a matter of seconds before someone shoves their fist down your throat.

5. **Do the whirly bird.** Pull your pants down and do the whirly bird with your cock. This move has been known to actually stop time, slow down the earth's rotation, and harden the nipples of Perez Hilton. While leaning back with your pants around your ankles, swing your pecker either clockwise or counterclockwise, whatever you've practiced at home, in a windmill-like motion. When people back away, staring and mesmerized by your spinning junk, make a break for any visible holes in the pit. If Perez happens to be there, you better move fast.

You might realize, once you're out of the pit, that you actually want to go right back in. Maybe you decide that you're not a pussy and somehow you have just found your true calling in life: running with a swarm of sweaty Berzerkers. I commend you on this accomplishment and since you are well on your way to becoming a real man, I'm going to share some of my super-signature moves that you will find extremely useful when you're in the mix—they may very well save your life.

Authors' Note: The fine editing staff at HarperCollins wanted us to cut the following moves from the book because we "crossed the line into promoting violence." Subsequent to their request, we sent Bubba to New York City to pay them a "visit" and discuss their reconsideration. After a very brief meeting, the staff happily complied with our request to keep the moves and was then transferred to the nearest urgent care center to have a size 14 boot removed from their backsides. That said, the authors and Bubba ask that you do not attempt a Bubba Bomb, or any of the following professional techniques, without proper training, a healthy physique, and keen knowledge of sexually transmitted diseases.

1. **The Bubba Bomb.** This one is great from behind. Get the menacing mosher into a wrestler's full nelson, where you reach both of your arms underneath their armpits and then clasp your hands tightly behind the back of their neck, applying a King Kong fuck-ton of pressure while you're at it. Then lift them into the air and fall into a seated position, driving their tailbone straight into the ground.

2. **The Bubba Cutter.** Reach around the back of your opponent's head and grab their jaw with your hand. Then as you pull their jaw back, forcefully drop with them to the floor, pulling their head into the ground. This way you crank their head and smash them into the ground simultaneously. Make sure to say, "You're welcome," before they go lights-out.

3. **The Standing-Release Powerbomb.** Lift your opponent, preferably by their throat, until they are seated on top of your shoulders and facing you. (This is also a great move for you and your old lady.) Then slam them onto the fucking floor with their back impacting first. (Most women will prefer you not do this part. However, in my profession there are a few who would refer to this as foreplay.)

4. **The Bionic Elbow.** Facing your opponent, proceed to smash your elbow onto the top of his head until he forgets his name, where he came from, or even what planet he

is on. Then when he wakes, you tell him that his name is Sharon Osbourne and that he fell off the stage while introducing Black Label Society, and that Ozzy is anxiously waiting on the tour bus for "her."

5. **The Senton Slam from the Stage.** First you'll need to use one of the previous moves to knock your opponent flat to the ground. Then, leaping off the stage in a swan dive, keep your body straight and arms extended, perform a front somersault, and land with your back on top of your opponent's chest and stomach, knocking the wind completely out of them and rendering them useless.

6. **The Overhead Belly-to-Belly Suplex.** Grab the opposing mosher underneath their arms and wrap your arms around their body, clasping your hands tightly against their back so that they can't escape. Crouch and jump backward, hurling him over your shoulder and onto his back, with your belly landing on top of his. On a personal side note, I used this move to get my wife into the sack for the first time. While my sex wasn't that impressive, she still scored me a solid seven for originality and flair. It must have worked, because she still asks me to use this move on her on a nightly basis.

Disclaimer: Remember, you're likely to be on the concrete or hard ground, and if you break someone's skull or your own, don't go pointing your finger at me. It's not my fault your IQ matches your tooth count; blame that one on your parents.

See you fuckin' Berzerkers in the pit.

Bubba

Team 3D

By the way . . . I also want all the fans to know that Zakk and I are not only about destruction and brutality, that we also have our sensitive sides. Not long ago we were going back and forth text-messaging about some kind of bullshit. Zakk was in his studio, the Black Vatican, and I was at home on the East Coast. About twenty messages into the conversation, I got an off-the-wall message from Zakk that said, "Do you want me to come tuck you in, little one? XOXO."

At first glance I went cross-eyed trying to interpret it as something other than the completely homo text that it seemed like, and I didn't text back. And then, several minutes later, I got another text from Zakk that said, "Oh my God, I'm so sorry, bro, that wasn't meant for you, it was meant for the Warden. But if you need me to come over, Schmoopie, I can tuck you in also."

So I answered back, "If the world only knew that the greatest guitar player and one of the greatest tag-team wrestlers of all time were exchanging text messages about tucking each other into bed, it'd be pretty funny."

Note from Zakk: Father Bubba, I don't find it funny at all. I really thought we had something special. Up until this point, the whole "Barb and the kids" gig was a complete sell—everybody was buying that I'm a married guy. Bubba, now you just went and fucked the whole thing up. Fuck it—I still love you, Schmoopie. I'm willing to risk it all. Let's be real; how much more gaping can my ass get? Looking forward to being Powerbombed—wrestling, I mean of course! Wink wink.

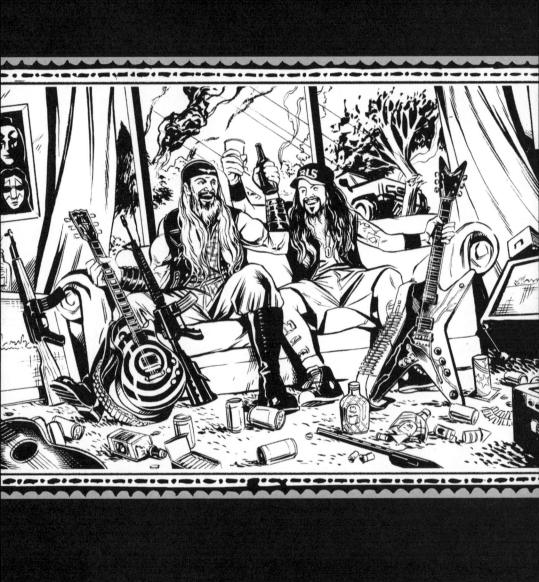

CHAPTER SIX

Psst! Don't Tell the Warden!

The Halls of Valhalla resounded with the songs of victory and stories of battle, and with boisterous tales of wanton maidens and housewives alike. And the wine and ale flowed freely, as did the bladders of the slumbering inebriates. The Berzerkers were celebrated and bound by stout brew, the effects of the bog myrtle, and the conquest of the campaign. Fattened by the spoils of war, and exhausted from the prizes of women, road-weary and scarred, we felt our hearts brim with the pride of the brave.

Our chronicles shall become rich with praise, for we have subjugated the foreboded beggars and fiends with triumph. We scoured the enemy with the steeled edges of our halberds and broadswords; hence they now lay as swine and in ruin, their carriages destroyed in our warpath. Our tales continued through the night with the ingredients of hops and barley. And as the eve moved to break of day, tens of lions became hundreds, and hundreds of Berzerkers became thousands.

And so concluded our noble Black Label Crusade, and once again our tribe returned home with swords and shields in hand, honored and celebrated by our adoring wives and children with great feast. Favors of fanciful fornication would be offered over a fortnight in reward for our bravery, determination, and glory. The Berzerkers were legends of the land, sea, and skies, set above the village in stature and in might, to protect those among us who are feeble and trivial, and to ensure the ongoing spread of the Black Label Order! It was a time of victorious revelry for all!

Note from Zakk: Brilliant, Father Eric, just brilliant. Your way with the literary kingdom is as remarkable as it is spiritual. You are truly a man of charm and moxie whose genius is way ahead of his time. Plato, Aristotle, Einstein, and Hendrikx are all synonymous names in my diary. I'm fortunate to have you as a best friend, blessed to have you as a brother, and privileged to have you in my life—respect.

Note from Zakk: The last "Note from Zakk" was not from me at all. Father Eric thought he would trick us all by using my commentary as a platform to tweet his own twat. We are not fooled at all, Father Eric. "Brilliant"? "Genius"? I think not. "Friend"? Are you fucking kidding me? More like idiot, tool, dolt—sweet fancy Moses, just make it stop.

Have a Drink on Me

I'VE KNOWN FATHER DAVE "SNAKE" SABO SINCE LONG BEFORE THE DAYS of Skid Row and my going on to roll with the Boss and Black Label. Father Dave used to work at this ass-kicking music store in Toms River, New Jersey, called Garden State Music. They had all the coolest gear, and as a young musician, it had a cool buzz about it and was a cool place for musicians to hang. Eventually, after I started to play with Oz and Davey went on to sell twenty gazillion records with his band Skid Row, whenever we'd hook back up out on the road, the booze, the good times, and the laughs would flow abundantly. So on this occasion, it was Father David and company out touring in support of their album *Slave to the Grind* with Guns N' Roses. Davey called me up at the compound, shot the shit with Barbaranne for a bit, and then said, "Hey, jackass, we're playing the Forum tomorrow night with Guns. Why don't you come down to the Riot House"—the nickname of the Hyatt Hotel on Sunset Boulevard, as Led Zeppelin and other legendary rock bands would get into good old family fun and shenanigans there and absolutely destroy the place; mind you, being the upstanding and respectful Metal gods they are, they always paid for the countless damages— "so we can hang and have a couple of adult beverages." Needless to say, I didn't have to ask Barb to join us after she said, "Tell Dave I love him. You two fucking idiots have a good time."

Lars Ulrich was also hanging out with us that night. Not only did all of us numb-nuts go out to the Guns and Skid Row show, but afterward, we all wound up at this one fucking rock bar together. All I remember is waiting in this never-ending crowd trying to get drinks for the guys, and I had to piss like a fuckin' racehorse! So I finally made it to the bar, just fuckin' sardined in among a ton of people, and yelled out my order of Jack 'n' Cokes and beers to the bartender, but by now, my bladder was swollen. I had to piss bad . . . real fuckin' bad.

As I was standing there waiting for my bladder to explode, I reached out and snagged up a few red plastic cups that were on the bar in front of me, snuck my dick out, and began filling them one by one. As each one reached the brim, I nimbly switched to a fresh cup and placed the piss-filled ones on the bar. I figured that after I was done, I would toss them in a fuckin' garbage can and be done with it. The joint was packed, so nobody saw me with my dick in a cup, and the plan seemed to be working just fine. But then, as I was standing there relieving myself, I saw a hand reach past me and grab the piss cups from the bar. I looked over and saw that it was fuckin' Lars, and he was reaching for the drinks as fast as I was fillin' them up. He had no idea they were piss-filled.

Of course he was standing there holding court with a bunch of guys who were all practically sucking his dick over how much they loved Metallica. He unknowingly handed all these dudes the piss cocktails and once everyone had a "drink," Lars grabbed his *real* cocktail and did a fucking "Cheers" toast! All these guys enthusiastically pounded my fucking piss, so ecstatic that they were drinking with the drummer from Metallica, yet so unaware of the fact that they were slurping down whatever I had to drink about two hours beforehand. It didn't take more than a few seconds for them to realize what the fuck had just happened, and that's when the shit hit the motherfuckin' fan.

Security showed up almost immediately and grabbed me to throw me outta there. I tried telling them that I was gonna toss the cups in the garbage, but they didn't listen. I mean, it wasn't like I was pissing on the bar or in their faces or anything like that (well, not directly in their faces anyway)! They apparently didn't agree with my evaluation of the situation and continued to escort me out of there. Dave saw what was happening but didn't know about the piss yet, and so he was a little confused about why I was being asked to leave.

It didn't really matter to me; once they kicked me out of the bar I figured I'd just head back to the hotel and continue the party there, and so I jumped in our van and told the driver to split. Next thing you know, Dave and Lars come hauling ass out of the fucking door. The two of them jumped in the van and Lars yelled to the driver, "Let's get the fuck outta here!" All of a sudden the van started shaking, and the guys who had just chugged my piss were outside, pounding on the windows and yelling, "I know you're fucking in there, Lars! You motherfucker! You fucking asshole!"

"Awww man, I think we just lost two Metallica fans," said Lars.

I was sitting there trying to figure out what the fuck Lars was thinking, but he'd grabbed those cups and didn't realize they weren't cold beers? As I was sitting there pondering the situation, someone opened a window and yelled out to these poor sons of bitches, "Hey, chill out, we got another case of that shit if you guys want some more!"

As the van sped away, I could hear them screaming after us. I don't blame them for being upset, but still, how they didn't realize the cups were warm is beyond me. We weren't in the Sahara fucking desert or anything like that. If someone handed me a cup that was heated up to body temperature, I would hope that I would question it before I simply choked it down. Funny thing about drinking—sometimes it can cloud your better judgment. Thank God the Immortal Beloved drank those eight Long Island iced teas right before I proposed to her.

𝔐𝔬𝔰𝔠𝔬𝔴 𝔓𝔢𝔞𝔠𝔢 𝔉𝔢𝔰𝔱𝔦𝔳𝔞𝔩 𝔟𝔦𝔞 𝔑𝔢𝔴 𝔍𝔢𝔯𝔰𝔢𝔶 𝔖𝔥𝔬𝔯𝔢
BY SNAKE SABO

MY FIRST REAL JOB WAS AT A PLACE CALLED THE GARDEN STATE Music Center in New Jersey. It took me an hour and a half and two bus rides to get to work each day, but I didn't mind because I just couldn't handle the thought of any kind of regular job. I'm thankful I was able to talk my way into that job, because it really turned out to be quite fortuitous for me later on in life.

Zakk used to come into the music store all the time. He was this eighteen-year-old kid who was really just kind of shy and unassuming. Once, he asked me if it was cool if he took down one of the guitars and tried it out. Of course I said that it was fine, and to my surprise he took down a classical guitar and started playing this unbelievable shit. It was fucking nuts! I've never heard an eighteen-year-old kid play like that. I was only a few years older than him, but he was so far ahead of me at that point. He was just killin' it. The guy always had that star presence about him, that "it" thing if you will. Everybody in town who was involved in music knew that he was *the guy*.

At the time he was playing in bar bands in front of a dozen drunks, and I had just started to put together Skid Row. We were both on the same path with the same dream, so we got to know each other pretty well. We soon realized that we had the same sense of humor and would say the same stupid remarks to each other, so we became friends pretty quickly. Of course, none of us had any money, so I'd throw him packs of strings and picks and do whatever else I could to help him out.

One day this music photographer, Mark Weiss, called Zakk and told him that Ozzy was trying out new guitar players and that he had been able to get Zakk an audition. Zakk was really, really nervous about it, but me and Scott Hill (the other guitarist for Skid Row) were positive that he was going to get the gig. I distinctly remember telling him, "Zakk, you're getting this gig, man, this is yours." And sure enough, we got word almost immediately that Zakk had landed it. It was nuts; our buddy Zakk was the new guitarist for Ozzy!

Right around the time Zakk joined the Ozzy Osbourne band, Skid Row was signed to a major record label, and so all of us were out there touring and playing arenas. We were on tour with Bon Jovi and Aerosmith, and Zakk was out with Ozzy. It was so awesome when we'd run into each other on the road and get to hang out, but we really didn't get to do it right, until Moscow.

In 1989, our manager at the time, Doc McGhee, had put together this massive festival with some of the biggest rock acts of the time: Ozzy, Mötley Crüe, Bon Jovi, Scorpions, Cinderella, and Skid Row. It was called the Moscow Music Peace Festival and was happening at Lenin Stadium, where the 1980 Olympics had been held.

The plane route went from Los Angeles to Newark, where I connected with Zakk, and then on to England, and then I think Moscow. We may have had a stop in Germany, but by the time we got to Europe, we were fucking crushed from all the drinking and partying. Now this was supposed to be a *dry* flight and performance because it was being sponsored by the Make a Difference Foundation. We ended up dubbing it the Make a Different Drink Foundation because we got plastered the whole flight!

Zakk and I hadn't gotten to spend much time together up until that point so we were probably the two most annoying people on board. Neither of us slept the entire way. We would wait for people to fall asleep, and when they did, we'd drink whatever booze they had happened to sneak onboard. I think we were pretty well hated after that flight; because we were so isolated over there, it wasn't easy to restock what Zakk and I had drunk.

When we landed, we were shuffled off to Moscow's version of the Hard Rock, where a big welcome party was being held for all of the bands. So we decided to go there for a bit and just go berserk. After a while, Zakk and I decided to head back to the hotel, which was called the Hotel Ukraine, in the middle of Moscow, right near Red Square. This hotel was really, really old and creepy—bats in the belfry and everything.

We had been up well over thirty hours by then, but we were just so excited to be hanging out that we couldn't sleep. So we went exploring from floor to floor, looking for something to do or someone to annoy. Finally we got up to the top floor, where we found this door ajar. The light was on inside, so we decided to go in and found ourselves in this big old room full of telephone-type operators who were monitoring the phone calls of every guest in the building. Even though it was the beginning of the end of the Cold War, obviously Communism was still in full effect.

It was funny because I didn't even know that the phones in our rooms could dial out! I mean our rooms were pretty broken down and overrun with cockroaches. There were so many roaches, in fact, that we were rounding up any aerosol spray cans we could find and lighting these nasty critters on fire. That was really crazy because we really were being overtaken by these suckers.

After that we went and hung out in KNAC disc jockey Tawn Mastrey's room. She was there covering the event for KNAC, God rest her soul, and we annoyed her until about five thirty in the morning before saying enough was enough and finally going to sleep. But for all the partying, Zakk was right up there with Ozzy the next day, just fucking killing it. There's this great, classic photo of all the bands coming out at the end of the show to jam out on Zeppelin's "Rock and Roll," and I'm up there on Zakk's shoulders. That's pretty much how that all ended, both of us wasted onstage, me up on Zakk's shoulders, jamming out killer tunes and lovin' life.

A Few Words About Alcohol

THERE IS NOTHING SEXIER ON GOD'S GREEN EARTH THAN THE CLINKING sound of fresh beer bottles, ice cold and smooth as a mountain goat. It's the sounds of Black Sabbath, Led Zeppelin, and those clanging bottles of hops and barley that warm the heart and soul. Ever quantify your drinking to figure out exactly how much it costs you? Me neither. But you can bet your ass that my wife and my manager did, and it wasn't pretty. In fact, I'll break it down for you to give you a better understanding of the effort I put into my drinking habit. Let's just say that if drinking was graded, I'd be the one setting the curve.

If you saw the alcohol and destruction bills I paid at the end of each tour, you'd agree that the name *Berzerker* fit those damn bills. One year we were out on Ozzfest only four weeks before I got a call from the Warden. She said that in just that one month we had already spent thirty thousand dollars on alcohol alone. Now, mind you, this was among ten guys on our tour buses, but only eight of us were real fuckin' boozers. Barbaranne told us that the party was over and she'd had "enough of that." So what did we do? The next month out, we just continued drinking and kept the Black Label pub open around the clock. At the end of the second month we had raised the alcohol bill to fifty-four thousand dollars. Let's just say good times were had by all, except for the Warden.

It isn't tough to rack up the bills, especially when you decide to cover the bill for a shit-ton of hell-bent boozehounds, like the kind of Berzerkers and Berzerkerettes who roll with Black Label. With album titles including *Sonic Brew, Alcohol Fueled Brewtality,* and *Hangover Music,* I can't say that the music discourages the behavior though. The booze bill was especially high when we decided to film for the DVD *Boozed, Broozed and Broken-Boned* at a classic watering hole in Detroit, Michigan, called Harpos. We shot the whole thing during a show with the Detroit chapter, so they could be in the video as well. And clearly, the Detroit chapter is one of the most heavily intoxicated of our clan. So it was fitting to have them there with us, enjoying every alcohol anthem of mayhem we played that night.

Things actually went fine as far as the shoot was concerned, and we ended up with a ton of badass footage. Everyone was working away, so I wasn't really paying attention to all that was going on, until we were wrapping up and I was ready to grab myself a case of cold ones for the road. I asked the bartender to set me up, but to my surprise my request was denied. There wasn't any alcohol left! That's right, the entire bar had been drained dry. There wasn't a fuckin' beer left in the place. The bartender himself couldn't even believe it, and he told me that it was the first time in the history of the place that it had run out of booze.

So if you ever find yourself getting into a drinking contest with the Detroit chapter of Black Label Society, I highly recommend that you pack yourself an extra liver, one or two spare pancreases, and a couple of semitrucks loaded with extra adult beverages. Chances are that you'll need all of that just to stay in the game! Good luck.

Well, that whole experience ended up costing me. I don't, or don't want to, remember how much that bar tab was! But let me assure you, in my good old inebriated heyday, it didn't take an entire chapter of boozers to run up a ridiculous tab. Now, one of the only other true vices I have besides a stiff drink is a prime cut of steak, and so the concept of the steakhouse is, in my mind, the single greatest culinary achievement in modern history. Unfortunately I can't eat much of anything before a show, and so I usually find myself out searching for a meal right after we clear out of the venue, and the steakhouse is the ultimate destination as far as I'm concerned.

During one particular food quest, myself, Mark Ferguson, Sean Peyton (my tech at the time), and our tour manager wound up at one of those higher-end steakhouses where, besides prime cuts of meat, they serve all sorts of liquor. I spied a bottle of Louis XIII that they were serving for a hundred and sixty bucks a shot in these fancy snifters. I had to order a shot for the guys to try.

We were eating, drinking beers, and enjoying sipping this cognac and it went down real smooth-like. The three of us sharing the shot didn't satisfy us at all, so I ordered up three of more of them, one for each of us. The more we ate, the more we kept drinking. It wasn't long before I wound up getting us all another round of the good stuff. Soon a couple of my friends, who always seem to show up when I'm buying drinks, arrived at the place, and another round got delivered. And of course the restaurant didn't stop us; I'm sure they figured that if us idiots wanted to power down Louis XIII like it was Jim Beam, that was our own deal. To show their appreciation for all of the money I was throwin' at them, the bar gave us the crystal bottle we'd been draining.

I was having a great time eating a delicious meal of steak,

BRINGING Metal TO THE CHILDREN

242

spinach and cream, and garlic mashed potatoes, and putting back these cognac shots. Everything was going splendidly, until I took that one last shot. There it was, that warm rush. That feeling I knew all too well. Everything was about to come up. I tried to fight it, but I wasn't kidding myself; I always lose that battle. And then it happened. The Floodgates of Doom opened and unleashed their fury.

I started puking right there on the bar. One of the guys reacted quickly and handed me one of the snifters. I filled that, and he immediately handed me another. There I was, hurling into glass after glass and setting them on the bar as I went. When I was finished there must have been eight or more glasses full of incredibly expensive vomit all lined up in a row, full of what looked like Irish stew . . . like *gravy*. I mean, you could see it all, the spinach, the beef!

Then Sean, being a fuckin' wiseass, leaned over and said, "Oh, Zakk, I see it was you that had some of my asparagus. I was wondering who else was eating it, I knew I didn't eat it all myself."

Needless to say, the cognac was all that and more. But the fact that I puked up over two thousand dollars' worth of alcohol wasn't very cool. In fact, it was really pretty nasty. Sometimes it's just cheaper to stay home and drink. Well, less expensive maybe, but not necessarily safer.

Back at the compound we always had a good time drinking, barbecuing, and taking full advantage of the rights that come with owning a mountain, kind of like how my manager takes advantage of my God-given talent for his own personal gain. Only in my case, I bought the mountain, so I should get to play on it with my friends. And what better toy to have for the rocky terrain than my black Ford F-350 Super Duty, or as it's come to be known, the Deathcore Warmachine.

Take the Mountain!

BACK IN 2005, MY BLACK LABEL BROTHER, COLLABORATIVE DOUCHE OF this book, and runner-up homecoming queen at his high school prom, Father Eric, was in town recording with his band. I invited him up to the compound to hang out, watch a game, and have a few cocktails. It's not that I actually liked Father Eric. In fact I still don't—nobody does. But since we were all out of booze I thought I'd invite him up, so long as he made a pit stop at the liquor store and brought a few cases with him. Was it worth it? It never is.

It was totally dark by the time he reached the dirt road that leads up to the compound. And the road branches off all over the fucking place, so if you don't frequent the compound, you can easily get lost. Also, if you're Eric Hendrikx, you could get lost in a brown paper bag. Fortunately, there's only one of him that we all have to deal with. When he showed up, we grabbed the beer, jumped in my truck, and took off to test it against the mountain. I wasn't driving. Another buddy of mine was, who also happened to be a stunt driver.

Within a few minutes we reached our target—the steepest fucking hill in the area, covered with desert brush and small trees. That's when we plowed the truck up the fucking mountain to see if we could make it to the top.

Note from Eric Hendrikx: What actually happened here was something I'll never forget. After jumping the truck off these massive tyrannosaurus dirt jumps that repositioned all of my internal organs, we stopped at the base of a steep-ass cliff and got out to take a piss. I was standing next to Zakk finishing my piss when he turned to me and asked, "Father Eric, do you know what time it is?"

"No, what time is it, buddy?" I was sucked into his antics.

There before me was something I had never seen before. Even with my bottomless and twisted sense of humor, I had never conceived this lewd act as a possibility. Zakk had stretched his dick around his wrist and was flaunting it like a Rolex watch. I'm not sure if I was frozen in a dead gaze like an armadillo on the highway or if time just completely stopped, but I couldn't remove his baby-arm wristwatch from my view.

"It's time to take the fucking mountain," he said, and then, with that sinister laugh of his, holstered his skin saber and jumped back into the cab of the truck.

If Zakk was a superhero, whipping out his cock-watch would replace the need for a freeze ray to stun his enemies. He could just use his super cock watch to stop time and defeat his nemesis:

"Excuse me, evildoer, do you know what time it is?" Super Zakk would say. His fierce nemesis would look down and take one glance at the fleshy bracelet and become completely perplexed. This confusion would be followed by a quick and deadly strike from Super Zakk's Black Label Five Deadly Venoms kung fu.

Game over.

Within seconds, the truck boosted its way up the incline, ripping out bushes and small trees, for a few hundred feet before it began losing speed and then sliding backward. The truck went fuckin' sideways on us and began tipping over. I'm not sure how we managed to keep right-side up—probably because we had a fucking stunt driver behind the wheel—but we still slid down the hill and had to adjust our approach to get more speed.

Again the truck bashed into the side of the mountain, pounding over boulders, shit flying all over the cab, beer foaming all over us; we were all cracking the fuck up! Well, at least I was cracking up. After about a dozen attempts and realizing that we weren't gonna make it up without completely annihilating my ride, we headed back to the compound.

We finished off most of the beer and then took turns riding my son Jesse John Michael's motorcycle around the property. It had to be two in the morning and we were ripping around on this thing right next to the edge of the mountain. It's a miracle one of us didn't go for a death roll off Dead Man's Curve just at the edge of the property. After that ended we continued drinking, storytelling, and listening to music.

Thank God I wasn't there when the Warden found Father Eric. But he later told me that she was fuckin' furious after finding the empty beer bottles and boxes. I can picture it now, Eric hungover as hell with eyes crusted with dirt from last night's motocross event, looking up at the Warden, who had fire and smoke coming out of her fuckin' ears!

A little later the Warden discovered what we did to my new truck. It wasn't long before the three of us were standing in front of the Deathcore Warmachine, looking over the deep scratches from the trees we ran over the night prior. The thing looked like a mating post for a fuckin' grizzly bear! So to calm Barbaranne I told her, "This will all come out with some wax; we can buff it out."

Barb looked at me in disbelief and then at Father Eric, and asked him if we could *really* get the scratches out.

"Oh, definitely," he told her, siding with me on this one. "That will come right out with a little buffing."

The two morals of this story are: Vehicles and alcohol never mix well (even when the driver is sober), and Eric Hendrikx is always a problem.

Note from Eric Hendrikx: Later that day I was back in the studio. Zakk called me and asked if I wanted to come back up to the compound that night to watch *Monday Night Football*. "Hell yes, buddy!" I said. "See you in a bit."

About ten minutes later the phone rang again. It was Barbaranne, calling to uninvite me to the house.

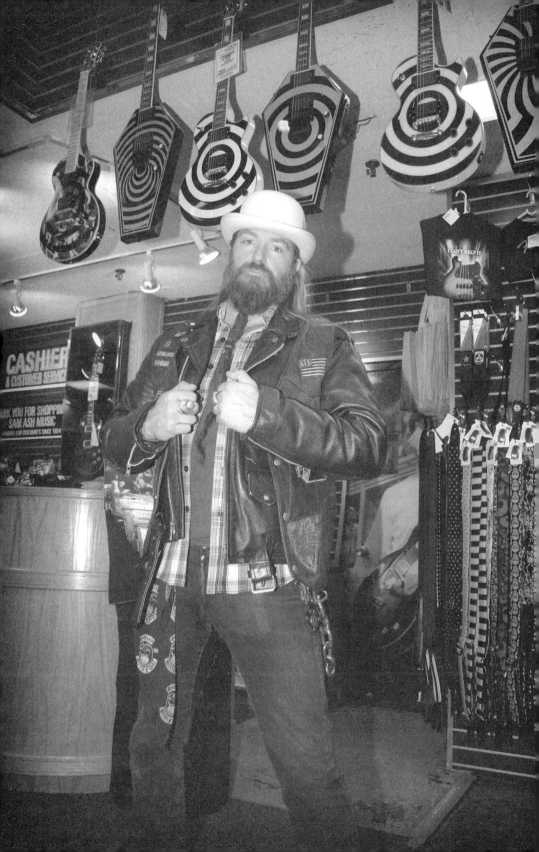

New York City Chickens

In 2003 I was out in New York for Ozzfest pulling double-duty shows with Black Label Society and Ozzy. My brother-in-arms Chris Jericho was also in New York to promote his band Fozzy and their new record *Happenstance.* So he and I did the right thing and met in the city at a pub in Times Square for a couple of beers. The joint we ended up in had a really cool vibe and a jukebox loaded with cuts from some killer bands like Zeppelin, Sabbath, the Stones . . . all the classics. We just drank beer 'til all hours of the morning listening to these cool tunes, just vibing on the music and shooting the shit. That's another thing I love about New York City: Most of the bars stay open until four A.M., so you can really get some damage done when it comes to drinking.

Once we left the pub, our plan was to walk down to a convenience store and get some more beer, then head to the hotel, knock out a few more cold ones, and chill. The shop we rolled into had these hard-boiled eggs at the counter (high in protein), so we wound up buying a bunch of them as well. Then we headed back to the Waldorf-Astoria Hotel, where Ozzy and I were staying. On the way, and I'm not sure whose idea this was (probably mine; Chris is generally smarter than I am), we decided to get into a game of traffic chicken. This is where you lie down in the middle of the street and wait for cars to come, and hope that they stop or go around you. Now, I can't speak for myself, since I was out of my wits and copping a really nice buzz by that point, but Chris always says that this is probably the dumbest thing he's ever done, especially since we were in midtown New York. But obviously neither of us had any problem with doing it at the time.

After annoying the hell out of countless taxicab drivers, we finally made it to the hotel. Now, Chris was thinking that he was in for a real treat as we headed up to the penthouse suite, hanging at the fanciest hotel in New York, where Ozzy Osbourne was staying. He thought we were about to head into a night loaded with some serious rock 'n' roll debauchery; there were going to be waterfalls of booze flowing down from the walls, groupies with our pictures and names on their tightly fitted baby-doll T-shirts, strippers snorting cocaine off each other's asses, midget sex in the bathrooms, the whole nine yards. I think he was in for a bit of a shock, not because of the amount of hookers and booze I was able to cram into my room, but because when we got to the door I told him that we had to be quiet because my daughter and her friends were inside sleeping.

As trashed as we were, we stumbled inside and were seriously trying to be quiet, so we decided to go into the bathroom and close the door. I sat on the side of the bathtub and Chris sat on the toilet, and there we were, whispering so we didn't wake up the girls. After about five minutes, we both just started laughing our asses off. I mean, here you've got one of the most famous wrestlers on the planet and my dumb ass, hiding in a hotel bathroom and talking in quiet voices, trying not wake up the children.

It's just so funny to compare what people think happens on tour and what actually goes down. If you told someone Zakk Wylde and Chris Jericho were getting together, they'd think it was gonna be a bender from hell, but instead you've got two complete idiots drinking in a shit closet with nowhere better to go. Chris and I always laugh about that, but even so, we were really fucking hungover the next day. Well, maybe Father Chris was; I never had a problem with hangovers. I don't even know what one feels like—I just wake up with a decent glow on, like we're still at the bar. We didn't leave the room until we absolutely had to. In my usual pure Black Label fashion I didn't shower, brush my teeth, change clothes, or even have a thought about a hairbrush. I'm not gonna lie, I absolutely reeked from sweating booze out of my pores all night and was still emitting the smell of the asphalt of New York from our game of street chicken the night before. Chris was appalled that I took no interest in washing up or getting ready; he follows a completely different daily regimen. He did ask me why the hell I wasn't going to take a shower, and I had to let him know that true Vikings don't worry about hygiene even when they're going to the fucking prom.

Yeah, but Vikings never stayed at the Waldorf penthouse in New York City with a showerhead that looks like it was made by Chinese monks—take a fucking shower, you scumbag.
—CHRIS JERICHO

Greasy Fingers
BY CHRIS JERICHO

MY BAND FOZZY WAS FILMING A TV COMMERCIAL IN L.A. FOR OUR record and so we were all in Los Angeles. We were invited to come up to Zakk's compound to hang, but as soon as Barbaranne saw us pull up to the house, she packed up the kids and left for a hotel. It's not that we ever did anything too crazy, but she knew that the night would involve two idiots drinking and being stupid until morning.

We got to the house, and my other guitar player, who has always been a huge Zakk fan, was so excited to be there and to possibly jam a little with him. Of course we were planning on enjoying ourselves, and all of us like to eat well, so we had brought a bunch of groceries up to the house to barbecue. We had no idea that Zakk didn't have a proper barbecue. He just had this old, round fucking Flintstones grill. One of those old-school ones you see Mr. Cunningham from *Happy Days* using. It just had this big bowl with a grill on top of it, where you can only really cook one thing at a time. All Zakk had for meat was this one-pound tube of hamburger that you squeeze out of the plastic. I tried to make patties out of it but it wasn't sticking together, so then I tried to cook it all at once, but it was just falling through the grill of

BRINGING **Metal** TO THE CHILDREN

the barbecue. There was one pound of meat to begin with, but by the time it was cooked we had more like 0.1 pound of beef. And so Zakk was there eating all the meat with his fingers right off the grill. He was a greasy masterpiece with oily crap all over his hands and beard.

As I mentioned, my bandmate was a big Zakk fan, and so he wanted to jam out on Zakk's guitar. After a while, Zakk took the guitar and started playing something, but he had all this fucking ground beef and grease still all over his hands. Then Zakk went and started playing his Randy Rhoads Concorde guitar, a Jackson pinstripe Flying V, a replica of the one that Randy actually played. And the guitar ended up looking like it had been in a butcher shop, with ground beef all over the stock, pickups, and strings. Here you had this holy grail of guitars and it was all covered in bits and pieces of beef.

After all of that, we decided, for some reason, that we were going to have a tricycle race around the compound. We grabbed a couple of Zakk's kids' tricycles and went for it. There we were, two six-foot grown men on tricycles. It wasn't exactly the fastest race but I was completely kicking his ass; I even lapped him. And as I lapped him a second time, I crashed into his ride with mine and dumped him into the bushes. So I won. When it comes to tricycle races, the score is currently Jericho 1, Wylde 0. Not only did I win, I knocked his ass right off the tricycle and left him lying in the bushes—the scumbag.

Had the night ended in a wrestling match, I believe Zakk would have been the victor, and here's why: When Zakk was drinking, his finishing move was just talking. He would talk so much and so long that if you were on the phone with him you could literally put the phone down, leave, go have a bite, take a dump, play a little guitar, play some video games, fuck your wife, come back, and he'd still be talking. You couldn't get a word in edgewise. If the phone rang at three in the morning and it was Zakk, it was like, "Oh no, here it comes," and Zakk would have these amazing fantastical stories, like "You, me, and Rich are gonna go to a desert island and we're gonna put on the colors and it's gonna be a desert island Sharks vs. Jets match. And we'll get Nikki Sixx and C. C. DeVille to come ashore and then we'll fight them and beat the living shit out of them, and then we'll cannibalize them. Brotha, you don't understand, it's gonna be great," and he'd come up with all these ridiculous plans for movies he wanted to make or fantasy stories he wanted to tell. So if he really wanted to take someone out all he had to do was start talking and everyone would just fall asleep or say, "Please, just leave, go away." He wouldn't even need to use any of his Viking physique; he could just use his voice and that deranged mind of his. Any of his friends will tell you the same thing, especially his wife!

The Pub Is Closed

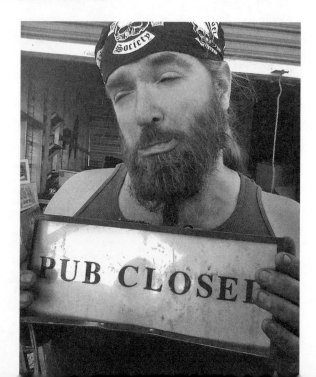

YES, UNFORTUNATELY FOR THE IRISH, GERMAN, AND DUTCH PARTS OF me, the pub is closed. But before its doors were closed for good, let me tell ya, good times were had by all. Which leads us into another episode of *Black Label Alcohol-Fueled Masterpiece Theater.*

World Tour Survival Technique: Trust No One

BEFORE I ACTUALLY QUIT DRINKING FOR GOOD, I HAD TO MAINTAIN A level of Black Label Special Operations when it came to drinking around the house. Barb was always worried about me and my health, and so when I wasn't on the road I'd hide my drinking as much as I could. Mind you, I wasn't drinking beers in the closet and shit like that (okay, maybe I did do that sometimes, fuck it—last time I checked it was my fucking closet). I mean, I was always the ruler of my roost and would drink a beer if I wanted to, but I didn't want her counting the bottles as I emptied them. What that really meant was a bunch of undercover missions to the liquor store and secret stashes around the compound. It was during one of these covert beer runs that I learned the first rule of hiding your drinking: *Trust no one.*

A buddy and I had hit up a liquor store nearby my house and grabbed a twelve-pack, nothing major really. After that it was time for me to go pick up my son before heading home. Of course when I got the little guy in the car he saw the twelver, and so I told him, "Son, whatever you do, do not tell your mother that I got this beer, okay?" He agreed, and everything was fine, or so I thought.

We got back to the compound, and after I successfully smuggled the beer in, I thought I was home free. This was not the case. It wasn't even ten minutes before I heard the Warden screaming through the place, "Zakk! What the fuck! Did you get beer?" I knew exactly what had happened. I just looked at my son and said, "What? You ratted me out? You threw me under the bus?" It was right then and there that I realized, when it comes to drinking, you can't trust anyone, not even that which cometh from your own loins!

Later that night, I dreamed that I was in the bathroom taking a long, relieving fuckin' piss. Then I woke up to Barb yelling at me, "What the fuck are you doing?" I had just pissed all over her back and down the crack of her ass. How much did I drink that night? Just the right amount.

In late 2000, Dimebag and I were scheduled to do a photo shoot for the cover of *Guitar World* magazine. I headed out with Nick Bowcott to Arlington, Texas, to meet up with him and knock out the session. Of course, when Dime and I would get together, we'd end up having more fun than what was usually legal. Such was the case with this felonious visit.

It started out before I got there. Dime had gone down to the army surplus store and bought a bunch of camouflage gear and makeup for the photo shoot. When I arrived, we went right into the bathroom and put this shit on our faces and got all the gear on. Rita was there laughing at us hysterically while filming the whole debacle. You could always count on Dime and Rita to have a video camera on hand to catch any drunken stupid move you made. And this was definitely one of those nights.

We drank and blew shit up all night, got our photos handled, and I even laid down some guitar and vocal tracks on the Damageplan record. My flight out of there was set for five o'clock in the morning, so Rita had called a car service to come take me and Father Nick to the airport. When the driver finally showed up, he came in the house to take a piss and left the SUV running out front. In a split second I jumped in the driver's seat, Dime sat shotgun, Father Nick got in the back, and off we went.

We tore up the entire neighborhood in this truck, running through fences, plowing through bushes and trees, destroying mailboxes, and spinning doughnuts in a park next to the police station. I even ran over a stop sign and knocked it clear into the street. (We took the sign with us. It's actually still in Rita's living room to this day.) This adventure ran clear into another county and back. We annihilated the undercarriage of the truck, tore off the mirrors, and you can imagine what it looked like after driving through endless barbed-wire fences.

The one thing I didn't know about the SUV was that it actually belonged to the driver. Instead of picking up a company cab to drive us to the airport, he had brought his own brand-new SUV for the trip. His new ride was fucking demolished. Thank God for Rita and Barb; they fixed all the horseshit with the destroyed SUV, the park we wrecked, and all the rest of the absolute insanity we brought into the neighborhood. We ended up hooking the guy up with some guitars and of course took care of the damages. We also had to give the police station a couple of guitars and mend a few fences and things around town.

And that wasn't the only time I got into trouble while in Dime country. Another time I was out there with Father Nick during the holidays. I had to make it back to Los Angeles and meet up with Barb and the kids. We were going back to Newark for the holidays, and she had the little ones in tow, with all the toys and diaper bags and crap that you have to carry when you travel with kids. So Dime and Rita dropped me and Nick off at the airport in plenty of time to catch our flight. A little too much time, as we soon found ourselves waiting it out in the airport bar. As was our habit, we spent the time most unwisely, and before long I was feeling no pain—mind you, I was thoroughly enjoying myself, enough to miss my flight to L.A. and then the next two flights after that.

The best part of the whole thing was Barb tearing Father Nick a new asshole over this ordeal. We were all supposed to be getting together in New Jersey for the holidays. "Nick, you better get his fuckin' ass, I need him fuckin' here with the family . . ." Finally, she was just like, "Fuck him! He's so wonderful, you can fuckin' keep him!" She left with the kids, took the rental car, and got them to Newark.

I got to the point of just saying, "Fuck all this," and went to a hotel room near the airport and passed the fuck out. Nobody knew where I was because I didn't have a cell phone or anything.

I just checked myself into a hotel and crashed. So I was completely off the grid, they couldn't find what hotel I was in, nothing. Dime and Rita had gotten me to the airport, I missed three flights while drinking at the fuckin' bar, and I was officially MIA.

I slept it off and eventually went back to the airport, got onto a plane, and made it down to Jersey. When I walked in, Barb was on the phone with Rita, and as I opened the door I could hear her say, "He just fuckin' walked in right now"; she was not a happy camper. It was like three o'clock in the morning or something. Drinking with Dime also meant that you had to be prepared to sleep in the doghouse for a while.

Whenever I hung out with Dime it was nothing but good times. Over the years, he and I spent endless nights hanging out whenever we could, mostly on the phone, talking about how much we loved Eddie Van Halen and Randy Rhoads, all the bands that we loved, and how much we loved music in general. I've also had some great times with Father Van Halen.

In 1998, Van Halen was performing at Budokan in Tokyo, Japan, while on tour in support of the *Van Halen III* album—the album with Gary Cherone singing on it. It was perfect timing, because I was also in Tokyo promoting the first Black Label Society album, *Sonic Brew*. Barbaranne and I were staying at the Four Seasons, and as it turned out, so was Eddie. I ran into him in the lobby, and we bullshitted for a bit and ended up in the bar together later that night with Father Anthony and the rest of the Van Halen crew, talking about war stories from the road and some of Ed's adventures from back when Van Halen toured with Black Sabbath. We were laughing our asses off and having a great time.

After a few cocktails, I had to go take a piss and Father Ed had to go too. As I got up, Ed started following me to the pisser. I told him that a guitar god should never have to walk himself to a bathroom, so I hoisted him up on top of my shoulders and headed through the lobby toward the restrooms. On our way, Ed punched me in the back of the head and told me to stop for a minute so he could light his cigarette on the candlelit chandelier above us.

Once we got into the bathroom I pulled out my dick and started pissing in one of the sinks. Eddie saw what I was doing, laughed, and said, "Fuck it, man," and pissed in the sink next to mine. Then Eddie was back up on my shoulders as we headed back to the bar for more drinks and storytelling with the rest of the Van Halen gang.

When the bar closed down, we went up to Eddie's room to check out some guitars and keep drinking. Eddie picked up my mirror Les Paul and put it on. The strap was so low, because I play with my guitars really low, and the guitar ended up down near Eddie's knees just like on Jimmy Page. He instantly started playing all these Led Zeppelin riffs. I was having the time of my life watching one of my guitar heroes, and my friend, act out his versions of Jimmy Page's stage moves. He was playing the guitar solo to "Heartbreaker" and all this other shit he knew—it was fucking awesome and absolutely surreal.

Later that night, after I went back to my room, the phone rang and Barb picked up. "Hello, Barb, it's Edward. If Valerie calls, you didn't see me at all tonight, okay?"

We had been up most of the night having a killer time. I had to be up at eight o'clock in the morning for press interviews. Lucky for Ed, he had a show that night, so he could sleep all fuckin' day. I remember doing my interviews half-asleep while switching between coffee to wake up and beer to keep my buzz going. But you know the Black Label code:

Drinking all night, hanging out with your guitar hero, and feeling like prison ass the next day—fuck it, MERCILESS!

That night Ed invited me and Barbaranne to the show and it was amazing. It was the first time I had actually seen him play live. His guitar solos were absolutely incredible, I mean all the chops, the tone, and everything was there that night. If you didn't play guitar, after seeing Eddie throw down, you were instantly inspired to learn how to play. He proved, hands-down, why he is the one and the only—King Edward!

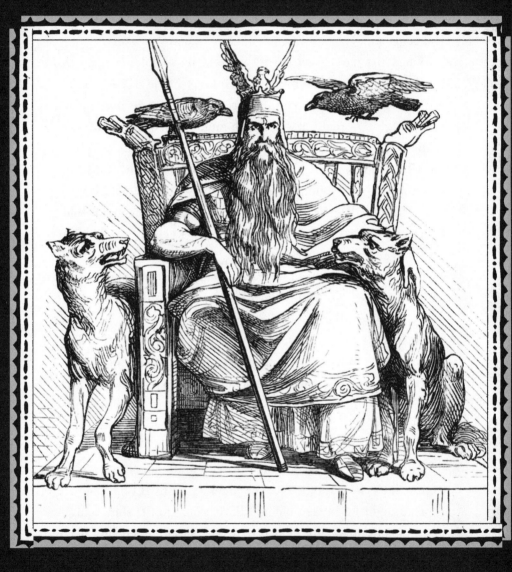

EPILOGUE:

One for the Road

Great Odin, hear my words of Praise and Thanks, for I am eternally blessed by Victory and with Family and with Brotherhood. I have seen thy visions, forged my steel, and called my arms. Your Berzerkers have laid siege to the World just as You bade me. And now my ranks rest, with knowledge I impart that soon enough the time shall come when we must take up arms and allegiance to your worship, smoldering the entrails of those who contest your sanctity and bonding by blood the almighty Order of the Black. For now we will enjoy the blessings of life, the loins of our women, and the warmth of our ale.

I swear to keep the edge of my axe sharp and the blade of my sword oiled and ready for war. I shall carry on my oath to the Children of Metal and bring to them the divine enchantments of Rock. And with haste I shall provide them with another text of Infinite Wisdom to enlighten their own paths to Valhalla!

Until you once more require my services in battle I shall enjoy my life, pondering your wisdom, atop mine own mountain, mine own Valhalla, and deeply plundering the pleasures of mine Immortal Beloved with the Crotchal Mjöllnir you have seen fit to bless me with! Hail Odin, great God of War and Metal!

I raise my glass in toast to you, Odin, and swear upon my sword to walk this earth a warrior, a harbinger of Metal, a Berzerker!

Note from Zakk: I gotta be honest with you—of all the musicians out there in the world, I'm just one of them. If you can make a living doing what you love, you'll never work a day in your life. And if you never have to read any of Father Eric's waxing-poetic horseshit ever again, God bless you. With any luck, Father Eric's next book will be an instruction manual on how to stick your peanut-butter-covered cock into a beehive, and we'll just never hear from him again.

So there you it have it, my battle-ready brethren in Metal, a tried-and-true blueprint for ultimate conquest and certain victory, and hopefully a little inspiration from some of my favorite war stories! Just remember to follow your dreams and passions with a sense of purpose. Make sure your concept is meaningful, your music is honest, and your dedication is true. Work your fuckin' balls off—and your ass and labia as well—and proudly carry your own set of colors into battle. Always remember the rules of the road, which I have laid out for you. Never get discouraged when things go wrong or take an unexpected turn, because you can bet that they will and you need to be able to adapt and solve problems, not freeze up like JD did when Barbaranne walked in on him conquering his wiener in the Pazuzu Loo.

You've got to shed blood to win a war. You have to bleed for it. This is the difference between being successful and not. Spilling your blood for your cause will keep your band from being one that experiences only moderate, short-lived success and one that stands the test of time and comes out with a lifelong career. Don't let anyone else tell you what to play or write; that's gotta flow from you naturally. If your sound is forced, then it just won't be believable. Believe me . . . Even I've been in situations where I seriously questioned why the fuck I was playing something I didn't have my heart in. But our band was being told by someone else that *that's* what we should be doing to make our dreams come true. It happens to all of us somewhere along the way. Nip that in the shitter right now and keep your music honest.

From Zeppelin to Sabbath, Kiss to Poison, Metallica to Pantera and Slayer, all of these bands, and ones like them, truly love and believe in what they do, and that's why they all made a success of themselves. The lesson to be learned from these bands is that regardless of anything, you have to believe in yourself and bleed what you do.

Build your own destroyer, take it out to sea, and annihilate everything in your path!

I hope that the knowledge I've imparted within these pages acts as some kind of lube to make things easier for you. Remember, you can be either laughing or crying when bullshit happens. Fuck crying, unless you're JD. Before I leave you to the work at hand, of forging your own sound and cutting your own unique path, I want to leave you with one cautionary tale—one for the road.

It was about eight years ago, after a Black Label mass. I was relaxing on the bus, unwinding after the show. Some of the guys brought these two smokin'-hot chicks on board to party with the band. So I came up to the front of the bus to be social, grabbed a beer, and set the ladies up with some drinks.

The whole time they were just whispering and giggling, so I finally asked them what the fuck was so funny. They told me that, back in the day, they both had a huge crush on me. Back when I was first playing with Ozzy and had the big poofy fuckin' hair. They were a bit younger than me, so when they told me they used to have pictures of me on their bedroom walls, I couldn't help but laugh. Of course I made a goof out of it, but in my head I was thinking, "Yeah . . . I've still got it!" (As if I ever had it.)

They were still laughing. I asked them again what was going on. Now, remember, these girls were slammin', and so when they told me, "We think you've got a fine ass, we've always thought you had a fine ass," my head swelled with mightiness and pride.

"You know what we would do to you?" they said to me.

Then I was just waiting for the big pat on the back. I was expecting to hear something like, "We want to suck and fuck the living shit out of you right now," or something to that effect. You know, the most insane *Penthouse* letter ever written—about me jackhammering them both into submission as I glue them to the ceiling with a mother lode of conquest—something only Peter North or a stable of steroidal horse cock would be capable of.

But what do I get? Me? The Al fuckin' Bundy of Metal . . .

"We think your ass is so hot. We'd like to put on *strap-ons* and fuck you up the ass."

So I did it. It actually hurt a little at first, but it reminded me of that deal I signed with Geffen Records. After they pulled out, it dawned on me—it couldn't have been a request for me to dominate and bathe them in my conquest. No, instead these two beautiful young girls wanted to fuckin' sodomize *me*! When people ask me if it's hard to be faithful out on the road, I just tell them that horrible tale. I mean, with opportunities like that, I have no problem being faithful! Thank God I'm married, because if I was single I'd have to be celibate. But I guess that's how it goes when one is keeping it intercontinental.

In this business, it seems *everyone* is trying to fuck you in the ass. At first I thought it was just the music attorneys and record labels, but later I found out that in this business, even your wildest sexual fantasies will turn on you and fuck you in the ass. It was just then, at that moment, I thought of changing my name to Snake River Canyon—as my ass was so gaping that even Evel Knievel couldn't fucking jump over it.

Well, I guess it's good-bye for now, my Black Label brethren. Remember to keep your fist raised high and your butt cheeks tightly clenched. Let the music you love guide you. Keep your eyes out for Black Label on tour, and we'll see you crazy fuckers soon! Again, thanks for everything, you are the best family on the fuckin' planet, and we appreciate you more than you know. In the end, we're all headed up to God's tavern, where the cocktails are overflowing, they've got the best jukebox in the universe, and we are all reunited as one massive Black Label family.

In the name of all that is pure, holy, sacred, and unlike JD . . . God bless.

Stay strong. Bleed Black fucking Label. And don't fuck it up by *going in heavy* with the mustard.

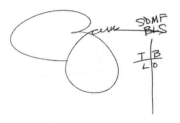

Acknowledgments

MANY THANKS, AS ALWAYS . . .

God.

Society Dwelling Mother Fuckers Worldwide.

Ozzy and Sharon Osbourne—I love you both always and beyond forever.

I would like to speak for my wife, Barbaranne, and thank me for all of the magickal years I have provided her with, as well as all of the incredible, pleasurable vagina-plowing and anus-stretching evenings of jackhammering her in the sack. She is eternally grateful to me for being bathed in her king's conquest of love. You can thank me again after you read this—while you're rubbing my feet.

I would also like to thank our children for having work ethics of doom, staying out of jail, and not being fuckups that would force me to start drinking again. Thanks for making me and your mother beyond-proud parents.

Father Chris Jericho for always being a great friend and Black Label brother. Thank you for your excellent hygiene, thus bringing balance and order to the world when we hang out, like yin and yang, peanut butter and jelly, donkeys and Tijuana hookers, or Pope John Paul II and Anton LaVey. By the way, Chris, you're Anton—and the hooker. Love ya, buddy!

Bob Ringe, Jim Baltutis, Carise Yatter, and Darren Edwards

for making it seem sensible for companies and promoters to pay me shitloads of money to do absolutely nothing.

The Black Label Society band and Doom Crew Inc. for keeping the Black Label Armada rolling.

Nick "E.T." Catanese for being the Ronnie Wood of Black Label Society. Keef needs his Ronnie.

Phil "How Ya Doin'" Ciulo and Jeff "Grim Cracker" Graham for keeping the Black Label world a safer place.

Mark "Field General" Ferguson for your fearless General Patton leadership.

Keith "Moby" Lanoux for the best damn back-and-foot rub a Guitar Deity could ever ask for—and for being the general in command of the Black Label guitar army.

Rita "Weety" Haney for the Black Label love always shared with you and Saint Dime.

Zack "Under the Wire" Fagan and Adam "Irish Catholic Rabbi" Klumpp for the killer studio and recording alchemy.

Rich Ellis and Ben Dewey for the kick-ass drawings.

Glenn B. Davis and Adam Korn for proving, after extensive hand-to-hand combat in the fashion of Bruce Lee's *Game of Death,* that an entertainment attorney and a literary agent can actually coexist . . . at least for now. It would be a great UFC pay-per-view, except in this match there would be no tap-out—it would be a battle to the death.

Father Eric and I actually wrote the original manuscript for this book in the Old Norse language and carved it into stone tablets. Many thanks to Will Hinton and Matthew Benjamin for strapping these heavy stones to their backs and hauling them down the treacherous sheer cliffs and peaks of Valhalla.

Bret Aita for proving that a man can survive on rice and beans for many days on end and still maintain a Berzerker level of creative editing genius (fuckin' twisted, but genius the same).

Forrest Griffin and Erich Krauss for their infinite wisdom on the subject of manliness and their superior expertise on . . . um . . . I got nothin'. Thanks, guys.

Dave "Snake" Sabo. I'm still drinking with you in my heart, my slithery brother. Who am I kidding, Davey, I'm a fucking pussy now—order me up another Shirley Temple.

Mark "Bubba" LoMonaco—the perfect Berzerker . . . three hundred and thirty pounds of massive Metal sex appeal. And don't forget the "wink wink."

Brad Tolinski and Jimmy Hubbard at *Guitar World* for permission to reprint their magazine covers, which I have used to get half-off entry at tit bars and gay bars across the country.

I would like to *un-thank* JD. I don't know why his name is on the roster of those whom I am actually grateful toward. I would actually be grateful if he would stop harassing me, being mean to me, and hurting my Black Label feelings. [Note to editor: Please remove JD from the acknowledgments, and if at all possible, from my life.]

Very special thanks to Hendrix Wylde and Stone Hendrikx—a couple of kids who are constantly subjected to the shenanigans of a couple of bigger kids. Hopefully neither of you will ever be exposed to this book, but if you are, it will be when you're old enough to truly appreciate phrases such as "plow her sugar walls," "dominate her baby-maker," and "bathe her in conquest." Follow your dreams, boys, and may the OdinForce always shine its glorious light upon thy faces.

Eric also thanks . . .

My son, Stone—Thank you for your eternal love and patience, for the seemingly endless hours driving back and forth between the Hendrikx and Wylde compounds at all hours, for all the nights spent on the Wyldes' couch so that your dad could accomplish his goals, and for your understanding and sacrifice of time made for me to focus on my writing. I love you forever.

Erich Krauss—Thank you for a lifetime of friendship, honesty, and guidance that brought me to this point in my career. Without your examples of loyalty and inspiration, this book, and many others, would not exist.

Adam Korn—Thank you for believing in an idiot with a lot of bad ideas and one good one. It's a rarity to have a friend as honest and loyal as you. Love you, buddy. P.S.: I just called your parents and told them that you're gay.

Rita Haney—Thank you for sharing so many wholehearted stories from your relationship with Dime, and for your authentic love and friendship. Also, Stone and I need to extend our sincere gratitude for the best enchiladas of our lives.

Neil Strauss—Thank you for your inspiration, your counsel, and your amity.

I am infinitely grateful to Zakk, Barbaranne, Hayley Rae, Jesse John Michael, and Hendrix—Thank you from the bottom of my heart for making space in your home for Stone and me, as if it was our own. Your love and kindness, counsel, and generosity have taught my son precious life lessons, for which I am forever thankful. We are blessed to have you in our lives. We love you.

ACKNOWLEDGMENTS

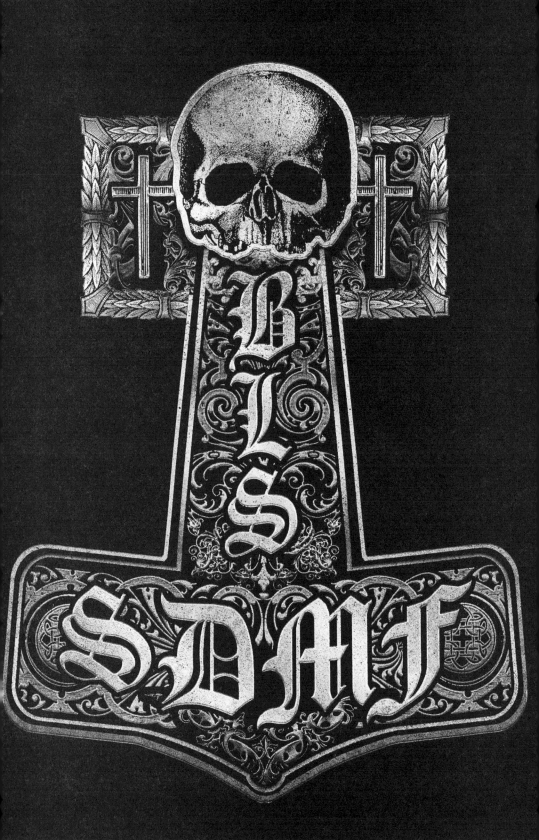

𝔄ppendix:

Bonus Material

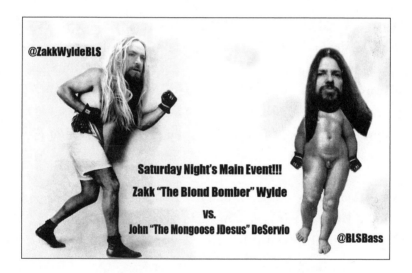

Saturday Night's Main Event!!!

HERE'S A LITTLE GAME THAT ME AND FATHER JDESUS PLAY. WHAT HAP-pens is, when we're on Twitter talking to our Black Label family, I'll take somebody's tweet and serve it up to JDesus, throwing in a little extra about how wonderful and fucking adorable I am. Then he swings for the fences to tell me what a fucking douchebag loser I am in his rebuttal. He never ceases to amaze. Enjoy!

Tweet: I swear @ZakkWyldeBLS is an angel.

Blond Bomber: I was wondering what was growing out of my back?? It's my Wings!!! :)xo

Mongoose: I wish it was a zip-tie, like on a hefty bag, for easy discarding of rubbish!!

Tweet: @ZakkWyldeBLS and you are our RULER, Oh Great One!!!

Blond Bomber: I thought Gretzky was the "GREAT ONE"?? Guess there's a NEW SHERIFF IN TOWN!!! :)xo

Mongoose: The sheriff is near!!!!! Lol

Tweet: @ZakkWyldeBLS I have 3 different guitar pics from your show in Medford, OR. You were right in front of me and it was the most amazing thing!

Blond Bomber: Not Amazing. . . . "MOST AMAZING"!!! Thank you ladies 'n gentlemen . . . :)xo

Mongoose: The only amazing thing is that these idiots still come to see you!!

Tweet: @ZakkWyldeBLS Damn Zakk, you're getting Gi-Normous

Blond Bomber: In every possible facet of Life!!!! :)xo

Mongoose: Especially the ego.

Tweet: @ZakkWyldeBLS 17 days, boss. The Brazil chapter and I thank you for blessing us with your presence- Thanks! † SDMF †

Blond Bomber: I appreciate doing it. Ya know, goose? :)xo

Mongoose: No. You really don't.

Tweet: @ZakkWyldeBLS :) So many treasures that I'm sure you've got there . . . you're my Guitar God, Zakk!! True living Leyend!!

Blond Bomber: Truly. . . . Truly, without question . . . :)xo

Mongoose: You are a leyend!! Whatever that fuck that is!!!

Tweet: @ZakkWyldeBLS One of the best guitarists . . . His chords touch my heart. It would be an honor if you follow me:)

Blond Bomber: My chords touch your heart too. Don't they JDiesel??? Don't they?? :)xo

Mongoose: They do something to my heart. They clog my ventricles!!

Tweet: Life is a loaded gun - love is a bullet that sometimes kills amazing lyrics by the awesomely powerful OVERLORD @ZakkWyldeBLS

Blond Bomber: "AWESOMELY POWERFUL OVERLORD" . . . I really am something, ain't I Goose??!!! :)xo

Mongoose: OH YOU'RE SOMETHING ALL RIGHT. And when we find out what exactly it is, we will terminate it.

Tweet: Listening to @ZakkWyldeBLS do a version of "Whiter Shade of Pale". Awesome! #hangovermusic

Blond Bomber: I am quite "THE AWESOME ONE," right, buddy?? :)xo

Mongoose: As I've said before.....THE BORESOME ONE!!!!!!!!!

Tweet: Zakk, YOU RULE!!! RT @ZakkWyldeBLS: BLACK LABEL FAMILY WORLDWIDE!!!! YOU RULE!!! †TBLO † SDMF

Blond Bomber: I kinda do, don't I Stallion?? :)xo

Mongoose: Rule?????? Cruel - definitely. Tool - obviously.

Tweet: @ZakkWyldeBLS Just saw you on Californication. Keep rocking! Brazilians love you!

Blond Bomber: How could anybody NOT Love Me!!!! C'mon man!! :)xo

Mongoose: Obviously the Brazilians are starving for good quality entertainment. So I guess you fill a void, kinda, but not really.

Tweet: @ZakkWyldeBLS You're a funny, funny guy. I like you buddy. I like you. Lol

Blond Bomber: Gosh darn it!!! I am funny 'n people DO LIKE ME!!!! Right JDiesel?? :)xo

Mongoose: Nah, not really bro.

Tweet: Hi, I'm a big fan of yours. I want to someday be as good as you on guitar. Ok, see ya!

Blond Bomber: Who doesn't? Right, buddy??!! :)xo

Mongoose: Um, John McLaughlin, Jeff Beck, Al Di Meola, Frank Marino, Paul Gilbert . . .

Tweet: Holy Shit Jesus Balls @ZakkWyldeBLS is following me! I can die and go to heaven now.

Blond Bomber: I have quite a profound effect on people. Don't ya think, Goose??? !! :)xo

Mongoose: Poor misguided soul.

Tweet: You should all follow the world's best guitarist @Zakk WyldeBLS

Blond Bomber: If you know what's good for ya!!! Ya know, Buddy??? :)xo

Mongoose: Follow him, just like in animal house when Stork led the band down the dead end alley. Idiots!!!

Tweet: @ZakkWyldeBLS OUR*TRUE**LORD**OF*METAL! A*LEGEND! #ZAKKWYLDEBLS

Blond Bomber: "LORD", "LEGEND"-care to add to this list my Black Label brethren?? :)xo

Mongoose: Yep – "Lord Lesion".

Tweet: @ZakkWyldeBLS Thanks for answering me! You are the guy.

Blond Bomber: I am quite "THE GUY" don't ya think, Goose?? :)xo

Mongoose: Quite the gay guy . . . not that there's anything wrong with that!

Tweet: @ZakkWyldeBLS You're good at doing everything you want! You can be a great Comedian! . . . You're a great Comedian! =)

Blond Bomber: I notice whenever you're around me you are always smiling!!!! :)xo

Mongoose: You are pretty funny! Just look at ya!!

Tweet: @ZakkWyldeBLS Huge fan of your work here. Haven't taken Order Of The Black out of my truck cd player- going on 3 months now. Lol!

Blond Bomber: He likes it!!!! :)xo

Mongoose: Mind you, he hasn't turned on his cd player.

Tweet: @ZakkWyldeBLS Just wanted to say you are fuckin' amazing and a huge inspiration! Thanks for being awesome:)

Blond Bomber: I do exude Awesomeness. Don't ya think buddy?? :)xo

Mongoose: Boresomeness!!

Tweet: Randy Rhoads, Eddie Van Halen, and @ZakkWyldeBLS are overrated??? #yeahright

Blond Bomber: Did you write this buddy??? :)xo

Mongoose: There's only one overrated douche on this list. Care to guess?

Tweet (from a Twitter name with a John Lennon reference): @ZakkWyldeBLS ZAKK WYLDE! You are the best guitar player, man!!

Blond Bomber: Amazing!!! A Beatle thinks this of me!!! Thoughts??? :)xo

Mongoose: Seeing as how he's been dead for 30 years, I don t think he is thinking too clearly!

Tweet: You are nothin' special, you act like a fuckin' kid and got daaaamn lucky. You're not superman, so shut the fuck up!!
Blond Bomber: Did you write this silly???!! :)xo
Mongoose: No, but he's dead on!

Tweet: I'm going crazy right now listening to @ZakkWyldeBLS stuff!! Oh man, he's one of the best fucking guitar players of all time!! Big Influence!
Blond Bomber: Just wondering buddy - How much do you listen to "Your" Buddy in the morning?? The Blond Bomber :)xo
Mongoose: Only when I'm on the toilet bowl, to gimme that extra push!!!

Tweet: @ZakkWyldeBLS The world becomes more influenced by the iconic Zakk Wylde when I have to fill them in on what I'm listening to. † GIFD †
Blond Bomber: And this is just my Bowel Movements!!! Some guys have all the *luck* and some guys have all the *pain*!!!! :)xo
Mongoose: Living with you - guess which one I have?

Tweet: @OfficialOzzy @ZakkWyldeBLS No More Tears (Album) is the soundtrack of my life. Thanks Mr. Ozzy and Mr. Zakk Fuckin' Wylde.
Blond Bomber: It is Quite the Soundtrack I might add . . . Don't you agree JDiesel?? :)xo
Mongoose: I haven't heard any Ozzy since Diary!! Was it good?

Tweet: @ZakkWyldeBLS Thanks for the inspiration, boss. I'm gonna learn this Les Paul inside and out because of you. TBLO. God Bless.

Blond Bomber: ZAKK WYLDE-Not only an All-Around Good Guy, but an "INSPIRATION" as well. . . . :)xo

Mongoose: Now you're self-imposing "all around good guy?" That's up for debate.

Tweet: @ZakkWyldeBLS you are my biggest influence to become a Heavy Metal Singer one day. I am just an amateur for now. You are the man Zakk Wylde!!!

Blond Bomber: In order to *be* the "MAN", you gotta *beat* "THE MAN"!!!! whooooooo!!!!! :)xo

Mongoose: In this case that won't be hard.

Tweet: @ZakkWyldeBLS is a fucking rock god. #allimsaying

Blond Bomber: You already know this but I thought you'd like to see this tweet buddy . . . :)xo

Mongoose: A fucking cock gobbler?

Tweet: The fact that @ZakkWyldeBLS adds smileys to his tweets only adds to his badass factor :)

Blond Bomber: I am quite the "BADASS," ain't I, Goose?? :)xo

Mongoose: You're just an ass.

Tweet: @ZakkWyldeBLS wearing my Wylde shirt and have had 6 people tell me how much they love you. Chicago misses you.

Blond Bomber: Want me to get you one Buddy?? You LOVE ME don't you JDiesel??? :)xo

Mongoose: I have one. I use it to wipe up the leakage from the garbage can outside my house. You know I love ya boss!!!

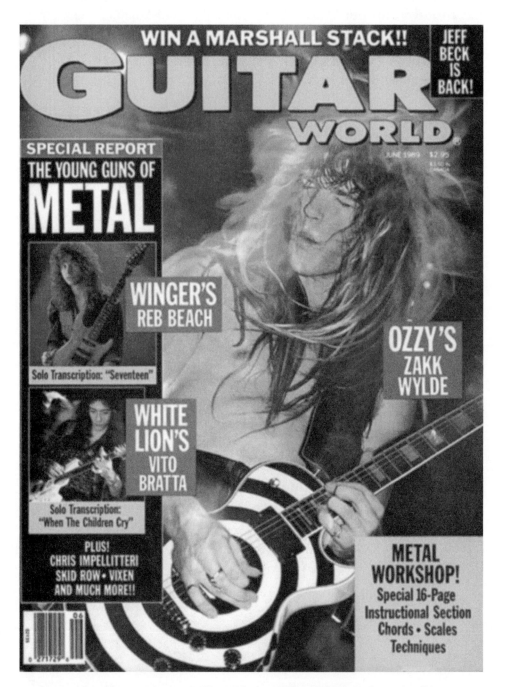

After this cover came out, Vito said to me, "You couldn't do the cover all by yourself, could ya?" I said, "Yeah, but at least I'm in a band that plays cool fucking music. And who's got the biggest picture? Go fuck yourself, douche."

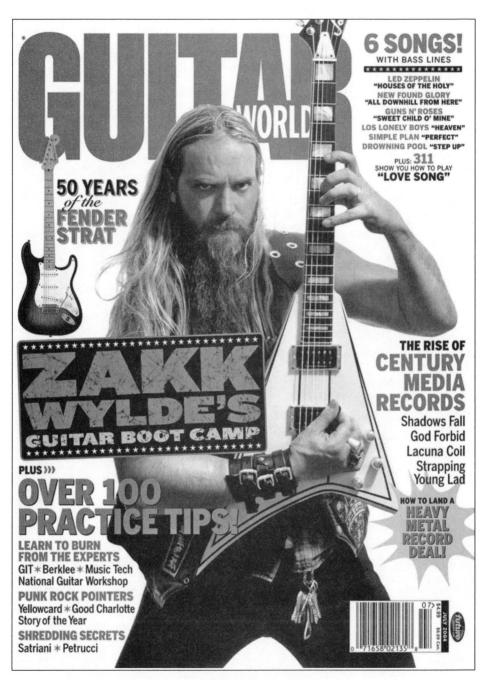

One of my prize possessions—my Randy Rhoads pinstripe concord made by Father Shannon, who made Randy's original. Mrs. Rhoads signed the back of the headstock. Love you, Mom!

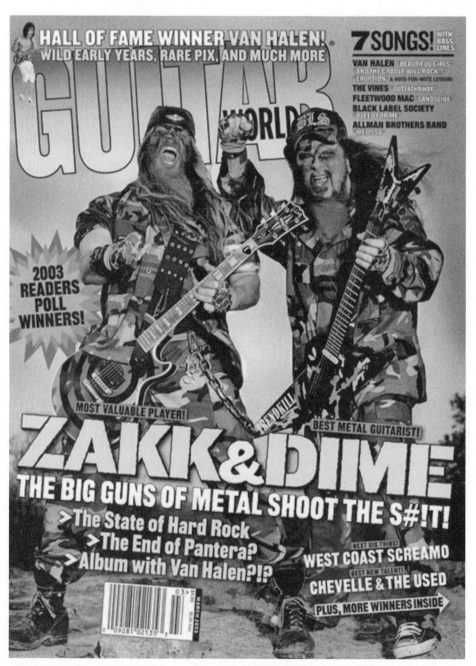

Dime rules! Nuff said.

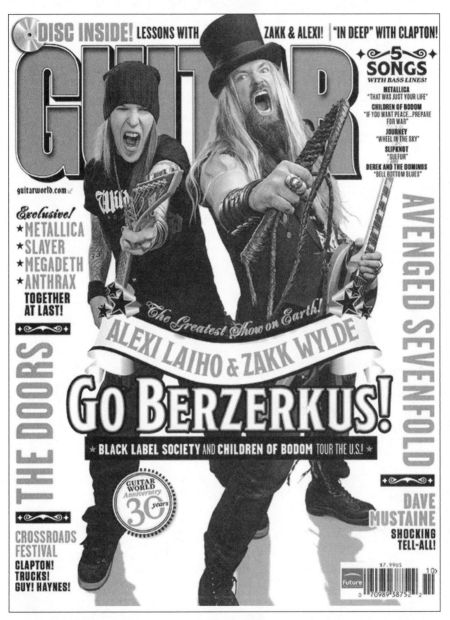

As always, we had a cool day with the gang down at *Guitar World*. Alexi is a cool kid and an amazing player. His publicist asked if it was okay if Alexi drank during the photo shoot, knowing that I don't drink anymore. I said, "No problem, I just smoked some crack-cocaine and mainlined some heroin." I enjoy my Shirley Temples as well. But when I'm around the guys, I only drink the Roy Rogers. 'Cause I'm a Baaaaad Man!

6x12x10

"GODSPEED HELLBOUND"

DESCIONS THAT KILL AND THE
BULLETS THAT FLY/LORDS OF INFERNO
THAT LITTER THE SKY/SHATTERED
CRIES OF THE PRAYERS NEVER HEARD
WAR OF THE GODS THAT DROWN
OUT THE WORDS

AS THE WORLD BURNS/BENEATH
THE GROUND/AS THE WORLD BURNS
GODSPEED HELLBOUND

THE GEARS THAT GRIND SHALL
NEVER BE STILL/THE GRUDGE THAT
BURNS OBSESSED TIL IT KILLS
SCHIZOPHRENIC POEMS OF DEATH
MACHINE EVERAFTER THAT NEVER RESTS

CRASHING BURNING ALL SHALL FADE
DEAD N DYING HERE TO STAY

AGAINST HIS MAKER/NO REGARD
FOR HIS FALL/THE WINDS OF THE
WEST BOW DOWN TO HIS CALL
FAMINE N MURDER RESIDE FROM
WITHIN/THE VULTURES GATHER
DEVOURING SIN

ABANDONEMENT

6x12x10

"DARKEST DAYS"

DIVIDED SOUL OF A TROUBLED MAN
THE FINAL FIGHT
THE FINAL NEED TO UNDERSTAND
THESE TANGLED ROOTS RIPPED
FROM THE GROUND
ABANDONMENT N WORRY
FOREVER TO BE FOUND

RAIN RAIN RAIN
TAKE THIS HAND OF SORROW
TAKE AWAY MY DARKEST DAYS
RAIN RAIN RAIN
TAKE AWAY MY DARKEST DAYS
RETURN ME FOR I FEEL I'M HERE
TO STAY

FOR JUST ONE MOMENT OF PEACE
I LONG TO KNOW
I CAN SEE THE STORMCLOUDS
CALLING ME BACK HOME
THE BLOOD OF THE HURRICANE
WHERE THE WATER IS NEVER
STILL
LIFE IS A LOADED GUN
LOVE IS A BULLET THAT SOMETIMES
KILLS

"JANUARY"

THE COLD THAT BURNS
THE tides that DRIFT AWAY
NO MORE talks ABOUT TOMMOROW
THE PAST IS GONE & ALL THAT
    WAS TODAY
I CAN't FORGET THE COLD THAT FELL
THAT JANUARY DAY —

SEASONS CHANGE
FOR the RAIN HAS WASHED AWAY
ALL the SMILES N THE TEARS
WHATS INBETWEEN ALL ONES HOPES
N FEARS —
I FEEL that JANUARY'S COLD SHALL
NEVER DISSAPEAR

~~RAIN RAIN RAIN RAIN~~
EMPTY SKY THE BITTERNESS UNFOLDS
ITS HARD TO HOLD A MEMORY WHEN THERE'S
NOTHING LEFT TO HOLD
RAIN RAIN RAIN
THE DESERT KILLS WHATS LEFT INSIDE
ITS HARD TO LIVE WHEN ALL U
WANNA DO IS DIE

THE BOOK IS DONE/NO MORE PAGES
LEFT TO TURN/NO MORE LETTERS
LEFT TO RIGHT/NOTHINGS LEFT
FOR WHOM it MAY CONCERN
JANUARYS COLD SHALL FOREVER
LIVE ON

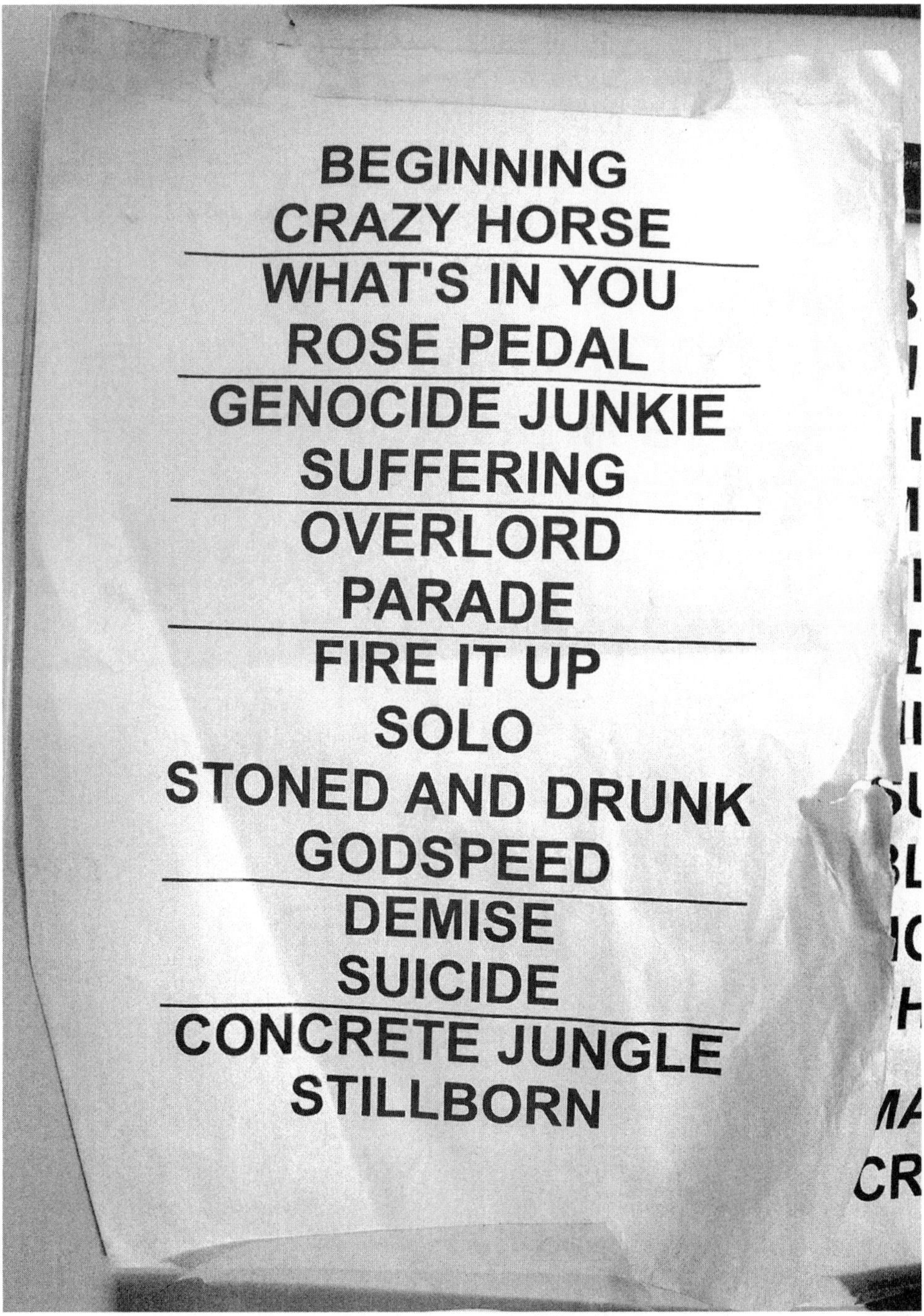

BEGINNING
CRAZY HORSE
WHAT'S IN YOU
ROSE PEDAL
GENOCIDE JUNKIE
SUFFERING
OVERLORD
PARADE
FIRE IT UP
SOLO
STONED AND DRUNK
GODSPEED
DEMISE
SUICIDE
CONCRETE JUNGLE
STILLBORN

BARK AT THE MOON
MR CROWLEY
NOT GOING AWAY
FLYING HIGH AGAIN
BELIEVER
I DON'T WANNA STOP
ROAD TO NOWHERE
SUICIDE / SOLO
I DON'T KNOW
NO MORE TEARS
CHANGE THE WORLD

MAMA I'M COMING HOME
CRAZY TRAIN
PARANOID

From the Desk of
John DeServio

DEAR READERS, FANS, AND BERZERKERS WORLDWIDE,

This is John DeServio. Not JDesus, *not* Meatball Lasagna, *not the* Italian Stallion—*it's JD, bitches. Let me tell you a little something about this self-proclaimed "Viking Berzerker" whom you all have come to know as one Zakk Wylde. First off, I'm going to let you know that you've completely wasted your time and money on his thoughtless book, which is full of countless self-appreciative (and overexaggerated) tales. I guess he's still trying to prove to himself that he has actually added some kind of value to the universe and that people really do want to hear what he has to say.*

He calls himself the Führer, the Great One, Sweetness. What the fuck? You think he makes this shit up himself? No chance. He basically steals nicknames from everyone else he knows and then regifts them to himself. Well, we, the members of the band and Doom Crew, have given him a few titles of our own over the years!!

Douchebag–*A perfect blend of jerk and asshole, reflecting that his overinflated ego, combined with his extremely low IQ, causes frequent maladaptive behavior.*
The Vortex–*A complete disaster where time stops altogether, absorbed by the infinite abyss created by his delusions of greatness.*
Nothin' for Nothin'–*I'm not even sure what the fuck this means, but he starts every sentence with it as if it gives credibility to everything he says . . . As in* "Nothin' for nothin', my calves are much beefier and sexier than that guy's." *As he points to one of his almost-naked-man magazines.*

This is a guy who grew up in fucking New Jersey but proclaims his love for NYC (mostly Christopher Street). We're talking major identity crisis here. He doesn't even go by his real name anymore. Wikipedia says his birth name was Jeffrey Wielandt, before Ozzy made him change it to Zakk Wylde. But I'm here to testify that this is a farce. When we were in grade school, Zakk's real name was Stewart McNutsac, or as the schoolkids called him, Stewie Nutsack.

That's actually the reason he got so good on the guitar. You see, I used to have to save his ass from a daily playground beat-down. And after school I would walk him home to make sure he didn't get jumped along the way. Stewie would run up to his room, lock the door, and after crying himself out, he'd pick up his guitar and practice for the rest of the day. He was terrified to leave the house for fear of receiving another ass-whoopin', and that's why he was able to put so much time into his playing. While the rest of us were out in the streets playing baseball and hockey, he honed his skills on his axe. I guess I don't blame him;

it was far less dangerous for him to wiggle his fingers around for six hours than to face the wrath of New Jersey street kids.

The Order of the Black *album was supposed to be my band Cycle of Pain's next record. Instead, the cocksucker drew me in by tantalizing me with a "co-producer" or "associate producer" credit. By the time we got into recording I began to refer to myself as the disassociate producer. I mean, do I really want to associate myself with a complete wanker like this? Anyway, he suckered me in. I soon started to realize that every riff I had already recorded and mixed for my album had mysteriously found its way off my computer and ended up being released as the new Black Label record. I'd like to see him do that to Zeppelin (who did that to Robert Johnson) . . . Oh wait, he already did! The phrase* void of originality *is a complete understatement when talking about this prick.*

Never mind the platinum albums, the Grammy, and all the other musical accolades this dipshit has piled up. My scumbag brother's actual crowning achievements in life are: not showering for seventy-seven days and being told by David Lee Roth, "Get the fuck off my stage!" while Zakk strutted around wearing George Lynch's wife's high heels (he still hasn't returned her kicks and proudly wears them whenever he works out in the Black Label gym).

And it's not only his music that makes me want to puke. Zakk's love for testosterone has led him to many horse stables around the country, a few bathhouses, and a plethora of same-sex marriage rallies. What kind of man plasters his own gym with oversized photos of nearly naked, muscle-bound men? Zakk does. I mean, if I'm in the gym getting my lift on, the

last thing I want to see is another man's steroidal glu-
teus maximus tightly wrapped in a banana hammock.
I also find it disturbing that he leaves his muscle
magazines around the tour bus, as if he is trying to
lure others to peek over the homoerotic hedge along-
side him. Strength in numbers, as he always says.

Zakk has never been sick a day in his life.
He's what we call a "carrier." His mere presence
has caused SARS, dengue fever, the bird flu, and
even some bad cases of gingivitis (don't ask me
how he spread the swine flu . . . "Squeal like a pig,
boyeee!!!"). Why do ya think I have three crucifixes
on me at all times? Just being in the same room as this
guy causes my immune system to weaken and bodily
fluids to begin seeping out.

Why do you think I smoke so much weed? It's to
keep my sanity in a world of Zakk preaching how
incredible he believes he is. And just for the record,
it's herb, *not crack!! Every crack that I've ever sniffed*
smelled like shit! But Zakk seems to like to talk about
crack, and for that matter ass, a little too much for my
liking.

What can I say about my brother that hasn't
already been said by millions around the globe? He's
a talentless hack, a repetition in redundancy, "Bombo
the Clown"—and these are what his closest relatives
and loved ones call him!!! Despite everything we've
been through though, I still love him like a brother.
He's the Tom Hagen of the DeServio family. Well, he
and his Irish Coalition brother Rob, and any other
drunken Mick we find along the way. It's no surprise
though; the Italians have had to keep the Irish in line
for years now, so we're used to it.

And while I'm on the topic of douchebags, meaning

talking about Zakk, let me tell you a little bit about Zakk's "coauthor," Eric Hendrikx. Here's a guy who can barely manage a legible text message. His writing is so bad that it only makes sense for him to pair up with an illiterate like Zakk to do a book about shitting and puking on the road. Seriously, guys, how much talk about excrement do you need to put into a book to get your point across? Hendrikx needs to have his head checked because I'm sure he has some sort of fecal fetish going on. I've heard rumors that he looks in the toilet bowl to see what kind of animal shape his dumps fall into. Who the fuck does that? His next book is probably going to be a how-to guide for stuffing Play-Doh up your ass and squeezing it out into the shape of a giraffe. This boy is not right in the head and he is completely unsafe to be around. I don't like him on the tour bus with us either. I can't sleep knowing that his disturbed mind is on board. I sleep with one eye open and my ass cheeks pressed firmly into the mattress.

Order of the Bass

We all know that my bass playing is the foundation for Black Label Society's heavy sound. I'm the mothafuckin' heart and soul of the band. I keep the band in time, lay down the fat rhythms that everybody grooves to, and keep Zakk from sticking a spoon into his own eye while he's eating. Zakk plays guitar to my rhythms; I don't play to his leads. Oh, and in the studio, you think he's coming up with all that shit on his own? Think again, buddy. If Zakk were left alone in the studio to make a record, he'd come out with finger paintings and a copped version of "Mary

Had a Little Lamb" squeaked out in a series of Auto-Tuned farts!

Oh, and just so you know . . . after these two jag-offs' feeble attempt at reaming me in their futile book, they offered me a back-of-the-book rebuttal. But in fear that my prose would dominate their own, I was given only two words to defend myself. How is it even possible to defend yourself in two words? So instead I directly contacted their editor, Matthew Benjamin, over at HarperCollins, who gave me a legitimate plat-form to defend myself, and without the consent of the aforementioned shitbirds. Thanks, Matthew!

Still want those two words for your book, fellas? Here they are . . . SUCK IT!

Thank you, bitches.
I Remain,
John "JD" DeServio
Order of the Bass
Cycle of Pain
†WEED†

Credits

All photography by Eric Hendrikx unless otherwise noted.

Cover photograph by Travis Shinn.

Back cover photograph by Eric Hendrikx.

Chapter illustrations by Rich Ellis and Ben Dewey.

Courtesy of Mark Ferguson: Black Label Special Ops, insert page 5.

Courtesy of Jeffrey Graham: Jeff Graham, Billy Gibbons, Zakk Wylde, insert page 4; Lucha Libre Wrestling Team, insert page 2; Ozzy's birthday, insert page 5; Zakk Wylde in front of church, book page 129.

Courtesy of Chris Jericho: Ozzfest—Chris Jericho, Zakk Wylde, JD, and friends, insert page 5.

Courtesy of Chad Lee: Dimebag Darrel, Zakk Wylde, and Kerry King, insert page 7.

Courtesy of Jimmy Hubbard: Pedicab with Jimmy Hubbard and Zakk Wylde, book page 214.

All *Guitar World* magazine covers courtesy of *Guitar World* magazine, Brad Tolinski, and Jimmy Hubbard.

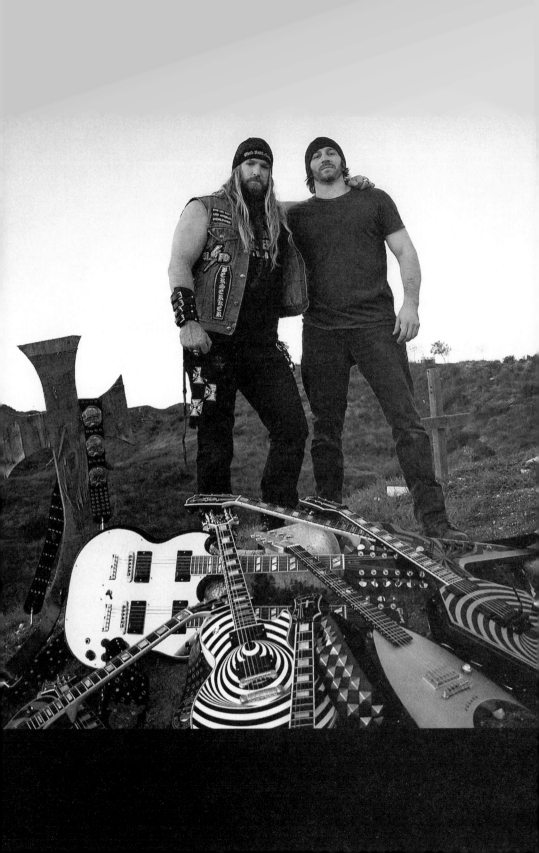

About the Authors

ZAKK WYLDE resides atop a mountain on the outskirts of Los Angeles, California, with his wife, Barbaranne, and their daughter, Hayley Rae, and two sons, Jesse John Michael and Hendrix. When he's not out on the Black Label Crusade, Zakk spends his days at home trying to convince his family that the year is AD 912 and that his mountain is Valhalla.

www.zakkwylde.com

www.blacklabelsociety.com

Follow Zakk on Twitter: @ZakkWyldeBLS

Writer and photographer **ERIC HENDRIKX** is a notable contributor to more than ten books, including the *New York Times* bestsellers *Got Fight?: The 50 Zen Principles of Hand-to-Face Combat* and *Be Ready When the Sh*t Goes Down: A Survival Guide to the Apocalypse* (both HarperCollins). Eric lives in Southern California with his son, Stone.

www.erichendrikx.com

Follow Eric on Twitter: @EricHendrikx

15 † 15 † 20 † 2